SHAKESPEARE NO DEERSTEALER

AMS PRESS
NEW YORK

SHAKESPEARE NO DEERSTEALER,

OR,

A SHORT ACCOUNT

OF

Fulbroke Park,

NEAR STRATFORD-ON-AVON.

BY

C. HOLTE BRACEBRIDGE,

SOMETIME HON. SEC. TO THE SHAKESPEARE HOUSE COMMITTEE.

LONDON:
PRINTED BY HARRISON AND SONS, ST. MARTIN'S LANE, W.C.

1862.

Library of Congress Cataloging in Publication Data

Bracebridge, Charles Holte, 1799-1872.
  Shakespeare no deerstealer.

  1. Shakespeare, William, 1564-1616--Biography
--Youth. I. Title.
PR2903.B7 1972   822.3'3 [B]   76-39517
ISBN 0-404-00921-2

Reprinted from the edition of 1862, London
First AMS edition published in 1972
Manufactured in the United States of America

International Standard Book Number: 0-404-00921-2

AMS PRESS INC.
NEW YORK, N. Y.   10003

TO

W. O. HUNT, Esq., of Stratford-on-Avon.

My dear Sir,

Permit me to address to you the following little Treatise which has resulted from some researches pursued from time to time, with a view to give an absolute and definite shape to the Deer Hunting (not Deer-Stealing) episode of Shakespeare's life. If I have succeeded, as I trust I have, in maintaining the poet's innocence, by shewing that he committed no illegal act, and in maintaining the truth of the tradition, while establishing a high probability of a long existing yearning towards the drama, and long converse with the chief actors of the day, previously to the incident which finally fixed his wavering determination, I may probably have gratified those who delight in protecting the material memorials of the world's poet which exist in and around the place of his birth, life, and death.

Among these, my dear Sir, you may be considered as the longest tried, the most persevering, and the most generous.

I am, my dear Sir,
Truly yours,
CHAS. HOLTE BRACEBRIDGE.

August, 1862.

The sketch of which the annexed lithograph is a fac-simile, was kindly presented to the writer by C. Knight, Esq., and will be placed in the Museum of the Birth-place at Stratford. Underneath the original sketch the following explanation was written by the draughtsman:

"GROVE FIELD, WARWICKSHIRE.
"THE DEER BARN.—*Drawn by W. Jackson*, 1798.

"This barn was originally appropriated to the use of foddering the deer belonging to the park which formerly surrounded this place of antiquity. Here it was where the immortal Shakespeare secreted himself after he had stolen the deer, the property of Sir Thomas Lucy. Charlecote is the name of the family seat of the Lucys, and there belongs to it a park well stocked with deer; but there remains a doubt in my mind whether it ever belonged to the park where this barn stands, as the river Avon runs close by the extremities of the present park, and that which originally (a park?) is now converted into farms."

Mr. Waldron, the well-known critic of Skakespeare's works, has added thereto the following remark,—"Since this drawing was made, the barn has, I believe, been taken down.
"F. G. WALDRON."

Grove-Field (Warwickshire).   (Drawn by Mr. Jackson 1798.)

SHAKESPEARE AT FULBROKE.

The following argument on the subject of an act of Shakespeare's early life, supposed to have greatly influenced his fortunes, if not indeed to have led him to that career which discovered to the world his great genius, and terminated in his happiness and his honour, can scarcely be deemed unimportant. It is to be lamented that we know so little of Shakespeare's life and private actions. He seems to have been without that vanity which leads men to record their acts, and push them forward in the great world if they can; or at all events to collect, correct, and republish their literary works when life and leisure shall have made it possible. The less we know of him, however, the more interesting it is to ascertain accurately what we do know; and if there be any act which, for want of explanation, may throw a slur on his character, or taint, however slightly, the moral atmosphere around his youth, that act should surely be examined minutely, to show if any blame really rest on him. To remove such blame cast upon him, and to dispel the taint by a close examination and arguments derived from facts legitimately proved, is unquestionably a duty we owe to one who has given us so much pleasure and instruction, and who has lived to the honor, not only of England, but of Europe.

Now the deer-stealing story attached to Shakespeare's youth, and generally assigned as the cause of his going to London by drawing upon him the anger of Sir Thomas Lucy, is precisely such a circumstance as above described. The tradition can neither be denied nor ridiculed as of no importance to his character as a mere boyish frolic. At that period deer-stealing was a very grave offence, and when proved was visited with severe punishment.* The ingenious and elegant writer who "will have none of it," only leaves the matter as it was—a tradition. The industrious inquirer and acute examiner of Shakespeare's annals, only reduces it to its original proportions. We are yet to decide whether Shakespeare, in boyhood or manhood, killed a deer, lawfully or unlawfully. If so, where the act occurred, and what were the consequences to him. In these consequences the English world had a deep interest, as it turned out, for they involved there being at Stratford a farmer and woolstapler the less, and in the world a poet the more, and such a one as has not since appeared.

The tradition variously told by Rowe, Malone, Drake, Stevens, and others, is more distinctly treated of by the two writers previously alluded to—Mr. Charles Knight and Mr. J. O. Halliwell; although, in their lives of Shakespeare, they in some degree take different sides of the question. The truth is, that the local tradition in the immediate neighbourhood of Stratford is most distinct. It has nothing to do with the legality of the act, or with its consequences; and as a simple spring of water is often better evidence of an historic fact than the works of man—architectural or literary—so, stript of all variations and literary tittle-tattle, the simple tradition of the simplest people is worthy of belief till refuted. We must especially guard against the additions of writers who, though living long after the epoch in

* Note A.

question, appear to us to be of weight, because they are remote from our own times. Thus, of late years, since Rowe, Malone, and Ireland favoured or troubled the world with their opinions and discoveries, the scene of the exploit has been as often laid at Charlecote Park as at Fulbroke Park, and the former has, by little and little, been preferred by the ignorant and unwary, perhaps because it still exists in perfection, while the latter has lost all appearance of park or forest for at least two centuries.

I trust, however, that I shall satisfactorily prove that Shakespeare killed the deer at Fulbroke, between the years 1583 and 1589, most probably in 1587; that by so doing he committed no offence either in law or morals; and further, that he nevertheless did incur the displeasure of Sir Thomas Lucy, which may probably have been the cause of his going to London at this particular time, although it was not his chief reason for betaking himself to the stage.

The tradition, as recorded by different writers, and as remaining in the neighbourhood, is varied in its incidents; and the verses cited as Shakespeare's are given in many or few stanzas; but what is the main feature of interest is the same in all versions of the story, viz., that the poet, in his youth, offended Sir Thomas Lucy of Charlecote, by killing a deer; that in consequence of some hostile proceedings taken by the Knight, he left Stratford and went to London, and that on his departure he wrote some scurrilous lines against Lucy, which was an aggravation of the first offence.

The chief variations in the story are:—that Shakespeare killed the deer in Charlecote Park, and was taken by the keepers; that the deer was killed at Fulbroke; that Fulbroke was a park, and was owned by Lucy; and that the poet nailed the lampoon to Charlecote Park gates. Mr. Halliwell considers that "we may safely accept the deer-stealing story, not in all its minute particulars, but in its outline, to be essentially true, until more decisive evidence can be produced which shall also explain equally well the allusions to the Lucys made in Shakespeare's plays."

Rowe's account is, that "Shakespeare fell into ill company, and engaged more than once in robbing a park belonging to Sir Thomas Lucy of Charlecote. For this he was prosecuted, as he thought, too severely, and revenged himself by making a ballad on Lucy. And though this, probably his first essay in poetry, be lost, it is said to have been so very bitter that it redoubled the prosecution against him, and he was obliged to leave his family in Warwickshire and take shelter in London." Many years after the appearance of Rowe's Life, published in 1709, part of the ballad referred to was published as being taken from the M.S. notes of Oldys, though Rowe distinctly states that the ballad was lost.

There is no evidence of any value in favour of the authenticity of this fragment, which runs as follows:—

"A parliamente member, a justice of peace,
At home a poor scarecrow, at London an asse;
If lowsie is Lucy, as some volke miscalle it,
Then Lucy is lowsie, whatever befalle it.
He thinks himselfe greate,
Yet an asse in his state
We allow by his eares but with asses to mate, &c."

One Jordan, of Stratford, afterwards professed to have discovered, in an old chest at Shottery, a complete copy of the ballad.

In Capell's account, published in 1779, we read that a Mr. Jones, who resided at a village eighteen miles from Stratford, and died in 1703, aged upwards of ninety, remembered to have heard the deer-stealing story from several people at Stratford, and he put down in writing the above stanza. Although this is no proof of authenticity, it is evidence in favour of the story being known in Stratford about the year 1700.

Mr. Knight, after reviewing the evidence as to the tradition, considers it unworthy of belief; and with reference to the ballad, is of opinion that the first stanza is an old forgery, and the remaining stanzas are modern ones. In fact, as Mr. Halliwell says, Mr. Knight "will, in no single instance, allow a blemish in Shakespeare's moral character, even in venial lapses, which would not lessen our respect for his memory."

Then in Sir Walter Scott's Diary, we read:— "April 8, 1828. Learning that the hall of Sir Thomas Lucy, was still extant, we went in quest of it. Mr. Lucy, a descendant of the worshipful Sir Thomas, came to welcome us in person. He told me that the park from which Shakespeare stole the buck was *not* that which surrounds Charlecote, but belonged to a mansion at some distance, where Sir Thomas Lucy resided at the time of the trespass. The tradition went that they hid the buck in a barn, part of which was standing a few years ago, but now totally destroyed."

Again, with singular pertinacity, Dr. Drake insists that the deer stealing occurred at Fulbroke, and that Fulbroke was at that time the property of Sir Thomas Lucy; while, in the Biography of Shakespeare, published in the present year, it is as strenuously maintained that the act took place at Charlecote, Fulbroke not being at that period the property of Lucy; the writer seeming to think it necessary to make Lucy the owner of the deer to account for his anger.

Let us first consider the period at which Shakespeare could have committed the act imputed to him. It was clearly between the years 1583 and 1589, and probably only between 1585 and 1587. He was married in 1582, at the age of eighteen; his eldest daughter was born in 1583; and the year but one after this the twins, Hamet and Judith, were born; and there is no reason to believe that he even temporarily abandoned his bride before this time.

Taking this into consideration with the fact which is universally believed, that he proceeded to London immediately after the act which gave rise to the anger of Sir Thomas Lucy, and remained there some years, he could not have taken the deer until 1585, the year in which the twins were born. In the year 1589 he is proved by the Dulwich papers, and the petition to the Chancellor Ellesmere, to be one of the Company of Queen's Players (in which Burbage, his friend and townsman, was the principal actor), and a shareholder in the Blackfriars Theatre. We cannot suppose he could become a shareholder in less than two years after joining a London Company, so that we may safely infer that he left Stratford not later than 1587, and not earlier than 1585.

Sir Thomas Lucy, who in 1558 rebuilt the manor-house of Charlecote as it now stands, imparked a considerable tract around it, on the left bank of the Avon in 1563, one year before the birth of Shakespeare; and it will be presently shown that from 1553 to 1592 Fulbroke Park was held *in capite* of the crown by Sir Francis Englefield, and that he was from 1558 to 1592 (when he died in Spain,) attainted, and his property sequestered, but the proceeds not appropriated by the Queen.* It follows, then, that Sir Thomas Lucy had no property in Fulbroke at this time; nor, indeed, had the Lucy family any right in the estate at any time previous to the last year of Shakespeare's life, when Sir Thomas (grandson of the knight above mentioned) purchased Fulbroke from the nephew of Sir Francis Englefield, the proscribed traitor, to whose mother, Margaret, the estate had been regranted after his uncle's death. Lucy's park, however, ran along the bank of the Avon for nearly a mile, and for about

* Note B.

the same distance Fulbroke occupied the opposite bank, a quarter of a mile higher up the stream. The river is shallow, and had a regular ford at Hampton-Lucy, situate at one angle of Charlecote Park, so that Lucy's deer were restrained by the fence alone, and by the same means only were the Fulbroke deer kept out of Charlecote Park, when the Fulbroke Park fences were broken down, as they must have been twenty-seven years after Englefield's leaving England. Now, had Shakespeare broken into Charlecote, and been found guilty of so taking a buck or doe, he would have been subjected to three months' imprisonment, to treble damages, and then to find bail for seven years, by the 5th of Elizabeth, cap. 21, sect. 3, the Act then in force.* The Act is clear, and it is incredible that Sir Thomas, with a park which had been enclosed but a few years previously, and with the ideas of his time, should have abstained from taking the satisfaction the law allowed for an offence looked upon at that period, by the gentry at least, very much as housebreaking is with us. But, in fact, Sir Thomas suffered no such wrong. He was a gentleman of ancient lineage ;† his ancestor had once held Fulbroke Park of the Crown during pleasure; and although that park had since 1553 been held *in capite* by Sir Francis Englefield, as before stated, yet as Englefield was abroad, a proscript, he, Lucy, no doubt still hunted there. He had his own park (Charlecote,) perhaps of fallow deer, or some prized sort, and was naturally jealous of their getting away to an adjacent forest, or of wild stags breaking in and spoiling his breed. He had been lately knighted, and as a justice of the peace he often went to Stratford on legal or state business, as we discover from the Borough Chamberlain's account-books.‡ We hear of Government imposts in letters of the period, so that it may have been of great importance to the Mayor and Cor-

* Note A.   † Note C.   ‡ Note D.

poration not to offend a gentleman of his position, and so near a neighbour. In this state of things Shakespeare would treat very lightly the warnings of the Charlecote keepers. Knowing, as a young lawyer, that he had as good a right as Sir Thomas to sport over Fulbroke, inasmuch as there was no legal park there, the owner, Englefield, being a banished traitor, and his land forfeited, though not seized by the crown, owing to the personal interference of the sovereign, yet he was incapable of delegating authority after twenty-seven years of banishment, even to maintain his fences, a legal essential for constituting a park.

Let us assume then, that Shakespeare and his friends—possibly a portion of one of the companies of players visiting Stratford in 1587—marched off to Fulbroke, about three miles from Stratford, on the Warwick road, with some hounds, picked up where they could,—not, probably, such a pack of the old English slot hounds as he accurately describes as the hounds of Theseus, Duke of Athens, in the "Midsummer Night's Dream."* He was, as we see from "As you Like it," well acquainted with the habits of deer. He must have found the park pales broken down, the rides grown over, and the little castle in ruins, having been left since Englefield's attainder in 1558, a period of about twenty-nine years. The lodge, being at the angle of the park farthest from Stratford, on low ground, by the then ruined church, he would not approach, and it was there only any inhabitants would be found. He would see the two old deer-barns, one on a hill side near the Avon, the other on high ground close to the paling along the Stratford and Warwick road, each at the end of a winding ravine, among the brush-covered hills and glens of this beautiful tract, the slopes of which descend gradually to the river. He would probably have sent forward to get some buck "pricked" into a thicket, or

* Note E.

would at all events bring some two or three brach-hounds to hunt up the lair. We can fancy him placing his men, choosing his wind, and laying on his hounds. Thus would he drive the deer into some open glade, and by a fortunate cross-bow shot bring down a buck or a pricket. A glen runs up from the meadows along the Avon to the Stratford road, through the very centre of the park. Some ancient trees still adorn it, and it widens and ends in the plateau along which runs the Stratford and Warwick road at that time bounded by the dilapidated park paling which the chronicler Rous, a monk of Warwick, describes. Nearly at the top of the glen, about two hundred yards from the Stratford road was the deer-barn, now replaced by a new brick cottage and homestead. The old wooden barn is well recollected, and was sketched for Mr. Knight's Biography of Shakespeare, and also mentioned in Mr. Lucy's conversation with Sir Walter Scott before referred to. Supposing the stag to have been killed in the glen, he would be dragged to this old barn to be broken up and prepared for the pack-horse. The horse may, indeed, have been tied in the barn during the chase, as the nearest point to the road.

Now, suppose the keepers of Sir Thomas, or one of his tenants, to have been looking for deer escaped from Charlecote Park, or seeking for some wild stag likely to break into the park and kill the young bucks (as often happens at certain seasons), but now harbouring at Fulbroke. They would come on Shakespeare's company, claim the buck, and assert that Sir Thomas had leave to hunt there; or even that the Lord Chamberlain allowed him to act as Ranger during Englefield's exile. Shakespeare, knowing the exact law of the case, would laugh at their claims, and probably, after a scuffle, succeed in carrying off his venison. The young men would make no secret of their successful day's sport, especially if they were of the company of players from London, under the

Lord Chamberlain's licence. The angry knight would go to Stratford, complaining and threatening generally, and especially Mr. Alderman John Shakespeare and Mr. Mayor. He would insist on putting a stop to such insolence of the townsfolk; and when resisted and told the law of the case, and that the Park Acts would not reach Will and his friends, and that his keepers had no more right in Fulbroke than they had, he might naturally enough say that which Shallow, in the play published fifteen years afterwards is made to say,* "I will make a Star Chamber matter of it," averring that the park was crown property. This invoking of that terrible tribunal might well frighten the rustics, especially as Fulbroke was an ancient park, at that time, and for more than twenty years before, forfeited by its holder, a traitor, though through special indulgence not yet seized by the Crown, as a fief held *in capite*. The great man would seek to bear down by authority and Shakespeare would reply with his newly-learnt law till Mr. Mayor would be thoroughly puzzled. As we see from contemporary letters, the town was afraid of national imposts, quartering of soldiers, &c., and had to pay for pikemen and furbishing their harness, in all which Sir Thomas, if outraged, might oppress them. What then so likely as that Mr. Mayor and old John Shakespeare should persuade young William to absent himself, and that he, seeing his father and the authorities refuse to maintain his obvious right, should, rather than humble himself to the great man, stick a scurrilous ballad on Lucy's park gate, and troop away with the players (probably with all their "properties" in their broad-wheel waggon) to London. Besides, the company included Burbage, Greene and Heminge his fellow-townsmen, and they would find it to their own interest to advise so sprightly a youth to join them, if indeed that had not long before been agreed on. As to the ballad,

* Note D.

the one stanza only before mentioned was probably written at the time either by Shakespeare or one of the company who may have shared his sports, and his feeling of anger and disdain towards the knight. The other stanzas seem to have been added afterwards, and indeed the evidence of the first appears to have been collected some sixty years after the events occurred.

The character of Lucy was indelibly stamped on Shakespeare's memory; and as Scott in his "Antiquary" drew Monkbarns from nature, so may Shakespeare have improved and enlarged on Lucy in his "Henry IV" and "Merry Wives of Windsor," not out of revenge for an old insult, but because his instinctive perception told him that such a country squire would amuse the courtiers, act as a foil to Falstaff, and by the more discerning part of his audience be accepted as a true sketch from nature.

Shakespeare had doubtless an inclination to go to London apart from the consideration of Sir Thomas Lucy's anger. We know that Jolope's, or as it was afterwards called King Edward's, Grammar School was carried on during the whole of Shakespeare's life in the two ancient rooms which it still occupies at Stratford, under the mastership of Hunt. Our poet, therefore, as the son of a burgess (afterwards alderman) must undoubtedly have been educated there, most likely from his tenth year, in 1574, until he was sixteen, in 1580. He may then have assisted his father for a short time on his farm, or in his trade. Probably the tradition of his having been apprenticed to a butcher arose from his having in a boyish freak killed a calf or a lamb in a mock heroic style, as he is said to have done. The years of his life after his marriage, at eighteen, till he was twenty-one or even twenty-three, he, in all probability, spent in the office of an attorney or scrivener at Stratford; and this calling he may have followed even afterwards in London, simultaneously with that of the stage ; for it seems impossible to reject the opinions of the poet Walter Savage Landor and Lord Campbell, after the proofs adduced by the latter in his "Shakespeare's Legal Acquirements," published in 1859, that Shakespeare had been long familiar with the legal practice of his time. During this short interval, from 1582 to 1589, viz., from the fifteenth to the twenty-fifth year of his age, he must have followed some literary pursuit, and thus have laid in such a store of reading as enabled him to compose his "Venus and Adonis" and "Rape of Lucrece," and some of his sonnets subsequent to his love song to Ann Hathaway. We have yet to find a cause for the excitement of his precocious intellect. This, after a perusal of Mr. J. O. Halliwell's extracts from the accounts of the Chamberlain of the borough of Stratford (still preserved in the archives of that borough), we shall be at no loss to do. The payments to various companies of players by the corporation show that from the time Shakespeare was five years old until he reached the age of twenty-three, Stratford was visited on no less than twenty different occasions by the first companies of players,* viz., the Queen's players, Lord Leicester's, Lord Warwick's, Lord Worcester's, Lord Essex's, &c., and these visits would naturally lead to intercourse between young Shakespeare and his townsmen, the two Burbages, Greene, and others. Here then is abundant excitement for the young poet's intellect, to say nothing of some of the marvellous shows he may have seen when eleven years old, during Queen Elizabeth's entertainment at Kenilworth, in 1575. It would, moreover, have been to the interest of at least one of the company of players, Richard Burbage, the celebrated actor, so commended by Lord Southampton, to induce Shakespeare to join his (Her Majesty's) company. So, at the age of 23, in 1587, during which year both the Queen's players

* Note F.

SHAKESPEARE AT FULBROKE. 13

and the companies of Lords Essex and Leicester were at Stratford, he might seriously have considered the question and determined to join them, if, indeed, he had not done so occasionally before that time. It is almost impossible to fix Shakespeare's removal to London later than 1587, in the twenty-third year of his age, and the fifth after his marriage, because, as there is absolute proof in the "Certificate of Her Majesty's Poore Players"* that he was a "sharer" in the company in 1589, only two years intervene before his attaining this rank. Now, in this same year, 1587, this company was at Stratford, and was paid twenty shillings by the Corporation, as appears in the Corporation account-books. Sir Thomas Lucy appears at Stratford in the previous year, 1586, and in these same accounts is a charge of twenty pence for wine and sugar for that knight "when he sat in commission on tipplers."† Lucy had been elected knight of the shire in 1585, and if we assume that his anger was the ultimate incentive to Shakespeare's determination, we must place the deer hunt in 1587. There is also another reason for so doing. In the records of the Corporation there is undoubted evidence that John Shakespeare was arrested for debt in April, 1587, in an action began in the preceding October, by one John Brown, and was brought up under a habeas in March; and again was defendant in actions brought by R. Sutton, in 1589, and by Adrian Quiney and others in 1591. So that we find the period of the appearance and probable overtures of the players coincide with the time of Lucy's anger and the poverty of the poet's father, three most powerful stimulants to seek more lucrative employment elsewhere; such as would be gratifying at once to his ambition and common sense views of life, as also to his good feeling towards his parents, who might ill support the rebukes Mr. Mayor would administer to please the great man then in the

* Note F.   † Note D.

height of his prosperity and power as Knight of the Shire, Justice of the Peace, &c. Nothing can be more likely than that Lucy's object in keeping all intruders out of Fulbroke, rightly or wrongly, was to establish a right by usage, so as the more easily to get the estate granted to him by the crown, as it had already been to his grandfather. This object was, however, frustrated by Elizabeth's steady adherence to her promise sent to Englefield when in Spain, that she would not use his effects, although an act was passed to render the forfeiture of his ancient property legal; and at Englefield's death Fulbroke was granted to the Clerk of the Signet, with reversion to Margaret, widow of Englefield's brother John, and mother to his heir.

It may here be remarked that to the years between 1559 and 1587, the fifteenth to the twenty-third years of Shakespeare's age, must be assigned any special law reading as a scrivener, any general literature; and, what belongs to our purpose, any practical initiation into woodcraft, which he obtained before entering the great world. The numerous passages in his works relating to rural scenery, flowers, &c., prove how much he had known of trees, fields, woods, and brooks; as other passages shew that he was intimately acquainted with what sportsmen designate "the noble science of the chase."* The Fulbroke deer hunt is clearly no solitary instance of Shakespeare's sporting, and therefore not likely to have occurred secretly, in the dark, but in the open forest, in daylight, with help of friends and hounds, just as a stag is hunted in the New Forest at this day, only that no leave was asked, there being no one legally entitled to grant it.

Having gone through the argument, which is fully borne out by the particulars given in the note on the ancient family of Englefield,† I may now indulge in a short history and description of the spot which, though interesting for its romantic scenery,

* Note E.   † Note B.

and the historic importance of its successive owners, is much more so as the scene of the incident which proved the chief cause of the successful career of Shakespeare, and of his world-wide renown.

From "Dugdale's Warwickshire," we learn that the Manor of Fulbroke was, in the year 1272, in the possession of Isabell, wife of William Gernune. Eleven years afterwards it was sold to William de Hynkelee, who, after holding it for a year, exchanged it with Nicholas de Warwick, Attorney-General, and follower of William Beauchamp, Earl of Warwick, for the Manor of Stoke Golding, in Leicestershire. In 1325, Lord Bergavenny left it to his son, by whom it was left to his widow Julian as her "dowrie." This Julian afterwards married William de Clinton, Earl of Huntingdon, and he was allowed to hold the estate of the king *in capite* on payment of six shillings and two-pence per annum. At his death it was granted to William Beauchamp, Lord Bergavenny, whose lady built a sumptuous gate-house and lodge thereon. It next passed into still more illustrious hands; John, Duke of Bedford, third son of Henry IV., holding it in 1432, by the fourth part of a knight's fee. "He," says Dugdale, "made the park and built the castle of brick and stone." Rous, the monk of Warwick, who lived near enough the time to have seen Richard the Third when living at Warwick Castle as Duke of Gloucester, with Ann, daughter and co-heiress of the great Earl of Warwick, says of Fulbroke, in his Latin Chronicle, "the church was destroyed, only the manor remained; the rest was enclosed by John, Duke of Bedford, brother of Henry the Fifth, who there built a square castle (but now it is almost nothing), and again by such enclosure the road, formerly safe, now screened by banks and palings, has become a lurking place for robbers, a very prison for honest men, a place of varied annoyances." This ruinous castle was pulled down by Sir William Compton in the beginning of

Henry the Eighth's time, and some of the materials removed to his new house at Compton Wyneat. After the decease of the Duke of Bedford, Fulbroke was granted by Henry the Sixth to John Talbot, Lord Lisle, for his life; and when it again reverted to the Crown, Edward VI., in 1462, granted it to the great Earl of Warwick, Richard Nevil, by whom it was held till he was killed at Barnet Field. The park was subsequently held by the Duke of Clarence, probably granted to his wife, the above Earl's daughter, and while in his possession we are told that the castle was in a ruinous state. This was in 1478. Henry VIII., in 1510, gave it to Thomas Lucy, sewer to the king, to hold during pleasure. John Dudley, Earl of Warwick, next received it from the Crown in 1547, and upon his attainder as chief delinquent in the Lady Jane Grey's affair, Queen Mary, in 1553, granted it to her Privy Councillor, Sir Francis Englefield, to hold *in capite*. At the death of this Sir Francis, Fulbroke, having previously reverted to the Crown by his attainder, was re-granted, but this time in *fee simple*, to Nicholas Faunt, Clerk of the Signet, with remainder to Margaret, widow of John Englefield, the brother of Sir Francis. Sir Francis Englefield, son of this Margaret, sold the estate to the third Sir Thomas Lucy, of Charlecote, in 1615, as is shewn by the original deeds which are still extant. We are informed by Dugdale that "this last Sir Thomas *renewed* the park, and by the addition of Hampton Woods thereto enlarged it much."

A writer on Warwickshire, soon after the time of Shakespeare, says, "the country is divided into woodland and fielden, and the latter is much frequented by an animal more destructive than the ferocious beasts of old, viz., the sheep." This alludes to the great sheep-walks made in the time of Henry VIII., Elizabeth, and James, when wool became valuable. Now the line of road from Warwick to Stratford, over the red sandstone hills on the right bank of the Avon, is precisely along this natural division. On the right are the woodlands of Hampton-on-the-Hill, Grove Park, Hatton, Snitterfield, Edston, and Welcomb, forming part of the oak woods of the forest of Arden, of which this is the south-western extremity. On the left are the meadows of the Avon and the rich valley of Wasperton, Charlecote, Alveston, and the alluvial and clay lands beyond, where the elm is indigenous and abundant. Fulbroke Park pales extended for more than a mile along the Warwick and Stratford road, in the time of Richard III. A lane still marks one boundary of the park, Hampton parish another, the N.W. and S.E. sides are formed by the before-named road and the meadows along the Avon. The ground breaks away from the red sandstone plateau in endless combes, gentle slopes, and rounded heights, to the meadows. In flood-time the bright waters appear below; Hampton Wood, with the little eminences near it, closes in the view; in a line with this wood the brick and lime fragments in a ploughed field even now prove where the castle stood. Farther on, by the river, is a substantial farm-house, with a moat, the ancient park lodge; and near this is the site of the church noted in Henry the Eighth's first survey, but which had disappeared before the last of his reign, commonly called the King's Book. A few large trunks of ancient living trees remind one of the self-grown oak forest still existing here in the year 1560, but most of the ground is under the plough. Three good farms and six or seven cottages contain the little population of Fulbroke, and among these is a new cottage and homestead built on the site of the traditional Shakespeare's deer barn, about 200 yards from the before-named turnpike-road, and opposite the lane leading to Snitterfield. The noble tower of Hampton church closes the scene on the

C

west, rising above the elms which conceal Charlecote from the view.

From the age of 15 to 23, Shakespeare must have frequented woodland scenery, and learnt something of the woodcraft and field sports which he occasionally describes.* Surely there is no place in the neighbourhood of Stratford which he is more likely to have chosen for his rambles, than these wilds within three miles of his home. Hence may he have taken his type for his Arden, the Duke's Forest, his Windsor Forest, his Grove of Titania, &c., &c.

Thus, to this beautiful but obscure little district, long denuded of its church and parochial rights (for its handful of inhabitants obtain the rites of the Church of England, and attend her services, on sufferance only, at Hampton-Lucy or at Sherborne), is due one of the great episodes of Shakespeare's life. To Fulbroke and to the pastime it afforded to the Stratford yeoman's son are to be referred passages of his works, as enduring as the records of the deeds of arms of its possessors, princes and sovereigns though they were. If the battle-fields of England, such as Edge Hill, which may be seen from the spot, claim the respect of Englishmen, for the sake of the great and the brave who there wove their fortunes with the history of their country, Fulbroke should do more. It should claim the sympathy and remembrance of all who speak the English tongue; for the incidents recorded of Fulbroke tended specially to form the poet's mind, to stimulate his fancy, and to mould his fortunes. One character of the time connected with Fulbroke, pourtrayed with art and stamped with reality by the poet's power, is handed down to posterity, and accepted as a portrait as truly drawn as is Richard III or Henry V. However closely Sir Thomas Lucy may have been connected

* Note E.

with Shakespeare's personal history, Justice Shallow is no less so with his works, for he is one of the best known of the *dramatis personæ* which exist as the enduring creations of the genius of Shakespeare.

Note.

The writer has to apologize for many, and probably some wearisome repetitions. Treating the arguments simply, without attempt at any rhetoric or elegance of language, his only wish has been that the facts should be contemplated from different points of view. Any emendations or remarks which may occur to the judicious reader, will be received with thanks if forwarded to the Custodian of the Birth Place, Stratford-on-Avon.

APPENDIX.

NOTE A.

Acts relating to Parks and Forest Laws.

3 Edwd. I, cap. 20.—Punishes offenders against parks with three years' imprisonment, besides requiring sureties for their future good behaviour.

1 Henry VII, cap. 7, and 31 Henry VIII, cap. 12.—Make it a felony to enter a royal park disguised, in pursuit of deer.

32 Henry VIII, cap. 11.—Enacts further severities towards offenders against the Park Laws.

5 Eliz., cap. 21, sec. 3.—Enacts that, "if any person, at any time by day or night wrongfully break into any park impaled, or other ground enclosed with a wall, pale, or hedge, used for the keeping, breeding, or cherishing of deer; and so wrongfully hunt, drive out, chase, or take, kill or slay, any deer therein, and be lawfully convicted thereof at the suit of our Lady the Queen, he shall suffer imprisonment of his body by the space of three months, and shall yield treble damages, and after three months expired shall find sureties for the space of seven years, or shall remain without bail or mainprize for seven years aforesaid."

This last-named Act continued in force from 1562 during the whole of Shakespeare's life, and its enactments were extended to parks made subsequently, and by provisions as to the use of bows, crossbows, and guns therein, by the 3 James I, cap. 13, and by 7 James I, cap. 13.

NOTE B.

SIR FRANCIS ENGLEFIELD.

Sir Francis Englefield, of Englefield, in Berks, a descendant of Hasculfus de Englefyld, of the time of Canute, Privy Councillor to Queen Mary, not complying with the change of religion on the accession of Queen Elizabeth, fled abroad, in 1559, rather than conform. His lands and goods were seized for the use of Queen Elizabeth for his disobedience in not returning home, and for consorting with her enemies.* In 1564, he wrote a letter of apology and explanation to the Privy Council, denying that he had consorted with the enemies of the Queen, and excusing his disobedience on the plea of conscience, promising at the same time " to conform himself to the Queen's devotion, and to reside wherever she might desire," and praying "that he might be spared as hitherto to enjoy that portion of living still left to him." He was indicted for treason in the same year, upon a paper written by him falling into the hands of the Lord Treasurer Burghley, containing a list of persons in England receiving pensions from the King of Spain, among whom he, Englefield, was named as receiving £84 per annum. He, however, induced Philip II, of Spain, to intercede for him that he might be allowed to live where he liked and enjoy the income of his estates. In reply to this request, Elizabeth, in 1567, informed Philip that "although upon Englefield's refusal to return, the profits of his lands were stayed by order of her laws, to be answered unto her, yet she never received, neither did dispose to any other person, any part thereof, saving only that she directed to his wife upon her lamentable petition (being an heir, and by whom Sir Francis had a great portion of living) a small part, to maintain her in no meaner degree than belonged to his wife. And the rest of all his living had been for anything she knew disposed by his friends and servants to the use of the said Sir Francis as he appointed." Notwithstanding all this, Englefield, in 1570, addressed a presumptuous letter to Robert, Earl of Leicester, against the Queen's authority, and six years subsequently he again offended by executing a deed purporting to make over his estates to his nephew Francis. His conduct led to his being attainted and convicted of high treason in 1586, and his possessions forfeited. Sir Francis died in 1592, at Valladolid, and in the year following an Act was passed confirming the Queen's title to the estates, 35 Eliz. cap. 5. The nephew above referred to, Francis Englefield, Esq., of Wotton Bassett, Wilts, and Englefield, Berks, was made a Baronet in the 10th year of James I, 1613, his uncle having died without issue. The chief portion of his uncle's estates were

---

* See Strype's "Annals of Reformation," (Elizabeth's reign), book i., ch. 3. Strype's "Memorials," ch. 46. "History of Reformation," chap. 36, ann. 1563. Coke's "Institutes," as to Englefield's right to make over his ancient property.

granted to him, but the Fulbroke property was granted to Nicholas Faunt, Clerk of the Signet, with remainder to Margaret, widow of John Englefield, the brother of the exiled Knight, and so came into the possession of her son, Francis, the holder of the rest of the estates. Fulbroke was, however, no longer held *in capite*, but in fee simple, and Sir Francis, having the power of sale, transferred that estate to Sir Thomas Lucy, the third of that name, in 1615, two years after the death of his mother, Margaret. The deed showing the completion of this purchase still exists, having been lately discovered among the title-deeds of the Lucy family at Charlecote; so that there can be no doubt as to the date or legality of the transfer.

The following extracts from the "Calendars of State Papers, Domestic Series, 1547 to 1580," having reference to Sir Francis Englefield, amply prove the traitorous proceedings of Englefield and his deep attachment to the Roman Catholic cause.

EXTRACTS *from* "*Calendar of State Papers. Domestic Series* 1547 *to* 1580." (Longman, 1856.)

A.D. 1555, May 6. Sir Francis Englefield to Earl of Devonshire.—Recommends Mr. Cordell to be joined with him in trust for the Earl's affairs.

1555, Nov. 16. Earl of Devonshire to Englefield.—Thanks him for conducting his affairs, gives directions as to raising money, &c.

1558, Sept. 30. Queen Mary writes to Sir Francis Englefield, as Master of the Wards.

1558, Dec. 5. (Elizabeth.) Englefield to Secretary Cecil.—Advises caution in removal of officers of Customs.*

1562, July 24. Anonymous to the Queen.—Has conveyed letters to Englefield, and held treasonable conversation with his servant, concerning the restoration of the old religion.

1562, July 24. John Payne to Sir Francis Englefield.—Has delivered the letter and remembrances from the Lady Abbess and the nuns of Sion, the Prior of Shene, &c.

1563. July 13. Brief declaration of all manors, lands, &c., in the counties of Berks and Wilts, whereof Sir Francis Englefield is seized in his own or his wife's right, .&c.

1563, July 13. List of manors, lordships, and hundreds held by Sir Francis Englefield in right of Lady Catherine his wife.

1564, April 8. Francis Englefield to Sir William Cecil.—Complains of malicious insinuations against him to the prejudice of his suit to Her Majesty. Professes loyalty and reverence;

* This was his last letter as Privy Councillor.

sends copy of assignment of his wife's revenue, which he entreats may be faithfully performed.

1564, April 8. Sir Francis Englefield to the Council.—States his circumstances and supplicates the Queen's forgiveness.*

1564, November. A valuation of all lands held in Wilts and Berks, being possessions of Sir Francis Englefield, held seized to the Queen, with annuities and pensions paid out of the same.

1572, June 26. R. Hogan to Earl of Leicester.—Solicits lease of Sir Francis Englefield's lands.

1575, May 28. Sir Francis Englefield to William Cotton.—Fears the news of their banishment may deter many from lending assistance in the cause.

1575, August 3. Francis Englefield to William Cotton.—Recommends the bearer, Thomas Evans, " who may be trusted, though a Welshman."

1575, October 11. Sir Francis Englefield to William Cotton.—Says that his services to Don John and the Cardinals have been acknowledged.

1575, Dec. 10. Sir Francis Englefield to William Cotton.—Has been obliged to change his residence on account of his health and safety.

1576, June 2. Sir Francis Englefield to William Cotton.—Gives directions for his guidance in some secret transaction. The plot is new, rare, and without precedent.

1576, June 9. Countess of Northumberland to William Cotton.—Speaks of Englefield's ill health.

1605. Grant to Francis Englefield of the reversion of the manor of Wotton Bassett, and others, in the county of Wilts.

1607. Revenue of wards and liveries in years from 4th Elizabeth to 4th James 1. Note of Lord Salisbury; date of his appointment as Master of the Court of Records, and date of Sir William Cecil's, Sir T. Parry's, and Sir Francis Englefield's appointments.

1607, Sept. 26. Lease to Nicholas Faunt, Clerk of the Signet, with *reversion* to Margaret Englefield,† of Fulbroke Park, in the county of Warwick, belonging to Sir Francis Englefield, attainted.

* This is the year of Shakespeare's birth, and the fifth or sixth of Englefield's exile and residence, either in the Low Countries or Spain, under the protection of King Philip.

† This lady was the widow of John, brother of Sir Francis, and mother of Francis, his nephew and heir, afterwards created a baronet by King James. She died in 1612, in the forty-fifth year of her widowhood, and is buried at Englefield, Berks; it is evident her son became possessed of Fulbroke at her death, for he sold it in 1615 to Sir Thomas Lucy, third of the name. In his necessities, King James converted tenures granted *in capite* to tenures in fee simple, as in this case, receiving, no doubt, the difference of value.

NOTE C.

The Lucy Family.

An elaborate account of this family is found in Dugdale's "Warwickshire." From that work it appears that William de Lucy, a descendant of Gilbert de Gaunt, the nephew of William the Conqueror, had confirmation of the lordship of Charlecote from Thurston de Mountfort, son and heir of Henry de Mountfort, but had his lands seized for being in arms with the barons against King John. On returning to his allegiance, his estates were restored, and descended, through his son William, to his grandson Fouk, who, being a follower of the de Montforts in the rising against Henry III, was deprived of his estates, which were, however, restored to him by the Dictum de Kenilworth.

The family appears in the "Baronetage of England," published in 1741, in which is a detailed account of many knights and gentlemen holding important offices under the crown between the time of the above-named Fouk, and Sir Thomas Lucy, Knight, who was one of the sewers to Henry VIII, and High Sheriff of the counties of Warwick and Leicester in the sixteenth year of that king's reign. This knight it was who, in 1510, held the park of Fulbroke during the king's pleasure. He died 3rd September, 1525, and was succeeded by his son William, at whose death, in 1543, Charlecote passed into the hands of his son Thomas. In 1558 this gentleman built the manor-house of Charlecote, of brick, as it now stands. He was knighted in 1565, and elected knight of the shire in 1571 and 1585. There is no record of the exact date of his death, but we know that he was living till 1594, as in that year he erected a monument in Charlecote Church to the memory of his wife Joyce, daughter of Sir Thomas Acton.* Thomas, son of the above, was knighted by Queen Elizabeth in 1594, during the lifetime of his father. He married first, Dorothy, daughter of Nicholas Arnold, Esq., and secondly, Constance, daughter of Sir Richard Kingsmill. At his death, which occurred in 1603, a sumptuous monument was erected at Charlecote Church, bearing the effigies of the knight, his wives, and fourteen children. Thomas, the eldest son of the last-named gentleman, by his second wife, Constance, also received the honour of knighthood, and was elected knight of the shire for the county of Warwick in six Parliaments, from the 18th year of the reign of James I. (1621) to his own death, which occurred 8th December, 1640, in the 56th year of his age. He married Alice, daughter of Thomas Spencer, Esq., second son of Sir John Spencer, of Althorpe. Another monument adorns Charlecote Church, erected to his memory and that of his lady.

* It is clear, therefore, that to this first of the three Sir Thomas Lucys must be referred all which occurred till the thirtieth year of Shakespeare's age.

APPENDIX.

This knight, the grandson of the Sir Thomas who lived during the first thirty years of the life of Shakespeare, purchased the estate of Fulbroke from Sir Francis Englefield in 1615, two years after Sir Francis obtained it on his mother Margaret's death, as is testified by a deed still in possession of the Lucy family, and as stated by Dugdale, "He renewed the park, and by the addition of Hampton Woods thereto, enlarged it much." And it should be remarked that this word "renewed," used by the accurate Dugdale, confirms the opinion, that although the park had been legally established by the great Duke of Bedford in 1432; its privileges under the forest and park laws had ceased during Englefield's exile and attainder, inasmuch as he, the owner, could not even have kept up the fences, an absolute necessity to the constitution of a park; nor could he have prosecuted, either by self or agent, any offender or trespasser therein.

The family of the Lucys still hold the Charlecote and Fulbroke estates. George Lucy, Esq., of whom we read in Scott's Diary, at his death, left both estates to his eldest son, George Fulke, who died shortly after his succession. By his decease the estates descended to his brother Spencer, the present proprietor, who was in 1859, High Sheriff of the county of Warwick.*

NOTE D.

THE JUSTICE SHALLOW OF SHAKESPEARE.

It is generally held that the character of Justice Shallow in two of Shakespeare's plays, "The Merry Wives of Windsor," and "Henry IV," is that of Lucy, written in revenge for his persecution. The annexed table of extracts from the Chamberlain's Accounts of the borough of Stratford, proves incontestibly that Sir Thomas Lucy was in the habit of attending to public business at Stratford on such occasions as required that his entertainment should be paid for by the corporation; from which it may be fairly inferred that on many other occasions the knight was in attendance at that town for transacting such business as

* Great praise is due to George Lucy, Esq., and his lady, with whom Scott conversed, for the taste, perseverance and munificence which they displayed in restoring, enlarging, and decorating the old manor house of Charlecote, in rebuilding its church and parsonage, and in erecting excellent cottages and farm-houses all over the estates of Charlecote, Hampton-Lucy, and Fulbroke. At Hampton-Lucy, the present rector, the Rev. John Lucy, has not only thrown an elegant bridge over the Avon, where it was much required, but restored and enlarged the church with such taste and at such great expense that it may be considered a unique little rural cathedral among the country churches of the county of Warwick.

pertained to his office, as justice of the peace, custos rotulorum, &c., and the acts in force against Popish recusants, tippling, mendicants, &c., would give ample employment to an active justice, living near a borough town. Shakespeare would, therefore, as a youth, have many opportunities of seeing Sir Thomas in his official capacity; the Guildhall, where the justices would sit in commission, being a portion of the building in which was and still is situated the Grammar-school where the poet received his education. So observant a youth would not fail to notice the character and peculiarities of the justice and the persons by whom he was surrounded, and the incidents being vividly impressed on his memory might well be made use of in his delineations of Shallow, even without any feeling of revenge against Lucy. Vide following extracts from " Merry Wives of Windsor" and " Henry IV."

" MERRY WIVES OF WINDSOR," published 1602.

Act i, Scene 1.

Shallow. Sir Hugh, persuade me not; I will make a Star Chamber matter of it; if he were twenty Sir John Falstaffs he shall not abuse Robert Shallow, Esquire.

Slender. In the county of Gloucester, justice of the peace and corum.

Shallow. Ay, cousin Slender, and *custalorum.*

Slender. Ay, and *rotulorum** too, and a gentleman born, master parson, who writes himself *armigero* in any bill, warrant, quittance, or obligation.

Shallow. Ay, that I do, and have done any time these three hundred years.

Slender. All his successors gone before him have done't, and all his ancestors that come after him may; they may give the dozen white luces in their coat.

Shallow. It is an old coat.

Evans. The dozen white louses do become an old coat well; it agrees well passant; it is a familiar beast to man, and signifies love.

Shallow. The luce is the fresh fish, &c.

* * o * *

Falstaff. Now, master Shallow: you'll complain of me to the King.

Shallow. Knight, you have beaten my men, killed my deer, and broken open my lodge.

Falstaff. But not kissed your keeper's daughter.

* The dog Latin of the Justice and his follower, means to express that he is one of the senior justices of his county, one of the custodes rotulorum—which are necessary to make the quarter sessions a court of record.

Shallow. Tut! a pin! This shall be answered.
Falstaff. I will answer it straight. I have done all this. That is now answered.
Shallow. The council shall know this.
Falstaff. 'Twere better for you if 'twere not known in council. You'll be laughed at.

* * * *

Evans. Pauca verba, Sir John. Goot worts.
Falstaff. Goot worts! good cabbage. Slender, I broke your What matter have you against me. [head.
Slender. Marry, sir, I have matter in my head against you; and against your coney-catching rascals Bardolph, Nym, and Pistol.

* * * * *

" HENRY IV." Part 2.

Act iii, Scene 3.

Falstaff. I do see the bottom of Justice Shallow. Lord, Lord, how subject we old men are to this vice of lying. This same starved justice hath done nothing but prate to me of the wildness of his youth and the feats he hath done about Turnbull-street; and every third word a lie, duer paid to the hearer than the Turk's tribute. I do remember him at Clement's Inn, like a man made after supper of a cheese-paring. * * *
It shall go hard but I will make him a philosopher's two stones to me.* If the young dace be a bait for the old pike, I see no reason in the law of nature but I may snap at him.

* * * * *

Act v, Scene 1.

Falstaff. If I were sawed into quantities I should make four dozen of such bearded hermits' staves as Master Shallow. It is a wonderful thing to see the semblable coherence of his men's spirits and his. They by observing him do bear themselves like foolish justices: he by conversing with them is turned into a justice-like serving man ; their spirits are so married in conjunction with the participation of society that they flock together in consent, like so many wild geese. If I had to suit Master Shallow I would humour his men with the imputation of being near their master: if to his men, I would curry with Master Shallow that no man could better command his servants. It is certain that either wise bearing or ignorant carriage is caught as men take diseases, one of another: therefore let men take heed of their

---

* This is the key to Shakespeare's treatment of Shallow—to strike the sparks of wit from two cold and hard flints.

company. I will devise matter enough out of this Shallow to keep Prince Harry in continual laughter.*

TABLE OF EXTRACTS FROM THE CHAMBERLAIN'S ACCOUNT BOOKS.

1578. To John Smith for a pottell of wine, and a quarterne of sugar for Sir Thomas Lucy .. .. .. xvj$d$

1584. Paid for a quart of secke, a pottell of claret wyne, and a quarterne of sugar for Sir Thomas Lucy, Knight, the 16th Januarie, 1583 .. .. ij$s$. jd.

1586. Paid for wine and sugar when Sir Thomas Lucie satt in commission for tipplers .. .. .. xx$d$.

1595. For sacke and clarett wine for Sir Thomas Lucie and my ladie, and Mr. Sherife, at the Swanne .. .. iij$s$.
Paid att the Swanne for a quart of sacke and a quartern of sugar burned for Sir Thomas Lucie .. .. xvj$d$.

1597. Pd. the 20th January, 1596, for wine and sugar that Mr. Rogers bestowed on Sir Thomas Lucye and another gent .. .. vj$s$. vj$d$.
Payd to Edward Aynge for a quart of sake and a quartern of sugar bestowed on Sur Thomas Lusy and Mr. Burgon at the Swanne .. .. xxj$d$.

1604. Paid to Mr. Baliefe for fishe that the maisters had when they went to welcome Sir Tho. Lucie into the countrie, Novemb. 16 .. .. vj$s$. viij$d$.

NOTE E.

EXTRACTS SHOWING SHAKESPEARE'S KNOWLEDGE OF SPORTING, WOODCRAFT, &c.

"MIDSUMMER NIGHT'S DREAM."

Act iv, Scene 1.

Theseus. Go, one of you, find out the forester; my love shall hear the musick of my hounds. Uncouple in the western valley;

---

* As Sir Thomas Lucy, the supposed prototype of Shallow, was elected knight of the shire for the county of Warwick, in 1571, and again in 1585, (in the twenty-first year of Shakespeare's life.) He may have been remembered in London, when this play was acted (probably) in 1601. By these dates, too, it is clear that Shakespeare in London could not have escaped the search of so public a man, had he been guilty of any act which could have legally been brought before the Star Chamber, or any lower court under the statute law. If the story be true, that when he first went to London, he employed boys to hold gentlemen's horses, who answered to the call of "Shakespeare's boy!" it proves that he let his name be publicly known immediately as connected with the theatre.

go—despatch, I say, and find the forester. We will, fair queen, up to the mountain top, and mark the musical confusion of hounds and echo in conjunction.

Hippolyta. I was with Hercules and Cadmus once, when in the wood of Crete they bay'd the bear with hounds of Sparta. Never did I hear such gallant chiding; for, besides the groves, the skies, the fountains, every region near seemed all one mutual cry: I never heard so musical a discord, such sweet thunder.

Theseus. My hounds are bred out of the Spartan kind, so flew'd, so sanded; and their heads are hung with ears that sweep away the morning dew; crook-kneed and dew-lapped like Thessalian bulls; slow in pursuit, but match'd in mouth like bells, each under each. A cry more tuneable was never holla'd to, nor cheer'd with horn, in Crete, in Sparta, nor in Thessaly. Judge, when you hear.

* * * * *

"Henry VI." Part 3.

Act iii, Scene 1.

Sinklo (a forester). Under this thick-grown brake we'll shroud ourselves,
For through this laund anon the deer will come;
And in this covert will we make our stand,
Culling the principal of all the deer.

Humphrey (another forester). I'll stay above the hill, so both may shoot.

Sinklo. That cannot be; the noise of thy cross-bow
Will scare the herd, and so my shoot is lost.
Here stand we both, and aim we at the best:
And, for the time shall not seem tedious,
I'll tell thee what befell me on a day,
In this same place where now we mean to stand.

* * * * * *

"Love's Labour Lost."

Act iv, Scene 1.

Princess. Then, forester, my friend, where is the bush,
That we must stand and play the murderer in?

Forester. Here by, upon the edge of yonder coppice;
A stand, where you may make the fairest shoot.

* * * * *

Act iv, Scene 2.

Holofernes. Will you hear an extemporal epitaph
On the death of the deer? And to humour the ignorant
I have called the deer the Princess kill'd, a pricket.

* * * * *

"AS YOU LIKE IT."

Act i, Scene 1.

Charles. They say he is already in the Forest of Arden,* and many merry men with him, and there they live like the old Robin Hood of England.

* * * * *

Act ii, Scene 1.

First Lord. To-day my lord of Amiens and myself,
   Did steal behind him, as he lay along
   Under an oak, whose antique root peeps out
   Upon the brook that brawls along this wood:
   To which place a poor sequestered stag
   That from the hunter's aim had ta'en a hurt,
   Did come to lanquish; and, indeed, my Lord,
   The wretched animal heaved forth such groans,
   That their discharge did stretch his leathern coat
   Almost to bursting; and the big round tears
   Cours'd one another down his innocent nose
   In piteous chase: and thus the hairy fool,
   Much marked of the melancholy Jaques,
   Stood on the extremest verge of the swift brook,
   Augmenting it with tears.

* * * * *

Act iv, Scene 3.

Jaques. Which is he that killed the deer?
1st Lord. Sir, it was I.
Jaques. Let's present him to the duke, like a Roman conqueror; and it would do well to set the deer's horns upon his head for a branch of victory. Have you no song, forester, for this purpose.
2nd Lord. Yes, sir.
Jaques. Sing it: 'tis no matter how it be in tune, so it make noise enough.

   " What shall he have, that kill'd the deer?
   His leather skin, and horns to wear,
    Then sing him home.
   Take thou no scorn, to wear the horn;
   It was a crest, ere thou wast born."
          &c., &c., &c.

* * * * *

---

* This is generally thought to mean the Forest of the Ardennes, near Aix-la-Chapelle, but Shakespeare, no doubt, selected the name as the same as that of the Forest of Arden, in Warwickshire, a very large tract of the oak-growing, red sandstone district, at the S.W. angle of which is Fulbroke.

THE "TAMING OF THE SHREW."

Induction. Scene 1.

Lord. Huntsman, I charge thee tender well my hounds.
Brach Merriman,—the poor cur is imbossed.*
And couple Clowder with the deep-mouthed Brach.
Saw'st thou not, boy, how Silver made it good
At the hedge corner, in the coldest fault?
I would not lose the dog for twenty pound.
  Huntsman. Why, Belman is as good as he, my Lord,
He cried upon it at the merest loss,
And twice to-day picked out the dullest scent.

* * * * *

Act i, Scene 2.

Lord. Dost thou love hawking?. thou hast hawks will soar
Above the morning lark: or wilt thou hunt?
Thy hounds shall make the welkin answer them
And fetch shrill echoes from the hollow earth.
  1st Servant. Say thou wilt course; thy greyhounds are as swift
As breathed stags,—Ay, fleeter than the roe.

* * * * *

NOTE F.

THE PLAYERS.

We learn from the account books of the Chamberlain of Stratford, which are still preserved, that the under-mentioned companies of Players visited Stratford at the dates given below, viz.:—

Queen's Players, in 1569, when Shakespeare was 5 years old.

Earl of Worcester's Players, in 1569, when Shakespeare was 5 years old.

Earl of Leicester's Players, in 1573, when Shakespeare was 9 years old.

Lord Warwick and Worcester's Players, in 1576, when Shakespeare was 12 years old.

Lord Leicester and Worcester's Players, in 1577, when Shakespeare was 13 years old.

---

* *Imbossed,* foaming at the mouth from over fatigue.

WITHDRAWN

HARVARD LIBRARY

WITHDRAWN

Religious Ethics and Constructivism

In metaethics, there is a divide between those (i.e., moral realists) who believe that there exist moral facts independently of human interests and attitudes and those (i.e., antirealists) who don't. In the last half century, the field of religious ethics has been inundated with various antirealist schools of moral thought. Though there is a wide spectrum of different positions within antirealism, a number of antirealist religious ethicists tend to see moral belief as a historically dependent social construction. This has created an environment where doing religious ethics in any metaphysically substantial sense is often seen not only as out of fashion but also as philosophically implausible.

However, there is a lack of clarity as to what antirealists exactly mean by "construction" and what arguments they would use to support their views. *Religious Ethics and Constructivism* brings together a diverse group of scholars who represent different philosophical and theological outlooks to discuss the merits of constructivism vis-à-vis religious ethics. The essays explore four different kinds of constructivism in metaethics: Kantian, Humean, Hegelian, and theistic constructivisms. The overall aims of these essays are to foster dialogue between religious ethicists and moral philosophers and to open the field of religious ethics to the insights that can be provided by contemporary metaethics.

Kevin Jung is Associate Professor of Christian Ethics at Wake Forest University School of Divinity, USA. He is the author of *Christian Ethics and Commonsense Morality: An Intuitionist Account* (Routledge, 2014) and *Ethical Theory and Responsibility Ethics* (2011).

Routledge Studies in the Philosophy of Religion

God and the Multiverse
Scientific, Philosophical, and Theological Perspectives
Edited by Klaas J. Kraay

Christian Ethics and Commonsense Morality
An Intuitionist Account
Kevin Jung

Philosophical Approaches to the Devil
Edited by Benjamin W. McCraw and Robert Arp

Galileo and the Conflict between Religion and Science
Gregory W. Dawes

The Arguments of Aquinas
A Philosophical View
J. J. MacIntosh

Philosophical Approaches to Demonology
Edited by Benjamin W. McCraw and Robert Arp

Eighteenth-Century Dissent and Cambridge Platonism
Reconceiving the Philosophy of Religion
Louise Hickman

Systematic Atheology
Atheism's Reasoning with Theology
John R. Shook

Does God Matter?
Essays on the Axiological Consequences of Theism
Edited by Klaas J. Kraay

Religious Ethics and Constructivism
A Metaethical Inquiry
Edited by Kevin Jung

Religious Ethics and Constructivism
A Metaethical Inquiry

Edited by Kevin Jung

Routledge
Taylor & Francis Group
NEW YORK AND LONDON

First published 2018
by Routledge
711 Third Avenue, New York, NY 10017

and by Routledge
2 Park Square, Milton Park, Abingdon, Oxon OX14 4RN

Routledge is an imprint of the Taylor & Francis Group, an informa business

© 2018 Taylor & Francis

The right of the editor to be identified as the author of the editorial material, and of the authors for their individual chapters, has been asserted in accordance with sections 77 and 78 of the Copyright, Designs and Patents Act 1988.

All rights reserved. No part of this book may be reprinted or reproduced or utilized in any form or by any electronic, mechanical, or other means, now known or hereafter invented, including photocopying and recording, or in any information storage or retrieval system, without permission in writing from the publishers.

Trademark notice: Product or corporate names may be trademarks or registered trademarks, and are used only for identification and explanation without intent to infringe.

Library of Congress Cataloging-in-Publication Data
A catalog record for this book has been requested

ISBN: 978-1-138-10341-2 (hbk)
ISBN: 978-1-315-10276-4 (ebk)

Typeset in Sabon
by Apex CoVantage, LLC

Contents

	Acknowledgments	vi
	Introduction KEVIN JUNG	1
1	Kantian Constructivism, Baseball, and Christian Ethics PAUL WEITHMAN	21
2	A Humean Account of What Wrongness Amounts To KEVIN KINGHORN	40
3	Constructivism in Ethics: A View from Hegelian Semantics MOLLY FARNETH	63
4	What Should Theists Say about Constructivist Positions in Metaethics? CHRISTIAN B. MILLER	82
5	Kantian Constructivism, Autonomy, and Religious Ethics CHARLES LOCKWOOD	104
6	On the Moral Significance of Nature: A Comparison of Hegelian Constructivism and Natural Law DAVID A. CLAIRMONT	128
7	Grounds of Normativity: Constructivism, Realism, and Theism KEVIN JUNG	178
	List of Contributors	205
	Index	207

Acknowledgments

This collection of essays developed out of the perceived need for a book which would address a number of philosophical and theological issues related to an ethical theory of growing importance in the field of religious ethics. It is the hope that this book will help engender and renew interest in metaethics among religious ethicists, while serving as a benchmark for further scholarship on constructivism in religious ethics. The goal has been to make the collection as representative as possible without being overly comprehensive.

I wish to acknowledge the support of the Dialogue on Science, Ethics, and Religion (DoSER) program of the American Association for the Advancement of Science (AAAS), which made possible the workshop "Constructivism and Religious Ethics" at Wake Forest University on September 30–October 1, 2016, on which this volume originally is based. I thank in particular Dr. Jennifer Wiseman, Director of DoSER, and Se Kim, Program Director, for their generous support.

I also thank all who participated in the workshop discussion and those who later joined the book project. All of them worked graciously, critiquing other's papers and being willing to revise their own papers multiple times in light of received comments. I wish to acknowledge two colleagues in particular who were very helpful in various developmental stages of this book project. Per Sundman, who co-chaired with me the Moral Theory Interest Group at the Society of Christian Ethics, helped convene a panel on constructivism in 2016 and subsequently made a meaningful contribution to the workshop discussion. Christian Miller provided valuable comments on my own writing in this volume. Finally, special thanks are due to my research assistant, Graham Lee, whose excellent and diligent editorial skills were instrumental in preparing the manuscript.

Kevin Jung
Winston Salem, NC
December 2017

Introduction

Kevin Jung

I. An Overview of Constructivism

Is mathematics discovered or invented? This rather simple question divides the opinions of contemporary theoretical mathematicians and physicists as well as philosophers of mathematics.[1] Those who are called "realists" support the view that math is discovered, often appealing to the uncanny ability of mathematics to explain certain natural phenomena with mathematical equations. If nature itself does not contain mathematical properties, they ask, how do we explain what Eugene Wigner calls "the unreasonable effectiveness of mathematics," the fact that mathematics has been so effective in building models that help us understand past and current natural phenomena and predict natural events in the future?[2] The theoretical physicist Max Tegmark even goes as far as to say that "our reality isn't just described by mathematics—it is mathematics."[3]

In contrast, those called "constructivists" argue that mathematical objects are human constructs that we use to suit our practical purposes. Some constructivists suggest that the evolution of mathematical ideas, whereby only those ideas that are able to solve new problems are selected, can explain the relative success of mathematics. Furthermore, other constructivists argue that mathematical reality is located in the physical world, albeit inside the human brain. The English mathematician Michael Atiyah says,

> If one views the brain in its evolutionary context then the mysterious success of mathematics in the physical sciences is at least partially explained. The brain evolved in order to deal with the physical world,

---

1. See Mario Livio, *Is God a Mathematician?* (New York: Simon & Schuster, 2010).
2. Eugene P. Wigner, "The Unreasonable Effectiveness of Mathematics in the Natural Sciences," *Communications on Pure and Applied Mathematics* 13, no. 1 (February 1, 1960): 1–14.
3. Max Tegmark, *Our Mathematical Universe: My Quest for the Ultimate Nature of Reality* (New York: Vintage, 2015), 254.

so it should not be too surprising that it has developed a language, mathematics, this is well suited for its purpose.[4]

On this view, there would be no mathematical properties or principles in the universe were humans not to exist.

One finds an analogous debate in contemporary moral philosophy. Therein the question is whether morality is discovered or invented.[5] Do moral facts exist independently of human attitudes, or are all moral facts human constructs? Constructivists about morality[6] (hereafter constructivists) believe that morality is something that is made or invented, rather than discovered, a construction that is dependent on the particular responses of the relevant respondent(s). Constructivism is often understood—though it need not be—as involving a procedure of construction whereby "there are answers to moral questions *because* there are correct procedures for arriving at them."[7] The basic idea for the proceduralist kind of constructivism is that there are no moral facts independent of a certain hypothetical or idealized procedure that determines which principles constitute moral facts.

Why an *idealized* but not an actual procedure? Some proceduralists may be concerned with moral relativism concerning truth—the view, roughly, that moral truths are relative to one's epistemic context—that might follow from articulating the principles from an actual procedure used by actual respondents. Other proceduralists may be motivated to distinguish moral facts from either *unreflective* evaluative attitudes or those evaluative attitudes that are neither logically nor instrumentally entailed from the whole set of other evaluative attitudes.[8] Also, idealizing the procedure of practical reasoning can in some way afford constructivism with a degree of the objectivity that it seeks (I will return to the topic of objectivity momentarily). On

---

4. Quoted from Livio, *Is God a Mathematician?* 243. Atiyah's view is echoed by Jean-Pierre Changeux, a neuroscientist who said that "mathematical objects exist materially in your brain. You examine them inwardly by a conscious process, in the physiological sense of the term. Our brain is a complex physical object. As such, it constructs 'representations' corresponding to physical states." Jean-Pierre Changeux and Alain Connes, *Conversations on Mind, Matter, and Mathematics*, trans. M. B. DeBevoise (Princeton: Princeton University Press, 1995), 13–14.
5. Admittedly, there are other options. For instance, nihilists simply deny that morality exists. According to nihilism, there are no moral facts, and thus, all ethical propositions are false. Nihilism, however, takes ethical statements to be truth-apt, even though there are no moral truths. It bears mentioning that nihilism can be made compatible with some versions of constructivism (e.g., fictionalism).
6. It should be noted that one can be a constructivist about a broad range of things such as knowledge, gender, and art. In this volume, we are mainly concerned with morality as a human or divine construction.
7. Christine M. Korsgaard, *The Sources of Normativity* (New York: Cambridge University Press, 1996), 36.
8. See Sharon Street, "A Darwinian Dilemma for Realist Theories of Value," *Philosophical Studies* 127, no. 1 (2006): 110–11.

the constructivist view, then, moral facts are fixed not by mind-independent but by mind-dependent facts. Constructivists hold to a kind of antirealism in the metaphysical sense, denying that moral facts can exist independently of the attitudes of the relevant respondent(s).[9] But not all antirealists are constructivists *proper*. In some important ways, constructivism accepts certain realist features of morality even as it parts ways with realism on some key issues. This helps differentiate constructivism from other antirealist theories.

Let me briefly identify several basic features of (non-theistic) constructivism by way of comparison with realism. First, (non-theistic) constructivism meets realism halfway concerning the function of ethical statements. Both consider ethical statements to represent moral reality, but unlike realism, constructivism doesn't find the need to postulate a realm of mind-independent moral facts in order to make such representation possible. Moral facts are not entities of a strange sort but are a function of moral judgments that are the outcome of correct procedures of practical reasoning. In this respect, constructivism, on a standard taxonomy, is to be distinguished from various forms of expressivism, which seek to explain the meaning of moral utterances in terms of their role in expressing the speaker's feelings or other conative states.[10]

A second feature of constructivism is that ethical statements are capable of being true or false; constructivism is a cognitivist theory about ethical statements.[11] Since constructivism views moral facts as a function of our attitudes, some ethical statements will be determined to be true or false according to the moral facts constructed. To be sure, constructivism and realism are not alone in insisting that ethical statements have truth-values. The moral error theory considers moral discourse to aspire to represent moral reality and takes a cognitivist approach to moral claims.[12] Yet the moral error theory concludes that all moral claims are false since there are no mind-independent moral facts or entities that would make the claims

---

9. Realism can be construed in different ways. Unless noted otherwise, I use the term *realism* in the metaphysical sense, in distinction from the semantic, epistemic, and explanatory senses. For more on various approaches to realism in general and to moral realism, see Christian Miller, "Introduction," in *The Bloomsbury Companion to Ethics* (New York: Bloomsbury Publishing, 2011), xxvi–xxx; "The Conditions of Moral Realism," *Journal of Philosophical Research* 34 (2009): 123–55.
10. The family of expressivism includes emotivism (Ayer and Stevenson), prescriptivism (R. M. Hare), quasi-realism (Simon Blackburn), and norm-expressivism (Allan Gibbard).
11. There is no single definition of cognitivism (or noncognitivism). Christian Miller provides the following helpful characterization of cognitivism:

    Moral judgments are or are expressions of cognitive mental states such as beliefs.
    Ethical statements are truth-apt or truth-evaluable.
    Ethical statements are factual.
    Ethical statements purport to represent the world as being a certain way.
    Miller, "Introduction," xxxi.
12. The moral error theory is a species of moral nihilism.

true. For the error theorist, ordinary moral judgments are not meaningless but false.[13] For example, moral judgments such as "torture is wrong" are treated as uniformly false. But the constructivist does not share this view of the error theorist, although the constructivist certainly takes her approach to be cognitivist.

As compared to constructivism, it is a bit difficult to locate where expressivism falls on the issue of cognitivism/noncognitivism. Expressivism is generally considered to be noncognitivist because it holds that the function of moral judgments is to express one's conative attitudes rather than to represent real states of affairs. This is certainly true of classic versions of expressivism such as emotivism and prescriptivism.[14] For instance, moral judgments such as "stealing is bad" are supposed to express the speaker's sentiment of disapproval toward the action. But this does not keep some contemporary expressivists like Simon Blackburn from arguing that their account of expressivism is cognitivist enough.[15] This is because the expressivist can employ a deflationary theory of truth that denies that truth is a metaphysically real property; it treats truth as a minimal or deflated property of truth-bearers.[16] On this theory of truth, the expressivist could argue that, if we deflate the truth-predicate, to say "S is true" is not to affirm "S's possessing the property of truth; it's rather more like just asserting S all by itself."[17] The expressivist's argument then goes like this: If truth is not a property that is ascribed to a truth-maker, to a relation between truth-maker and truth-bearer, to a relation among truth-bearers, or to pragmatic utility,[18] why can't we *ascribe* truth to an ethical statement?

13. See J. L. Mackie, *Ethics: Inventing Right and Wrong* (New York: Penguin, 1991), 40.
14. For emotivism, see A. J. Ayer, "Critique of Ethics and Theology," in *Language, Truth, and Logic* (New York: Dover Publications, 1952), 108; C. L. Stevenson, "The Emotive Meaning of Ethical Terms," in *Logical Positivism*, ed. A. J. Ayer (Glencoe: Free Press, 1959), 269. For prescriptivism, see R. M. Hare, *The Language of Morals* (Oxford: Clarendon Press, 1952); *Essays in Ethical Theory* (New York: Oxford University Press, 1993).
15. Simon Blackburn, *Essays in Quasi-Realism* (Oxford: Oxford University Press, 1993), 6.
16. All deflationary theories of truth deny that truth is a metaphysical property. According to them, the truth-predicate has only a logical, performative, or grammatical function; it does not add any substantial information to what is already asserted in the statement. Deflationary theorists therefore believe that the question of what truth *is*, is uninteresting. Blackburn subscribes to the minimalist theory of truth (a deflationary theory of truth) that takes truth as a minimal (or deflated) property of propositions. So does Allan Gibbard. See Allan Gibbard, *Thinking How to Live* (Cambridge: Harvard University Press, 2003), 18–19. For discussion of the minimalist theory of truth, see Paul Horwich, *Truth* (Oxford: Clarendon Press, 1998).
17. Matthew Chrisman, "Ethical Expressivism," in *The Bloomsbury Companion to Ethics* (New York: Bloomsbury Publishing, 2011), 41.
18. Deflationary theories of truth are not theories about what truth *is*. They deny that truth is a property of propositions (the correspondence theory of truth) or that truth consists in the agreement of a proposition with some other specified set of propositions (the coherence theory of truth). Nor do they support the view that truth is the name of what is expedient or useful by way of accepting a proposition (the pragmatic theory of truth).

A third feature of constructivism is its commitment to the idea that some degree or some kind of moral objectivity is possible. In general, the realist believes that moral objectivity requires the existence of mind-independent facts. These would be facts that exist independently of what we happen to care about or what we would counterfactually care about. Their existence is independent of the contingent needs and interests of individuals and societies. A standard realist claim is that mind-independent facts can ultimately justify our moral claims and give sufficient reasons for action. Meanwhile, the constructivist holds that realism so understood is not a necessary condition for moral objectivity.[19] It isn't a necessary condition, according to some Kantian constructivists, because

> it might be thought that even if there is no such thing as a mind-independent moral reality, morality can make inescapable claims on us in virtue of the fact that a commitment to some moral claims is a necessary feature of sound practical reasoning.[20]

Very briefly, the basic idea is that, if norms of morality are logically entailed by agency, we are necessarily bound to these norms as long as agency is something we cannot escape. Kantian constructivists, in particular, usually consider the *inescapability* of agency as an important requirement for moral objectivity.

In comparison, Humean constructivists are far less sanguine about the prospects of a Kantian account of constructivism that seeks to underwrite moral objectivity as an intrinsic feature of moral agency that all rational agents are necessarily bound to accept on pain of irrationality (see Chapters 1 and 7). Instead, many Humean constructivists think that "there are no facts about normative reasons apart from the standpoint of an agent who is already taking things to be reasons" (see Chapter 2 for a Humean constructivist account of deontic facts).[21] On this Humean view, all moral values are entailed from within the practical point of view of each individual, although it is possible that there are some overlapping values among us since we share similar biological tendencies and desires that motivate us to pursue certain objects. As Sharon Street puts it, "this secures all the moral objectivity one could ever sensibly want or hope for, and is likely to view normative facts of the kind posited by the realist as naturalistically incomprehensible and not to the point anyway."[22]

---

19. Hallvard Lillehammer, "Constructivism and the Error Theory," in *The Bloomsbury Companion to Ethics* (New York: Bloomsbury Publishing, 2011), 56–7.
20. Ibid., 57.
21. Sharon Street, "Coming to Terms with Contingency: Humean Constructivism About Practical Reason," in *Constructivism in Practical Philosophy*, ed. James Lenman and Yonatan Shemmer (New York: Oxford University Press, 2012), 48.
22. Sharon Street, "What Is Constructivism in Ethics and Metaethics?" *Philosophy Compass* 5, no. 5 (May 1, 2010): 380.

6 *Kevin Jung*

Meanwhile, Hegelian constructivists[23] also agree with Kantian constructivists that mind-independent facts can never give sufficient reason for action. But Hegelian constructivists do not think that there is a structure of practical reasoning that inescapably commits us to some substantive moral values. For this brand of constructivism, moral objectivity is not an intrinsic feature of moral agency,[24] for example, how we constitute our agency—but "a feature of the structure of discursive intersubjectivity" that transcends the attitudes of practitioners.[25] In this view, objectivity is given "an essentially *social* construal," although it is irreducible to communal agreement (see Farneth's essay in this volume for more details).[26]

In short, various constructivist approaches to moral objectivity try to give some account of it, despite however unsatisfying it may appear to the moral realist.

Earlier, I briefly characterized constructivism as the view that morality is something that is made or invented, a construction that is dependent on the particular responses of the relevant respondent(s). But some constructivist positions are more ambitious in trying to account for the normative in general. This raises the question, "Exactly what is it that constructivists believe can be constructed?" Perhaps the most obvious candidates for construction are *facts*. In a non-theistic version of constructivism, any moral facts obtain only because we humans have constructed them in a way that reflects our attitudes or interests, albeit through some hypothetical process of practical reasoning. But what facts are subject to our construction really depends on the aim and the method of construction itself. As Carla Bagnoli notes,

> the metaphor of construction leaves open the question of whether there is more than one way in which rational agents can proceed in thinking of themselves and others, and thus in following the procedure that constitutes the norms or values of morality.[27]

---

23. For the purposes of this book, I take social constructivism as the view that involves at least one of the following claims: a metaphysical claim, an epistemic claim, or a semantic claim. The metaphysical claim says that what there is, is socially constructed; the epistemic claim states that what we believe or know is a matter of social construction; and the semantic claim states that meaning of any terms is socially constructed. Hegelian constructivism is sometimes known as social constructivism, but some Hegelian constructivists may object to their kind of constructivism being lumped together with social constructivism because of the latter's possible connotation of epistemic relativism. Hegelian constructivists provide a much more nuanced account of truth and objectivity (see Farneth's essay in this volume). For this reason, I distinguish social constructivism from Hegelian constructivism in this book.
24. Korsgaard believes that a sufficient ground of moral objectivity is entailed from the conditions for self-constituting agency. See Christine M. Korsgaard, *Self-Constitution: Agency, Identity, and Integrity* (New York: Oxford University Press, 2009).
25. Robert Brandom, *Making It Explicit: Reasoning, Representing, and Discursive Commitment* (Cambridge: Harvard University Press, 1994), 599; *Articulating Reasons: An Introduction to Inferentialism* (Cambridge: Harvard University Press, 2000), 196–8.
26. Brandom, *Making It Explicit: Reasoning, Representing, and Discursive Commitment*, 599.
27. Carla Bagnoli, "Introduction," in *Constructivism in Ethics*, ed. Carla Bagnoli (Cambridge: Cambridge University Press, 2013), 2.

Some constructivists restrict the scope of construction to some class of moral judgments, such as deontic judgments about right and wrong,[28] while others extend the scope to encompass evaluative judgments about what we ought to be or do.[29] Hence, depending on the constructivist, facts that are said to be constructible could be about a whole range of normative (both deontic and evaluative) judgments or only about some limited class of moral judgments.

Another candidate for construction, though by no means universally accepted by constructivists, is *meaning*. The idea that the meaning of normative terms can be constructed by us could be particularly appealing to a broad group of social constructivists, including Hegelian constructivists, who take both the meaning of moral terms and moral facts to be a social construction. A crude form of constructivism about meaning may simply assert that all meaning is socially constructed because the meanings of linguistic expressions can only be explained in terms of their *use* and because the use of linguistic expressions is, in the final analysis, no private matter but depends on social practice. On a more refined form of constructivism about meaning, it has been argued that meaning *is* normative. The basic idea is twofold: first, the meaning of a word is not independent of its relations to other words and sentences but, instead, is determined by the inferential relations; second, the key to understanding the inferential relations between words (or sentences) is to articulate inference rules by elucidating the attitude of assigning a normative significance to someone. To put this in Brandomian language, one can explain semantic contents only by identifying inferential relations in linguistic practices that structure and assign specific roles to intentional states and expressions, and the inferential articulation of semantic contents requires the social and discursive articulation of what Brandom calls deontic scorekeeping attitudes.[30] Since "this social articulation of scorekeeping practice is essentially normative in force," meaning is

---

28. "Restricted" constructivism is only interested in giving an account of the correctness of certain moral claims. For restricted constructivism, see Ronald Milo, "Contractarian Constructivism," *Journal of Philosophy* 92, no. 4 (1995): 181–204; Thomas M. Scanlon, *What We Owe to Each Other* (Cambridge: Harvard University Press, 1998); *Being Realistic About Reasons* (Oxford: Oxford University Press, 2014); Thomas E. Hill, "Moral Construction as a Task: Sources and Limits," *Social Philosophy and Policy* 25, no. 1 (2008): 214–36. For unrestricted (or thoroughgoing) constructivism, see Onora O'Neill, *Constructions of Reason: Explorations of Kant's Practical Philosophy* (Cambridge and New York: Cambridge University Press, 1990); Korsgaard, *The Sources of Normativity*; Carla Bagnoli, "Moral Constructivism: A Phenomenological Argument," *Topoi* 21, no. 1–2 (2002): 125–38; Sharon Street, "Constructivism about Reasons," *Oxford Studies in Metaethics* 3 (2008): 207–45.
29. "Unrestricted" (or "thoroughgoing") constructivism gives an account of the correctness of any normative claims. For the distinction between restricted and unrestricted forms of constructivism, see Street, "What Is Constructivism in Ethics and Metaethics?" 367–70.
30. In a nutshell, these are Brandom's ideas of inferentialist semantics and normative pragmatics.

said to be normative.[31] Therefore, those, such as Hegelian constructivists, who are persuaded by this kind of semantics may be inclined to see meaning, in addition to normative facts, as subject to human construction.

II. Constructivism and Religious Ethics

Having briefly outlined some major features of constructivism, I want to say a few words about why the discussion of constructivism is relevant to religious ethics since this book is about constructivism in religious ethics. Traditionally, many religious thinkers in the West have been moral realists. But this may no longer be the case today. In the last half century, the field of religious ethics has been inundated with various antirealist schools of moral thought. Strongly influenced by these schools of thought—from deconstructionism to pragmatism—contemporary religious ethicists often implicitly, if not explicitly, endorse antirealism. In fact, it is not difficult to find scholars in contemporary religious ethics who argue that the justification of moral belief and the normativity of action are ultimately grounded in historical traditions and their social practices. Moreover, some religious thinkers have questioned whether metaphysically robust theories of truth and value are necessary for doing religious ethics.[32] Some have gone further, agreeing with Michel Foucault that "what counts as knowledge is constituted within networks of power—social, political, and economic" and nothing more.[33] To use the term *construction* rather loosely, many contemporary religious thinkers see religious morality as a human construction that reflects the contingent needs, interests, or attitudes of religious practitioners.

However, there is a great deal of unclarity as to what these religious thinkers would mean by "construction" and whether they are aware of all of the philosophical implications of such an approach to religious ethics. Unlike in the field of philosophical ethics, there has been virtually no general overview of or in-depth investigation into different forms of constructivism in religious ethics. Nor have there been any rigorous philosophical and theological appraisals of the various forms of constructivism by religious ethicists. This is where this book enters. It brings together a diverse group of scholars representing different philosophical and theological outlooks to discuss the merits of constructivism vis-à-vis religious ethics.

---

31. Brandom, *Making It Explicit: Reasoning, Representing, and Discursive Commitment*, 627.
32. See, for instance, Stanley Hauerwas, *The Peaceable Kingdom: A Primer in Christian Ethics* (Notre Dame: University of Notre Dame Press, 1983), 17–34; Jeffrey Stout, *Democracy and Tradition* (Princeton: Princeton University Press, 2005), 246–69; G. Scott Davis, *Believing and Acting: The Pragmatic Turn in Comparative Religion and Ethics* (New York: Oxford University Press, 2012).
33. James K. A. Smith, *Who's Afraid of Postmodernism? Taking Derrida, Lyotard, and Foucault to Church* (Grand Rapids: Baker Academic, 2006), 85.

This book presents four accounts of constructivism in order to introduce and discuss the following forms of constructivism: Kantian, Humean, Hegelian, and theistic forms. I will not attempt to elucidate these forms of constructivism here. Instead, I will let the contributors to this volume explain the kinds of constructivism they respectively advocate. Admittedly, each of these forms has more than one version, yet the versions represented here will be helpful at least for getting a broad idea of what each form of constructivism tries to emphasize.

II.1. *Four Accounts of Constructivism*

Kantian constructivism has established itself in contemporary philosophy as one of the most important metaethical alternatives to moral realism and skepticism about the existence and nature of normative truths. Despite this, it has received relatively little attention from religious ethicists. In Chapter 1, Paul Weithman makes a case for Kantian constructivism to those who may still be skeptical of the compatibility of constructivism and Christian ethics. The kind of constructivism he articulates and defends is a restricted version of constructivism, one that seeks to account for the authority of principles of distributive justice. For Weithman, constructivism is concerned with accounting for the validity of outcomes in a given domain. In order to ascertain the validity, the constructivist begins with a conception of correct reasoning about a particular domain under consideration by specifying an ideal procedure for reasoning about the domain. Such a procedure, however, is not to identify the outcomes that hold true independently of the procedure. Rather, being the outcome of the idealized procedure is what *makes* the outcomes valid. But how is it that an idealized procedure for reasoning can deliver correct answers to questions in a domain?

In anticipation of this question, Weithman poses an analogy between the idealized procedure and the rules of baseball to explain the conception of sound reasoning involved in such an idealized procedure. Imagine that there is a "ludic" constructivist who is concerned with the validity of rules in games. To show how the rules of a game are valid, the ludic constructivist must show how the rules are a rational solution to given practical problems and why they are authoritative for the participants. He or she can do so by first coming up with certain conditions the rules would have to meet in order for the players to be able to play the game under the rules adopted by them. The constructivist can then show that the rules have authority insofar as the would-be players commit themselves to rational participation in the play of the game. The point of the game analogy is not that the would-be players arrive at a particular way of playing the game that is antecedently valid. Rather, it is that we can "account for the bindingness of norms by showing how they could be arrived at through a procedure of construction—that is, through a procedure of sound reasoning about the matter at hand" (p. 24). If this ludic constructivist view of the authority of practical reason is correct, we need not postulate a source of authority external to the procedure of sound reasoning itself.

Can the authority of *all* norms be accounted for by ludic constructivism? Weithman acknowledges that the idealized procedure of practical reasoning may presuppose the bindingness of some other norms such as norms of hypothetical reasoning as well as norms of equality and freedom. Thus, Weithman is content with proposing ludic constructivism not as a complete account of normativity but as one more modest, that is, constructivism about distributive justice.

Weithman likens the practices involving distributive justice to a game he calls the social cooperation game. This game is similar to the game of baseball in that both involve a hypothetical procedure in which the rules that would be arrived at by a process of sound reasoning are taken as a rational solution and as enjoying the authority of practical reason. But unlike baseball, the social cooperation game is inescapable: it is impossible to live a fully human life without being committed to playing this game, given the human condition. While ludic constructivism cannot claim authority for those not committed to playing the game which is governed by prior norms such as the freedom and equality of would-be participants, it does show that the principles, as the outcome of an idealized procedure, enjoy the authority of practical reason for those who *are* committed.

Finally, Weithman also anticipates some Christian objections to constructivism. Despite these possible objections, he thinks that constructivism can be made compatible with Christian ethics. Very briefly, constructivism can be a powerful ally to Christian ethics because of its ability to meet the feasibility condition of morality, meaning that it can help Christians identify valid moral principles and show their capacities to honor them. It can also help Christians respect a variety of ends people choose to adopt. In so doing, constructivism can lead to the support of "a tolerant, morally pluralistic community," which, in turn, allows for "the conditions under which faith is freely developed" (p. 37).

Constructivism, when understood as a metaethical position, is often taken as the view that all normative facts are entailed from within the practical standpoint of the valuing human agent. But there are also other ways of construing constructivism. For instance, one could be a constructivist only about *some* normative facts. In Chapter 2, Kevin Kinghorn provides a hybrid account of normative facts with a Humean flavor, in which he gives evaluative and deontic facts different explanations for their normativity. According to this account, it is only deontic facts, not evaluative facts, that should be considered constructivist about the nature of normative truths.

Kinghorn considers truths about the goodness or badness of states of affairs to be fundamentally distinct from truths about the rightness or wrongness of states of affairs. Evaluative facts—which are concerned with what is valuable—are stance-independent, meaning that the nature of goodness is not dependent upon the evaluative attitudes of the valuing agent. In contrast, deontic facts—which are concerned with what is obligatory or permissible—are stance-dependent. Kinghorn argues that "one's positive mental states are the only things that noninstrumentally contribute to one's welfare" (p. 41). According to this view, the sole bearers of intrinsic value are the mental states of a being whose phenomenal experiences of pleasure or pain affect its sense of well-being. What is intrinsically good for someone, in this sense, is not reducible to facts about whatever evaluative attitudes individuals or societies choose to endorse under some idealized conditions.

But the nature of deontic facts is quite different. Kinghorn maintains that what determines deontic facts is fixed solely by "facts about some individual's or group's intent to sanction" those who perform some action that the individual or the group deems too costly to the person in question after some cost–benefit analysis (p. 47). Thus, only deontic facts can be properly taken as the Humean constructivist's facts since they are constituted not by some non-natural facts but by facts about the normative stance individuals or societies take toward those who perform some action, in view of what is good or valuable in terms of expedience.

Kinghorn objects to some Christian theists who try to ground deontic facts in non-natural properties, the latter often presupposed in a moral argument for the existence of God or used to defend objective morality. He is aware that his Humean approach to morality may be at odds with a traditional Christian conception of God that understands God as the author of a universal moral law. But, rather than appealing to non-natural properties as part of a metaphysical conception of divine commands in which these properties serve as an ontological basis for divine commands, he suggests that we use divine commands to help us focus on facts about the conditions of human flourishing. The basic idea is that divine commands "help us identify good states of affairs and how to attain them," revealing to us the scope and the kind of relationship into which God invites us and disclosing "the kinds of measures he intends to take as he draws us into maturing relationship with himself and with others" (p. 60).

While recent debates in philosophy concerning metaethical constructivism have largely been about Kantian and Humean varieties, another strand of constructivism, Hegelian constructivism, is also beginning to take shape in and outside of religious ethics. In Chapter 3, Molly Farneth presents Hegel as a constructivist about the meaning of concepts and about rational entitlement, seeking to flesh out major features of Hegelian constructivism in order to bring to light its unique significance.

Unlike its Kantian and Humean counterparts, Farneth explains, Hegelian constructivism assumes the semantic task of explaining the meaning of normative terms as relevant to normative tasks, such as showing one's rational entitlement to normative judgments and giving an account of moral truth. Hegel's work, in this regard, is worthy of attention because in it he attempts to explain that formal reason alone, "abstracted from an account of practical *reasoning*, understood as an ongoing social practice," is unable to provide determinate content (p. 67). Without an explicit semantics, no candidates for moral truth can acquire determinate content since the meaning of a proposition is dependent on the concepts used in the proposition, the inferential relations among those concepts, and the persons holding one another accountable for their uses of concepts and inference making. Related to this view is Hegel's insistence that the determinate content is inseparable from the social practices and forms of community that content-users participate in. In other words, without an explicit semantics—"a socially and historically attuned semantics"—the construction of normative truths remains abstract because these truths lack content (p. 70).

The same is also true of the activity of showing rational entitlement. In Hegel's view, formal reason alone cannot determine whether people are rationally entitled to their normative commitments. The normative status of rational entitlement requires not merely that the determinate content of concepts and principles pass the tests of universalizability and non-contradiction but also that "we track the commitments of those with whom we interact, in our effort to make sense of what they say and do" (p. 72). Since conceptual content and inferential relations already imply the ongoing social practices of licensing and endorsing commitments, it is necessary to see the process of determining rational entitlement itself as a discursive social practice. In this view, both the determinate content of and inferential relations involving a moral principle (or ethical norm) and the rational entitlement to the principle emerge from social practices.

Farneth argues that Hegel also offers an insight into the way we account for truth. He is known for rejecting a model of truth that is premised on a subject–object dichotomy, which characterizes the divide between the *absolute* as the object of cognition and the cognition by the subject. In this model, the absolute is independent of cognition so that the model fails to account for the fact that the concepts people use in cognition are dependent on the users themselves, in addition to the things they care about. Yet, Farneth cautions that Hegel's account of truth and that of conventionalism are not to be conflated. The conventionalist account of truth—"the view that conformity to the norms actually accepted by some community is enough to make those norms correct or true"—depends on the dichotomy that Hegel rejects (p. 74). The conventionalist takes moral truths to be the result of social convention or agreement, privileging the community, rather than the individual, as having a God's-eye view of truth. Hegel, in contrast, takes moral truths to involve no division between the absolute and cognition of the absolute since the absolute is the self-sufficient and authoritative product that emerges from ongoing social practices and relationships that involve discursive accountability.

Farneth builds on the Hegelian view of truth by drawing out a distinction between an epistemological account of truth and an ontological one. Following Robert Brandom and Jeffrey Stout, Farneth wants to preserve our ordinary use of the concept *true* not by reducing truth to a communal agreement but by recognizing the process of self-criticism that is built into our social practices of concept-use and judgment. Yet, such an epistemological account of truth does not entail the existence of truth as a property in the ontological sense. One can be a so-called minimalist or deflationist about truth, who denies that truth is a metaphysical property but doesn't give up on the ordinary use of the concept. The point is not that Hegel, in fact, holds a minimalist account of truth but that those who follow Hegel on semantics and epistemology might find such an account not only plausible but also helpful for understanding the changes in and critiquing any actual form of ethical life.

Given the unique insights that Hegel's semantics and account of rational entitlement offer for the way we think about the nature of normativity and truth, Farneth argues that Hegelian constructivism should reopen the conversation about the relevance of semantics to metaethical constructivism.

Constructivism, especially in its Kantian and Humean forms, probably isn't the first metaethical theory that would come to mind for many religious ethicists when they try to explain the religious basis of morality. As Christian Miller notes in Chapter 4, this is true of many theistic philosophers whose attention constructivism has largely escaped. But could there be some forms of constructivism that may prove useful to a theistic conception of morality? Miller addresses this question in his chapter by exploring the possibility of theistic forms of constructivism.

Miller pursues two questions from a theistic perspective. The first question is concerned with the plausibility of secular types of constructivism, and the second with the plausibility of theistic types of constructivism, both construed as accounts of the metaphysical basis of normative facts. His answer to the first is negative, as he finds a number of objections from a theistic perspective that can seriously challenge attempts by secular constructivists to deliver moral truths through some sort of idealized procedure of construction. Miller also finds many versions of theistic constructivism implausible, with the exception of a version that grounds only deontological moral properties in a divine construction procedure. In his view, various contemporary counterparts to divine command theory—such as divine intention, desire, and motivation theories—can be understood as involving some form of a divine construction procedure.

Still, theists should curb their enthusiasm about extending theistic construction to all normative domains or all the normative properties there are. Miller points out, for instance, that theists would likely reject constructivism about God's goodness since theists typically consider God's goodness to be metaphysically primitive, not in any way dependent on God's own self-valuation. Similarly, theists can reject constructivism about axiology in general. On a traditional monotheistic conception of God, God does not value things in the world simply because such valuation accords with that of human beings (real or hypothetical). Many theists are also inclined to believe that other normative properties like God's moral traits (e.g., perfectly loving, just, forgiving, merciful) and God's intellectual traits (e.g., rational, reasonable, wise) belong to God necessarily. For these and other reasons, Miller contends that theistic constructivism should be restricted to deontological moral properties. But here, too, a caveat is in order. Theists would be hesitant to think that God is under any moral obligations, given belief in God's sovereignty and freedom, and so the deontological properties in question apply to moral agents other than God.

To be sure, theistic constructivism is not the only option for theists seeking to ground deontological properties. Miller leaves open the possibility that a realist approach could turn out to be more plausible than the constructivist alternative. Be that as it may, he wants to investigate what issues a theist would need to address if she were to opt for a theistic constructivist approach. The first thing a theistic constructivist would need to do is choose what she considers to be the most plausible form of constructivism that grounds deontological properties in divine acts. There are four leading options in the literature: divine command theory, divine motivation theory, divine intention theory, and divine desire theory. Or she could develop a different option. Next, she would have to offer arguments for and answer objections to her preferred option. Miller then suggests that the theistic constructivist specify the dependence relation between deontic properties and the divine act; leading options include meaning equivalence, identity, causality, or (nonreductive) constitution. Eventually, when it comes to deontological moral facts, theists will have to consider the merits of theistic constructivism vis-à-vis those of moral realism.

II.2. Critiques of Nontheistic Constructivism

As the "Kantian" label implies, Kantian constructivists, in general, see themselves as furthering the legacy of Kant, who they believe argued that practical reason can deliver at least some normative facts through an idealized procedure of moral reasoning. They attribute to Kant, among other things, the idea that, in order to account for the objectivity of obligations, morality must be viewed as a product of a self-legislative activity of human beings without any metaphysical commitment to the existence of an independent order of value.

In Chapter 5, Charles Lockwood challenges Rawls's constructivist reading of Kant that, given Kant's commitment to a morality of autonomy rather than heteronomy, it is best to understand his account of morality in constructivist and non-theistic terms. According to this constructivist reading of Kant, we are bound to a law and its normative content only because we have given the law to ourselves. Also, we must be bound to the law if and only if the law was the outcome of our own construction, following a certain idealized procedure that reflects a certain conception of ourselves as self-legislators. The moral law is binding on all of us not because there is a prior moral foundation that justifies the procedure of constructing moral first principles but because the certain procedure of construction we can conceive of is capable both of mirroring a particular conception of ourselves as legislating members of a possible kingdom of ends, and of generating the content of the moral law. Kant is here seen as tying the autonomous procedure of construction to a practical conception of humans as free and equal persons who can govern the procedure as reasonable and rational beings, in order to avoid deriving the content of the moral law from an independent moral order.

Lockwood finds Rawls's constructivist interpretation of Kant problematic on several levels. Consider, for example, the following. Rawls's project of grounding normativity through a purely constructivist procedure will eventually have to face either the problem of infinite regress—in which he has to justify the normativity of the procedure through another procedure without having to justify the latter's normativity by appealing to yet another procedure—or the problem of introducing normativity in the procedure itself without fully justifying it. Lockwood thinks that Rawls succumbs to the latter. Rawls mistakenly believes that a commitment to autonomy entails a constructivist view of morality. He reads Kant as saying that autonomy requires that the content of our moral first principles cannot be derived from any source other than our own procedure of construction, but Kant himself appears to hold that "autonomy is fully compatible with the claim that morality is not simply constructed by us" (p. 110). On Lockwood's reading, Kant is more concerned with the source of moral motivation than with the source of substantive moral content when he distinguishes between hypothetical and categorical imperatives. In fact, it is quite possible to interpret, as John Hare and others do, autonomy as involving one's *endorsement* of the authority of moral principles discovered in a prior order of value, even *as* our own.

One reason to think this the correct way of reading Kant is that the moral community—that is, the kingdom of ends—that Kant envisions includes both human beings and God. Although both, as rational beings, must consider themselves as lawgivers in the kingdom, God is portrayed as the sovereign, whereas humans are mere members of the kingdom. Not only is God's "holy will" necessarily in harmony with the moral law in virtue of the fact that God has no inclinations that might conflict with God's rational nature, but as the sovereign, God is also not subject to any moral law that is purely a human creation. Yet this does not imply that it is then simply a matter of God's will to arbitrarily construct a moral law without any connection to our wills, in which case God's will would interfere with our autonomy. Lockwood argues, instead, that we can, as Kant does, take the moral law as the expression of our own essential, rational nature—grounded in an independent order of value that neither we nor God create arbitrarily but both share—and autonomously endorse it. If so, there need not be a conflict between autonomy and moral realism, on one hand, and between autonomy and theism, on the other.

As mentioned earlier, constructivism is often contrasted with moral realism, and one important area of disagreement between them has to do with the metaphysical existence and nature of entities such as moral facts. In this regard, constructivists and realists often find themselves at odds with each other over the question of the moral import of nature. In Chapter 6, David Clairmont probes one of the central questions in religious ethics: What is the significance of nature, if any, for ethics? He poses this question as a way of comparing and contrasting Hegelian constructivism and natural law theory as each is conceived in the work of Jeffrey Stout and Jean Porter, respectively. Such a comparative analysis would be helpful for not only understanding the differences between these two approaches to the question but also laying bare common mischaracterizations of natural law positions by some constructivists. In particular, constructivists often identify natural law view with the physicalist position that natural processes are themselves normative or with the absolutist position (known as the New Natural Law) that defends the intelligibility of basic human goods to practical reason and the self-evident nature of absolute moral norms derived from these goods. Clairmont, however, argues that these two natural law positions reflect a distinctly modern understanding of natural law shared neither by certain key medieval theologians nor by other natural law thinkers today.

In Stout's Hegelian constructivism, moral values and norms are integral to the process of an immanent critique within a particular historical community. This process involves "social practices of assessing claims to truth which address both the subject and the object side of the knower and what is known" (p. 136). The standards of knowledge and rationality both emerge and inhere in social practices where the subjects and objects are engaged in a dialogical and purposive activity. Hegel's term *spirit* is understood as the "context of evolving social practices that encompass both the subjects of knowledge and whatever is known by them" (p. 136). His other term, *absolute spirit*, is described as "the expanded epistemic context required to theorize the standard of knowledge self-sufficiently" (p. 137). Briefly, the idea is that the justification of normative claims and commitments belongs to the social practices of given historical communities, while truth itself belongs to the all-encompassing epistemic context unfolding in time and space. In this Hegelian view, the conditions for the possibility of knowledge are all socio-historical. No knowledge is possible without the dialectical process that characterizes the evolving social practices within historical communities.

Also in Stout's constructivism, nature acquires meaning and significance only through social practices. "The natural world is itself an object of inquiry and other forms of practical attention within the practices," as the concepts we use to refer to things in the world have meaning by virtue of the roles they play in those practices (p. 138). In fact, nature has no inherent meaning, value, or purpose apart from human engagement. Stout's point, however, is not that nature stands on the opposite side of human beings as the object of human discovery but that nature, insofar as its evolutionary history is concerned, has "harbored spirit, the realm of human practices, as a yet-unrealized possibility" (p. 139). Thus, Stout's reading of Hegel on nature appears to avoid a subject–object dichotomy between human beings and nature, although his emphasis on the importance of social practice remains consistent: "nature acquires moral significance to the extent that it can be taken up into the realm of human social practice" (p. 140). It should be noted, however, that Clairmont finds Stout's reading of Hegel only partially accurate since Clairmont takes Hegel to have a much more nuanced view of the relationship between nature and human beings. In Clairmont's view, Stout's reading of Hegel mirrors a reading by some scholars who tend to read Hegel's thoughts on ethics and history apart from the wider context of Hegel's metaphysics. The difference is crucial if Hegel really thought that nature has its own intelligibility and therefore if nature, since its structure and processes are widely shared by human beings, has moral significance independently of our attitudes.

Whereas Stout views nature as having no inherent teleology on its own and lacking intelligibility apart from human purposes, nature receives a different appraisal in Jean Porter's revisionist account of natural law. Compared to Stout's narrow, if not inaccurate, understanding of natural law, Porter "maintains the intelligibility of nature to be of central importance for understanding nature's moral significance" (p. 155). She holds that the intelligibility of nature "is flexible enough to support both specific norms necessary for any coherent understanding of nature's moral significance while recognizing the various ways that moral languages mediated through social practices interpret individual placement in a species-specific ethic" (p. 156). Utilizing the medieval scholastic conception of "nature as reason" (distinguished from that of "nature as nature"), Porter advances the view that human reason is capable of discerning particular purposes of creatures and that the realization of these purposes could lead to flourishing proper to the kinds of creatures they are. In this view, there are purposes in nature discernible to human reason that are not reducible to social practices (or even the dialectical process thereof) or to the satisfaction of basic desires. Nature has normative significance to the extent that there is "value of a specific kind of life, the form of life appropriate to a given kind of creature when it is flourishing in accordance with the intrinsic principles of its existence" (p. 159).

To say that nature is intelligible, however, does not imply that natural law, reflecting the intelligible purposes of nature, must be conceived as a prearranged or deductive metaphysical system that is independent of the historical conditions of moral reasoning or that yields infallible moral beliefs. Clairmont argues, as Porter does, that natural law can remain "open to the ways that social context changes, thereby revealing both new ways that human beings can flourish and new threats to longstanding social institutions that have made flourishing possible" (p. 170).

In Chapter 7, Kevin Jung offers critiques of Christine Korsgaard's Kantian and Sharon Street's Humean versions of constructivism from a realist perspective. Jung questions their central claim that normativity can be sufficiently grounded in facts about us, the valuing agents, and articulates a realist and theistic alternative for grounding evaluative facts.

As constructivists, Korsgaard and Street share the view that only subject-given facts—that is, facts about the evaluative attitudes of the valuing agent—can give us reasons to act, although they disagree over what sorts of subject-given facts are to be considered normative. In Korsgaard's Kantian version of constructivism, we see an attempt to underwrite normativity in the practical domain through a conception of practical identity, which informs and specifies conditions for an idealized procedure of practical reasoning. It is the conception of practical identity in which we see ourselves as rational beings who necessarily value themselves as ends in themselves in and through any acts of valuation. This conception also allows us to see ourselves as capable of conferring value on other things, thus making autonomy—the capacity for reflective endorsement—the source of all normativity. Her point is neither that actual human agents necessarily make their normative judgments through such an idealized procedure nor that normative facts are dependent on the attitudes of actual human beings. Rather, the idea is that we can give a plausible account of how to ground normativity through a conception of practical identity alone without any appeal to any mind-independent facts.

In contrast, Street denies that the practical point of view as such is capable of delivering any normative facts without some preexisting evaluative attitudes. In her view, substantive moral facts can be entailed only from within the valuing agent's contingent evaluative attitudes. Thus, all normative facts are dependent on the contingent facts about each agent's evaluative stances. Yet Street, too, takes normative facts to be an outcome of some idealized procedure of practical reasoning, which demands normative judgments able to withstand the scrutiny of the agent's entire set of normative commitments. Normative judgments are constructions of hypothetical, rather than actual, agents in the sense that the standards of correctness are determined not merely by what one happens to value but by what one can value in light of the entire set of one's own contingent evaluative commitments.

Jung raises several objections to the arguments advanced by these two thinkers. In response to Korsgaard, for instance, he calls into question her claim that our practical identities as reflective valuers not only confirm ourselves as the source of all value but also entail our having intrinsic value. He also challenges what is often referred to as the inescapability condition of agency: (roughly) the idea that since we, in virtue of being agents, cannot but accept the conditions of agency, we are also necessarily bound by the norms of rationality that follow from agency. The problem with the inescapability condition, however, is that it fails to recognize the fact that inescapability neither guarantees nor entails motivational commitment to the norms of rationality. Another of Jung's criticisms, leveled against Street's constructivism, has to do with how to account for normative error. If Street is correct about the nature of normative error, any normative error can only be the result of procedural error—failure of logical or instrumental entailment from within one's contingent evaluative attitudes. But it seems counterintuitive that all normative errors are due to a failure of the logical or instrumental entailment of our evaluative attitudes.

If we can't ground normativity in facts about us, where should we look for its grounds? With a narrow focus on evaluative facts, Jung introduces two ways of grounding them. One is a realist account—which grounds evaluative facts in mind-independent (or response-independent) facts—and the other a theistic account that grounds moral goodness in God's will. While one account does not entail the other, Jung maintains that they can be made compatible with each other. Borrowing John Duns Scotus's distinction between God's willing and God's willing for our willing, Jung contends that theists could understand the latter to be God's intentional endorsement of certain things that are intrinsically good or bad—those states of affairs that are intrinsically good because they are necessary for the flourishing of all human beings (and others), independent of their contingent preferences or attitudes.

Bibliography

Ayer, A. J. "Critique of Ethics and Theology." In *Language, Truth, and Logic*. New York: Dover Publications, 1952.

Bagnoli, Carla. "Introduction." In *Constructivism in Ethics*, edited by Carla Bagnoli. Cambridge: Cambridge University Press, 2013.

Blackburn, Simon. *Essays in Quasi-Realism*. Oxford: Oxford University Press, 1993.

Brandom, Robert. *Making It Explicit: Reasoning, Representing, and Discursive Commitment*. Cambridge: Harvard University Press, 1994.

———. *Articulating Reasons: An Introduction to Inferentialism*. Cambridge: Harvard University Press, 2000.

Changeux, Jean-Pierre, and Alain Connes. *Conversations on Mind, Matter, and Mathematics*. Translated by M. B. DeBevoise. Princeton: Princeton University Press, 1995.

Chrisman, Matthew. "Ethical Expressivism." In *The Bloomsbury Companion to Ethics*, 29–54. New York: Bloomsbury Publishing, 2011.

Davis, G. Scott. *Believing and Acting: The Pragmatic Turn in Comparative Religion and Ethics*. New York: Oxford University Press, 2012.

Gibbard, Allan. *Thinking How to Live*. Cambridge: Harvard University Press, 2003.

Hare, R. M. *The Language of Morals*. Oxford: Clarendon Press, 1952.

———. *Essays in Ethical Theory*. New York: Oxford University Press, 1993.

Hauerwas, Stanley. *The Peaceable Kingdom: A Primer in Christian Ethics*. Notre Dame: University of Notre Dame Press, 1983.

Hill, Thomas E. "Moral Construction as a Task: Sources and Limits." *Social Philosophy and Policy* 25, no. 1 (2008): 214–36.

Horwich, Paul. *Truth*. Oxford: Clarendon Press, 1998.

Korsgaard, Christine M. *The Sources of Normativity*. New York: Cambridge University Press, 1996.

———. *Self-Constitution: Agency, Identity, and Integrity*. New York: Oxford University Press, 2009.
Lenman, James, and Yonatan Shemmer, eds. *Constructivism in Practical Philosophy*. Oxford: Oxford University Press, 2012.
Lillehammer, Hallvard. "Constructivism and the Error Theory." In *The Bloomsbury Companion to Ethics*, 55–76. New York: Bloomsbury Publishing, 2011.
Livio, Mario. *Is God a Mathematician?* New York: Simon & Schuster, 2010.
Mackie, J. L. *Ethics: Inventing Right and Wrong*. New York: Penguin, 1991.
Miller, Christian. "Introduction." In *The Bloomsbury Companion to Ethics*, xiv–lii. New York: Bloomsbury Publishing, 2011.
Miller, Christian B. "The Conditions of Moral Realism." *Journal of Philosophical Research* 34 (2009): 123–55.
Milo, Ronald. "Contractarian Constructivism." *Journal of Philosophy* 92, no. 4 (1995): 181–204.
Scanlon, Thomas M. *What We Owe to Each Other*. Cambridge: Harvard University Press, 1998.
———. *Being Realistic About Reasons*. Oxford: Oxford University Press, 2014.
Smith, James K. A. *Who's Afraid of Postmodernism? Taking Derrida, Lyotard, and Foucault to Church*. Grand Rapids: Baker Academic, 2006.
Stevenson, C. L. "The Emotive Meaning of Ethical Terms." In *Logical Positivism*, edited by A. J. Ayer, 264–81. Glencoe: Free Press, 1959.
Stout, Jeffrey. *Democracy and Tradition*. Princeton: Princeton University Press, 2005.
Street, Sharon. "A Darwinian Dilemma for Realist Theories of Value." *Philosophical Studies* 127, no. 1 (2006): 109–66.
———. "Constructivism About Reasons." *Oxford Studies in Metaethics* 3 (2008): 207–45.
———. "What Is Constructivism in Ethics and Metaethics?" *Philosophy Compass* 5, no. 5 (May 1, 2010): 363–84.
———. "Coming to Terms with Contingency: Humean Constructivism About Practical Reason." In *Constructivism in Practical Philosophy*, edited by James Lenman and Yonatan Shemmer, 40–59. New York: Oxford University Press, 2012.
Tegmark, Max. *Our Mathematical Universe: My Quest for the Ultimate Nature of Reality*. New York: Vintage, 2015.
Wigner, Eugene P. "The Unreasonable Effectiveness of Mathematics in the Natural Sciences." *Communications on Pure and Applied Mathematics* 13, no. 1 (February 1, 1960): 1–14.

1 Kantian Constructivism, Baseball, and Christian Ethics

Paul Weithman

It is possible to be a constructivist about any or all of a number of domains: about mathematics or some part of it, about physics, about morality or some of its parts, about reasons or about normativity.[1] My topic here is moral constructivism and, more specifically, constructivism about distributive justice. The emergence of this kind of constructivism is one of the most exciting developments in moral theory in recent decades, yet it seems to have received almost no attention in the literature on Christian ethics. I suspect that this neglect is not born of ignorance but, rather, of skepticism that an ethical view that is seemingly so humanist in its motivations can be responsive to the deepest concerns and commitments that Christian ethicists bring to their discipline. My own view is that constructivism offers a powerful and attractive account of an important part of morality. If that account is not only powerful and attractive but also true, then it cannot contradict the truths of Christian ethics. My aims in this chapter are to show that constructivism is a plausible view about the authority of that part of morality and to rebut some reasons for skepticism about its compatibility with Christian ethics.

I. What Is Constructivism?

Here is one way of thinking about constructivism. Constructivism answers the question, "What accounts for the validity of outcomes in the domain under consideration—geometry or morality, for example?" To answer this question, the constructivist starts with a conception of correct reasoning about the subject matter of interest to her—a conception of the conditions any purported outcome must meet if it is to be adequate, of what inferences are valid when reasoning about that subject matter, of what considerations are to be taken into account in arriving at conclusions and of how those considerations are to be weighted, and of how conflicts among reasons are

---

1. I am grateful to Neil Arner, Kevin Jung, Christine Korsgaard, Jean Porter, and Samuel Freeman for helpful comments on an earlier draft.

to be resolved. Using this conception of correct reasoning, the constructivist specifies an ideal procedure for reasoning about the domain. As a first cut, a treatment of a domain is constructivist if correct outcomes in that domain—theorems of geometry or valid moral or political principles—are identified with those that could be arrived at using that procedure.[2]

The first cut is just a *first* cut because it is misleading. For it is compatible with the thought that the constructivist's procedure is a reliable method of discovery. It is compatible, that is, with the thought that the procedure is a means of ascertaining or identifying theorems or principles that hold independent of the procedure. And it is this thought that the constructivist denies. She claims instead that the theorems or principles hold in virtue of their being the outcomes that would be reached using the idealized procedure. That is what makes them valid. To use the defining metaphor for the view: what makes the theorems or principles valid is that—given a problem or a question in the relevant domain—they are the answers that would be constructed were we to use the procedure to solve it.

The inspiration of contemporary moral and political constructivism is found in the work of Immanuel Kant, but it has its more proximate origins in the theorizing of John Rawls. Rawls first made his constructivism explicit in his Dewey Lectures "Kantian Constructivism in Moral Theory," and he explained and qualified both his own and Kant's constructivism in later work. A number of philosophers have since followed Rawls's lead and developed constructivist views. But Rawls's theory of justice is an especially prominent member of the constructivist family. His derivation of his two principles of justice makes a useful example of constructivism because of its familiarity.

Instead of starting with the construction of Rawls's principles of justice, however, I shall start with what might seem to be a quite different set of rules: the rules of baseball. I show how constructivism accounts for their authority over those who play the game. I contend that the account is plausible because it accords with our pre-theoretic intuitions about that authority. The practical undertaking for which norms are constructed in the example and the procedure by which they are constructed share important features with the practice governed by norms of distributive justice and with the procedure for constructing those norms. The similarity of the cases should help to make constructivism about distributive justice seem plausible as well.

---

2. John Rawls, *Lectures on the History of Moral Philosophy*, ed. Barbara Herman (Cambridge: Harvard University Press, 2000), 238–9. The image of construction might seem to have more literal application in the geometric than the moral domain because truths about geometry, unlike moral principles, might seem—as they did to Kant—to depend on what figures we can construct with a compass, a straightedge, and a pencil; see Michael Friedman, "Kant's Theory of Geometry," *The Philosophical Review* 94, no. 4 (1985): 455–506. I discuss the propriety of applying the constructivist image to morality later.

II. Ludic Constructivism

Suppose we want to understand why the rules of baseball bind those who play it. According to the constructivist about games—someone we might call a "ludic" constructivist—we can answer that question by imagining people coming upon a stick, a ball, and four square bags in a large field. Wanting to while away the time, they ask how they might amuse themselves with these items. They realize fairly quickly that the best use they can make of the items is to play a game with them. How they are to play is their problem. To solve it, they set about devising some rules for the game, relying on a conception of sound reasoning about such matters.

What is that conception? How might it lead to the rules of baseball? And how does showing that it leads to the rules of baseball account for the authority of the rules? To answer these questions, let us first see how the would-be players would arrive at the rules:

- The would-be players have some idea of what conditions rules have to meet if the rules are to play the role in the game that rules must play: the rules have to be such that the players can understand them and can see that they are generally honored, the rules have to provide final settlement to disputes—including disputes about under what conditions someone gets the rewards and penalties such as runs and bases—and the rules cannot privilege anyone by name but, instead, apply to players just as such.
- The would-be players want the game to be well suited to their natural capacities. This imposes some constraints on the content of the rules at which they arrive. The rules do not, for example, call for putting the bases 100 yards apart, nor do they call for putting the pitcher's mound 20 feet from home plate.
- The would-be players recognize that some considerations ought not count in favor of a rule. There is no concept of deserving to win that they bring to the game, so there is no antecedently favored outcome that the rules are designed to bring about. There may be some athletic accomplishments which the would-be players want the game to bring out. But they don't want the rules to favor the speedy or the powerful just as such. Rather, if a rule is adopted that confers an advantage on the speedy or the powerful, it will be justified by the fact that that rule—in conjunction, perhaps, with other rules that favor the fleet of foot or the strong of arm—leads to a good and fair game in which the desired achievements are elicited and rewarded. In this way, incentives in the game are structured so that the distribution of athletic gifts is treated as a common asset which produces a better game for all who appreciate the achievements the game is designed to showcase. If there is any doubt about whether such a rule ought to be adopted, players can ask those who favor the rule whether they would do so even if they did not know whether they were strong or swift or could throw hard.

- However candidate rules are proposed to the would-be players, the procedure by which they finally settle on rules will almost certainly be iterative or recursive. For the would-be players may provisionally arrive at a rulebook only to find that one or more of its rules need to be revised in light of predictions about their likely consequences or of trial plays of the game. Different rules will then have to be proposed, considered, provisionally decided on, and subjected to trial. And so the procedure for sound reasoning about rules, however it is specified, will have to be complex enough to allow for provisional adoption, reflection, debate and amendment.

By working through the procedure sketched here, which I assume approximates sound reasoning about rules, we can see how the group we have imagined could reason their way to the familiar rules of baseball.

To say that the would-be players *could* arrive at the familiar rules is not to say that they *would*. For, although the rules of baseball as we know them specify a good way to play, they may not specify a uniquely good way to play.[3] There may be a number of rule books, all of which could be arrived at through the procedure I have described. Indeed, since the rules of baseball set distances between the bases and since distance is a continuous—and hence infinitely divisible—quantity, then, if there is one rule book that would work reasonably well, there is in principle an infinitely large set of rule books *all* the members of which would work reasonably well. But many of these rulebooks could presumably be grouped into equivalence classes whose members are not distinguishable in practice. And so I assume that there is at most a small set of distinct classes of rule books for baseball that satisfy the purposes of the would-be players. If none of the classes can be singled out as best, then this set is the output of the procedure.

I implied earlier that constructivism attempts to account for the bindingness of norms by showing how they could be arrived at through a procedure of construction—that is, through a procedure of sound reasoning about the matter at hand. We have now seen how the rules of baseball, or a set of rulebooks for baseball, could be arrived at that way. How does this account for their authority?

Showing that the rules would be arrived at by a process of sound reasoning shows that they are a rational solution to the practical problem facing the would-be players: the practical problem of how creatures with our physical natures and mental constitutions are to play using the materials at hand. Showing *that* shows that—given the would-be players' commitment to rational participation in the practice of baseball—the rules enjoy the

---

3. However—I puckishly suggest—Rawls may have thought otherwise; see John Rawls, "The Best of All Games," accessed April 12, 2017, http://bostonreview.net/rawls-the-best-of-all-games.

authority of practical reason. They enjoy that authority whether or not anyone actually conducts the procedure by which the rules would be selected. For constructivism uses the procedure for selecting rules to represent an important fact about the rules: by representing the rules of baseball as the outcome of a procedure for arriving at rules, constructivism displays how the rules for the practice are connected to practical reason and therefore enjoy its authority.

Moreover, according to the constructivist, if the rules of baseball have the authority of practical reason, there is no need to postulate an extra-procedural source of authority, to lay out a method for discovering it or to represent the rules as uncovered by such a method. That is why, as I noted at the outset, the constructivist procedures are not depicted as ways of discovering outcomes whose validity is independent of the procedures for arriving at them. If the rules of baseball can be shown to have the authority of practical reason, they are shown to have authority enough.

It may be objected that while I have said that the constructivist account of the rules' authority depends on the would-be players' commitment to the game, it depends on far more. In particular, it presupposes the bindingness of other norms. Some of the norms that are presupposed govern hypothetical reasoning. Others are moral norms the role of which would be more obvious if the procedure for arriving at rules were further specified. Such a specification might make explicit that all the would-be players are to have an equal voice in decision-making somehow understood and that decisions are to be made free of coercion. That the procedure presupposes these norms would be problematic if ludic constructivism were proposed as a complete account of normativity. It is therefore important that the account is limited in its ambitions: it is an account of the bindingness just of the rules of baseball. How the authority of other, prior norms is to be accounted for is a question that is left open.

It may also be objected that the metaphor of construction is ill applied to the rules of a game, since rules do not seem to be the sort of thing that one *constructs*. I think that the way to dispel this misgiving is to stress that the rules are not the terminus of the procedure of construction. With the rules in hand, we can develop an account of the excellences that can be shown by those taking part in the practice. Some of these excellences are exercised by complying with the letter and the spirit of the rules and by displaying the appropriate attitude toward infractions. Others are exercised by playing the game especially well. An account of these excellences, in turn, can be used to articulate the ideal of a game that is well played. An ideal *does* seem to be the sort of thing that can be constructed. So when practical reason is employed to work out the rules of play, what it ultimately constructs is a ludic ideal. This response to the objection gains some credence from its fit with Kant's constructivism. For realizing the ludic ideal is—to use a familiar phrase—"the object of the game." And so in working out rules of play, practical reason—now to use a Kantian phrase—really constructs and thus causes, its own object.[4]

III. Constructivism About Distributive Justice

I—and I expect many other people—find it intuitively plausible that the rules of baseball are valid or binding because they are a good or a rational way to play a game we wish to play. I take it that vindicating this commonly held intuition about what makes the rules valid tells powerfully in favor of constructivism about baseball. Moreover, I see no relevant difference between the rules of baseball and those of many other games. I—and I expect many other people—have the intuition that the rules of other games are binding because they specify good or rational ways to play, and I believe constructivism can vindicate those intuitions in much the same way it vindicates the intuition about the rules of baseball. Constructivism about the rules of games—what I have called "ludic constructivism"—is therefore a very plausible account of the rules' validity.

Our intuitions about what grounds the norms of distributive justice may be much less firm than those about what grounds the rules of games. But the later Wittgenstein taught us that there are no necessary and sufficient conditions for applying the concept of a game. Rather, he contended, playing together cannot be clearly demarcated from other of the practices that constitute living together. And he showed that likening other human practices to paradigm cases of games can yield valuable insights. We can read the constructivist about distributive justice as building on Wittgenstein's argument. For we can read her as likening the practices by which necessary goods are produced and distributed to a game—call it "the social cooperation game." It is an especially important game because its ongoing play consists in the continuous activities of producing and distributing goods that everyone needs.

The social cooperation game, like the game of baseball, needs rules. If the social cooperation game is indeed relevantly similar to baseball, then would-be players of the social cooperation game should be able to arrive at rules for it by a constructivist procedure that is similar to that which would-be players used to arrive at the rules of baseball. And so they can:

- Would-be players know what conditions the rules will have to satisfy if the rules are to play their role: the rules have to be such that those subject to them can understand them and can see that they are generally honored, the rules have to provide final settlement to disputes—including disputes about the conditions under which someone gets the rewards such as opportunity, income, and wealth—the rules cannot

---

4. Paraphrasing a passage quoted at Rawls, *Lectures on the History of Moral Philosophy*, 215.

Constructivism, Baseball, and Ethics 27

privilege anyone by name, and the rules must apply to participants in social cooperation as such, rather than as members of a select group.
- The rules of the game have to be suited to would-be players' natural situation: to the fact that goods are moderately scarce, that people disagree deeply about religious and moral questions that seem to bear on distribution, and that commitment to the rules will be hard to honor if they place extreme burdens or strains on some of us.
- The would-be players recognize that there are some considerations that ought not to count in favor of a rule. There is no concept of deservingness which they bring to the game, so there is no antecedently favored distribution which the rules are designed to bring about. There may be some accomplishments that the would-be players want the game to bring out or think they need to bring about for a well-functioning society. But they don't want the rules to favor one race or religion or the talented just as such. Rather, if a rule is adopted that confers an advantage on the talented, it will only be justified by the fact that that rule—in conjunction with all the others—leads to a good and fair game. That is, the distribution of talents is treated as a common asset to make the game better for all. To remove any doubt about whether rules unduly favor one group over another, players adopt rules in ignorance of their natural capacities and place in society.
- However candidate rules are proposed to the would-be players, the procedure by which they finally settle on rules will—like the procedure for settling on rules of baseball—be iterative or recursive. For the would-be players may provisionally arrive at a rule about the distribution of income and wealth, for example, only to realize that it needs to be revised to allow inequalities to function as incentives. Different rules will then have to be proposed, considered, provisionally decided on, and subjected to trial. And so the procedure for sound reasoning about rules, however it is specified, will have to be complex enough to allow for provisional adoption, reflection, debate, and amendment.

We can, I hope, see how would-be players could reason their way to principles governing the distribution of necessary goods by working through the process sketched here.

As with baseball, so, too, with the social cooperation game; there may not be a single set of rules at which players *would* arrive. Instead, there may be several sets at which they *could* arrive, perhaps because the conditions of sound reasoning about distributive justice—and hence the procedure for arriving at rules—admit of different interpretations that lead to different results. If so, then the output of the procedure will be a family or set of rulebooks for the social cooperation game. There may, however, be features common to all the members of the family of constraints that any admissible rule book must satisfy. If those constraints can be represented as the object of a choice by would-be players, then even if there is no first-order set of rules that the would-be players would choose, there is still a single set of principles they would give themselves—namely, the higher-order constraints.[5]

And as with baseball, so, too, with the social cooperation game, showing that the first-order rules would be arrived at by a process of sound reasoning shows that they are a rational solution to the practical problem facing the would-be players: the practical problem of how creatures with our physical natures and mental constitutions are to produce and distribute needed goods.[6] Showing *that* shows—modulo a qualification I shall mention shortly—that the rules enjoy the authority of practical reason. Their authority does not depend on the actual conduct of the procedure for choosing rules. Indeed, it does not depend on the possibility of conducting that procedure, for there may be conditions—such as devices that assure the impartiality of the parties by ensuring their ignorance—that make the procedure an impossible one to conduct. The procedure for selecting a rule book for the social cooperation game, like the procedure for selecting rules for baseball, is thus a "device of representation."[7] It is introduced to represent an important fact about the rulebook with clarity: the fact that the rules for the practice are connected to practical reason and therefore enjoy its authority.

There is one important difference between baseball and the social cooperation game. We saw in the last section that our commitment to sound reasoning commits us to playing by the rules of baseball only given the commitment to playing the game. We might choose not to play baseball, thereby escaping the grip of the rules. But some games are inescapable. Our circumstances and powers are such that none of us could live very well on his own. It is therefore necessary for us to enter the social cooperation game—a game in which all of us find ourselves caught up from birth anyway.

The conclusion that the social cooperation game is a game we cannot but play has been widely endorsed in the history of political philosophy. In the first book of the *Politics*, Aristotle famously argued that it is natural to human beings to live in a polis,[8] by which he meant that *eudaimonia* is available only in that social setting. While it is not impossible to live outside a polis, it is impossible to live a fully human life outside it. Aquinas largely concurred with Aristotle, though he would add some qualifications about the kind of flourishing that is available anywhere in this life. While Augustine expressed doubts about whether human beings would live under political authority in the absence of original sin, he seems to have regarded

---

5. I explore the implications of this possibility in Paul Weithman, "Autonomy and Disagreement About Justice in *Political Liberalism*," *Ethics* 128, no. 1 (2017): 95–122.
6. See Christine Korsgaard, "Realism and Constructivism in Twentieth-Century Moral Philosophy," in *Philosophy in America at the Turn of the Century* (Charlottesville: The Philosophy Documentation Center, 2003), 116–17.
7. The phrase was coined by Rawls, who uses it to describe the original position; see John Rawls, *Political Liberalism* (New York: Columbia University Press, 1995), 27.
8. Aristotle, *Politics*, ed. Carnes Lord (Chicago: University of Chicago Press, 1985), 1253a19.

subjection to such an authority as an inescapable fact of our fallen condition.[9] Hobbes, of course, thought that escaping the state of nature and entering commonwealth was a rational necessity.[10] Kant thought leaving the state of nature and entering a civil condition was morally obligatory.[11] Rawls takes it for granted that those he addresses live under the basic structures of modern states.[12] Locke thought that there were at least some states into which it would be rational for those in a state of nature to contract—though unlike others cited here, he explicitly held out the possibility that it would be rational to remain in a state of nature if the only alternative were a civil society that is sufficiently dangerous.[13] Thus—modulo Locke's qualification about life in dangerous states—the assumption that we must play the social cooperation game is common ground among a variety of thinkers who assume it for quite different reasons.

In the last section, we saw that the rules of baseball bind the players, not just in virtue of their commitment to play baseball but also in virtue of other norms that are presumed to hold. I said that those include norms of hypothetical reasoning as well as norms of freedom and equality. There are philosophers, such as T. M. Scanlon, who try to extend constructivism to all of morality.[14] There are others, such as Christine Korsgaard, who try to extend it to all forms of normativity.[15] For a number of reasons, I am presenting a more modest constructivism here, one that purports to account only for the authority of principles of distributive justice.[16] I can therefore presuppose

---

9. For Augustine and Aquinas on political authority, see Paul Weithman, "Augustine and Aquinas on Original Sin and the Function of Political Authority," *Journal of the History of Philosophy* 30, no. 3 (1992): 353–76.
10. Thomas Hobbes, *Leviathan*, ed. Richard Tuck (Cambridge: Cambridge University Press, 1991), chapter XVII.
11. Immanuel Kant, "On the Common Saying 'This May Be True in Theory, But It Does Not Apply in Practice,'" in *Kant: Political Writings*, ed. Hans Siegbert Reiss (Cambridge: Cambridge University Press, 1970), section II, paragraph 1.
12. The most explicit indication is at John Rawls, *A Theory of Justice* (Cambridge: Harvard University Press, 1999), 127, where Rawls says that if the parties in the original position do not reach agreement, they would live in a society of general egoism rather than in a state of nature.
13. John Locke, *Second Treatise of Civil Government*, ed. by C. B. Macpherson (Indianapolis: Hackett Publishing, 1980), chapter 7.
14. Scanlon first sketched his version of constructivism in T. M. Scanlon, "Contractualism and Utilitarianism," in *Utilitarianism and Beyond*, ed. Amartya Sen and Bernard Williams (Cambridge: Cambridge University Press, 1982), 103–26.
15. Christine Korsgaard, *Sources of Normativity* (Cambridge: Cambridge University Press, 1996).
16. To cite just one reason, it seems appropriate to liken a society's production and distribution of goods to a game because both seem to me to be collective undertakings: a group of players undertake to engage in them as equal participants pursuing at least some common purposes, and the participation of all as equals requires that the rules that govern the activity should be justifiable to all who take part. I do not want to take a stand on the question of morality or the activities governed by it are collective undertakings in this sense.

that some norms—such as the norms of rationality are already in place, as I did in presenting ludic constructivism.

In presenting ludic constructivism, I also assumed that the constructivist procedure was governed by prior norms concerning the freedom and equality of the would-be players. Some philosophers might say the same of constructivism about distributive justice. Ronald Dworkin, for example, might say that it presupposes a prior norm of equal concern and respect. The version of constructivism that I am summarizing here builds in freedom and equality differently. It assumes that would-be players of the social cooperation game are committed to playing it in a certain way: as free equals. It represents them as free equals in the constructivist procedure—by, for example, making all equally ignorant of their talents—so as to arrive at rules of the game which allow them to play that way. The assumption about how would-be players are committed to playing limits the constructivism presented here in a second way: it does not purport to account for the authority of principles over those who are not committed to playing that way. But by representing those principles as the outcome of a procedure which incorporates the strictures of correct reasoning about distributive justice, it shows that the principles enjoy the authority of practical reason over those who are so committed.

I said that the ultimate outcome of ludic constructivism—what finally gets constructed—is the object of the game: the ideal of a well-played game that calls forth certain moral and athletic excellences. What finally gets constructed by constructivism about distributive justice is the object of the social cooperation game. It is an ideal of a society in which players relate to one another as free equals by acting from the principles and from the moral and intellectual excellences such relations call forth. That ideal, if fully worked out, would provide players of the social cooperation game a picture of how their institutions and practices might be, and of how they and their fellow players might conduct themselves. The availability of that ideal can transform the self-understanding of the players, for it allows them to see themselves as possible players in a well-conducted game. The more reflective of them can then incorporate that ideal into their own practical deliberations by asking what, if anything, they can do to improve the game they are actually playing so that it better conforms to the ideal. Those most powerfully committed to playing the social cooperation game as free equals may regard realizing that ideal as their calling.

IV. The Appeal of Constructivism

I claimed that ludic constructivism is vindicated by its ability to account for and deepen pre-theoretic intuitions about why the rules of games are binding. Those intuitions are (1) that there are no independently obtaining facts about baseball in the world that the rules should express or represent and (2) that the rules of baseball are binding simply because they are a good or a rational way to play a game to which the players are committed. These intuitions explain why players' reasoning about the rules of baseball is not represented as a process of discovering rules that are antecedently binding.

We may have no comparable pre-theoretic intuitions about the authority of principles of distributive justice. Indeed, many people have views which sharply conflict with the constructivist account. If the parallel I drew in the last section holds—if, that is, principles of justice are rules for playing a game—then the constructivist account of the principles' authority would be vindicated by parity of reasoning. I find the Wittgensteinian claim that games cannot be sharply distinguished from other practices of living together, and the assimilation of production and distribution to games, to be quite compelling. I consider it a virtue of constructivism that, by assimilating production and distribution to games, it offers a unified account of the validity of the two sets of practice rules. And so I am strongly drawn to the view. I believe the burden of proof is on those who think that the parallel or the assimilation fails and that some other account is called for.

But there are other attractions to constructivism besides the unity of its treatment of practical authority.

An account of justice, or of morality more generally, should shed light on the interest we take in its subject matter.[17] Part of the appeal of constructivism is the elegant way in which it does that. Unfortunately, I can only mention one of the ways it does so here. Consider one of the most fundamental puzzles about our interest in the subject matter of a theory of justice: it is not at all obvious what the desire to do the right thing is a desire to do or what the desire to be a just person is a desire to be. What *is* the desire to be just?

The constructivist answer is that, just as the desire to play baseball fairly is not different from the desire to act on rules for the game that have been fairly arrived at, so the desire to abide by the demands of distributive justice is not different from a desire to act on the outcome of the procedure of construction. Moreover, recall that that procedure incorporates the features of sound reasoning about principles of justice and that the principles are the outcome of the procedure. Then the desire to act from the principles is not different from the desire to act on the outcome of such reasoning. That is, it is not different from the desire to be a practically rational person or to live up to the demands of practical reasoning, in this important subdomain of morality. And so, as Rawls implies, what seem like three different desires—the desire to satisfy the demands of distributive justice, the desire to act on the outcome of the constructivist procedure and the desire to express one's practical rationality in one's relations with others—are really desires for the same object under three different descriptions.[18] As Kant might say, though Rawls

---

17. T. M. Scanlon, "The Appeal and Limits of Constructivism," in *Constructivism in Practical Philosophy*, ed. James Lenman and Yonatan Shemmer (New York: Oxford University Press, 2012), 226–42, 231.
18. Rawls, *A Theory of Justice*, 501.

did not, the equivalence of the three descriptions is a synthetic truth that we arrive at by philosophical reasoning. It is synthetic a priori. The equation of the three descriptions enables us to give a substantive or illuminating characterization of moral motivation or of this instance of moral motivation.[19]

Moreover, I take it as given that the desire to satisfy the demands of distributive justice is a desire that can be had by people of very different fundamental convictions. The constructivist's characterization of that desire implies that it can be, for it implies that human beings with a wide variety of religious beliefs, or those having no religious beliefs at all, can be moved by considerations of justice.[20]

Finally, a constructivist account of distributive justice shows how we can act autonomously while acting on the demands of justice. Most obviously, it shows that the principles of justice are rules we give to ourselves through the procedure of construction. Less obviously, it shows that when we act on the desire to be just, our will is not determined by the causal power of something external to our own reason. To see this, recall why the label "constructivism" appropriately applies to the ludic constructivist account of baseball despite the oddity of describing rules as "constructed." What is ultimately constructed, I said, is the ideal realization of that which is the object of the game. That is why the practical reason of the players can be said to construct its own object. Similarly, in Rawls's account of justice, what is ultimately constructed is not a principle of justice but the ideal that participants in the social cooperation game realize when their activity satisfies the principles—the just conduct a well-ordered society. Thus, the desire to be just admits of still another description: it is a desire to do one's part in the ongoing realization of that ideal. Because the desire to be just admits of this description and because that ideal is ultimately constructed by our practical reason, the object of the desire to be just is one that practical reason gives itself. And so when we are moved by that object, we act autonomously.[21]

V. Christian Ethics and Constructivism: Some Objections

Ideally, having gestured to the sources of constructivism's appeal, I would now show that constructivism is relatively appealing by comparing its appeal to that of other views of morality, but I will not do that here in any systematic way. Instead, in deference to the constraints of space, I briefly anticipate objections that I think Christian ethicists would make to constructivism.

There are a number of reasons Christian ethicists might object to constructivism as I have characterized it. The most interesting objections would

---

19. Ibid., 418.
20. For a neglected expression of skepticism about Rawls's account of motivation that will be of special interest to religious ethicists, see John Courtney Murray, SJ, "The Problem of Mr. Rawls's Problem," accessed April 7, 2017, http://woodstock.georgetown.edu/library/Murray/1964d.htm.
21. See Rawls, *Lectures on the History of Moral Philosophy*, 252.

not, I think, query whether the constructivist procedure incorporates the constraints of practical reasoning about problems of justice or whether there is a unique solution to one of those problems that is given by, for example, Rawls's two principles of justice. For, as interesting as these objections are, there are others that cut deeper. The motivation for developing a constructivist account of justice, and claims about its appeal, depend on metaethical assumptions that Christian ethicists would want to query quite aggressively. They press their most interesting objections to constructivism by questioning those assumptions.

The most obvious such objection begins from the fact that, according to constructivism, God's will, God's commands, and God's goodness have nothing to do with the content of morality or with our knowledge of morality and our motivation to follow it. Christian ethicists, as their label suggests, assert an important connection between God and the norms of human behavior and may think it objectionable that constructivism seems not to do justice to that connection. But as objectionable as it may be to make God extraneous to morality in these ways, the extraneousness of God also betrays the deep motivation of constructivism. For constructivism is motivated by a desire to show how we can follow the dictates of morality autonomously. And many contemporary constructivists think that if God were not extraneous to morality's subject matter and to our motivation to follow it, we could not honor its demands autonomously. So God *has* to be assumed extraneous. Thus, it may be said, the deep motivation of constructivism is what is really objectionable about the view, because it implies that the defining commitment of Christian ethics is false.

Contemporary constructivist writing has a pronounced humanist flavor. The thought that God is the source of morality does not seem to be on the radar screens of most constructivists, except as a historically interesting metaethical option that has long since been discarded. But this does not imply that constructivism is orthogonal or antithetical to Christian ethics since we should be careful about taking the denial that God is extraneous to morality as definitive of that enterprise. For anyone who takes the theist metaethical option to be a live one must confront the Euthyphro dilemma. One horn of that dilemma, of course, is that the precepts of morality are endorsed and promulgated by God because they are independently valid, where what their validity is independent *of* is God's rational and volitional activity. Moral realism provides one account of that independence. But constructivism can be taken as another.[22] If we take constructivism this way, then—while some will think this is not the horn of the Euthyphro dilemma to grasp—I do not see that the view is inherently any more hostile to Christian ethics than any other view which grasps it. If it is more objectionable than those views, it will be for other reasons than that it makes God extraneous.

---

22. See Christine Korsgaard, *Creating the Kingdom of Ends* (Cambridge: Cambridge University Press, 1996), 62–3.

34   Paul Weithman

Realists may assert a connection between moral and natural properties which they think constructivists deny. Whether they do, in fact, deny it depends on the nature of the connection that is said to hold. Constructivists need not deny that the injustice of institutions is connected to the property—which I take to be a natural property—of being such that they give rise to inequalities of opportunity among the similarly talented and motivated. Quite the contrary, that an institution has one of these properties may—depending upon the content of the constructivist's principles—be among the grounds of the constructivist's judgment that the institution is unjust. More important for present purposes, the realist who claims that constructivism is incompatible with Christian ethics—because it denies the connection between moral and natural properties that the realist asserts—shows that Christian ethics is committed to the realist's connection. But it is hard to see why Christian ethics, just as such, is so committed.

Another objection begins from the observation that constructivists and Christian ethicists seem to differ on the point of identifying moral principles. As a result of the way constructivists think of that point, they deny that valid moral principles can demand the selflessness—the total self-giving—that is characteristic of the precepts of Christian ethics. Those precepts will not, therefore, be the outcome of a constructivist procedure. Thus, from the viewpoint of Christian ethics, the way constructivists construe the point of morality leads them to mistake its content.

One way to develop this objection would be to draw out the parallel with games that I introduced earlier. I said then that the point of formulating rules of a game is to solve a problem. It is to identify and adopt rules that can coordinate the activity of those who want to play. If rules are to play this role, they must satisfy a feasibility condition: they must be such that players can follow them. And so proposed rules will have to be assessed for feasibility before being adopted. Proposals which players cannot follow—because the sacrifices they enjoin are too demanding for the nature or talents of the players—are rejected as rules of the game.

Similarly, it may be said, constructivists think that the point of identifying rules of right, like the point of finding rules of a game, is to arrive at principles capable of playing a social role. The role of the rules is to coordinate activity and serve as a mutually accepted basis of accountability and justification. So constructivists, like those framing rules of a game, impose a feasibility condition on principles: principles of right must be such that we can use them to play that role. What it is to use them is itself complicated, but as a first approximation, they must be such that we can honor them if—though perhaps not only if[23]—we think others will and such that failure

---

23. On this score, Rawls is not as clear as we might wish; I discuss the unclarity briefly in my *Why Political Liberalism? On John Rawls's Political Turn* (New York: Oxford University Press, 2010), 338.

to follow them engenders feelings of shame and guilt.[24] To enforce the feasibility condition, constructivists build the condition into the procedure by which moral principles are identified.[25]

Christian ethics assigns morality a very different role. The point of identifying the principles of Christian ethics, it may be said, is to identify rules which accord with the teachings of the Gospel. The difference in point may give rise to a difference in content. There may be moral principles that Christian ethics is committed to but that constructivism cannot account for. As I shall say at greater length in the following, the inability to account for *some* moral principles is not problematic since the constructivism I have sketched here aims to account only for a part of morality. It *would* be problematic if Christian ethics were committed to moral principles that the constructivist is committed to denying. But in the absence of any examples, I shall lay this possibility aside and focus on a different one.

The Christian ethicist's description of morality, unlike the constructivist's, does not naturally suggest that we test principles for validity by asking the feasibility question the constructivist does: whether we can follow that principle provided others will. In fact, the Gospels seem to imply that such a test would fail to pick out the right principles. For when Jesus tell us to love those who hate us, he, in effect, enjoins us to follow the injunction to universal love on the assumption that others won't. Moreover, it may be objected, the imposition of a feasibility test would be out of place. For if reflection on human nature shows that we are incapable of abiding by the injunctions of the Gospel, it would be impious to conclude that the moral principles of the Gospels are invalid. We should conclude instead that human beings are sinful. Indeed, our inability to live up to the teachings of the Gospel might

---

24. How principles of distributive justice engage our moral sentiments is a complex matter that I cannot pursue here. What matters for present purposes is this. Principles of distributive justice play a role in social practices of morally justifying distribution and of holding people morally responsible for their distributive choices and activities. If the principles cannot engage our moral sentiments, they cannot be used to play that latter role. That is why the principles' ability to engage the moral sentiments of shame and guilt is built into the feasibility condition.
25. This reading of constructivism seems to be confirmed by Kant's "Kingdom of Ends" formulation of the categorical imperative, according to which we must ask whether our maxim could be a "universal law[] for a . . . kingdom of ends." For this formulation seems to imply that if a maxim or a principle cannot play the role a law would have to play in such a kingdom, it fails Kant's test. Clearer confirmation can be found in Rawls's *A Theory of Justice*. Rawls begins that book by identifying the social role of principles of justice; Rawls, *A Theory of Justice*, 3–6. Later, he requires parties in the original position to consider whether proposed principles could stably fill that role or whether, on the contrary, agreement on a principle would be undone by the strains of commitment; Rawls, *A Theory of Justice*, 153–4. Rawls's feasibility constraint is clearly tied to the defining features of constructivism at Thomas Nagel, "Moral Conflict and Political Legitimacy," *Philosophy and Public Affairs* 16, no. 3 (1987): 215–40, 220–1.

be an important source of that self-knowledge which is the beginning of wisdom.[26]

I believe constructivists are committed to the claim that moral principles must be such that we can use them to play a social role. And so I think a feasibility constraint is ineliminable from constructivism. But as I have argued elsewhere, the constructivist is not thereby committed to a naturalistic account of how our compliance with moral principles is possible. Indeed, she might hold that the various desires—with which I identified the desire to be just—are not normally *effective* desires: something in our nature keeps us from achieving their object. And so the constructivist could accept the propositional content of the principles of Christian ethics, hold onto her claim that compliance with those principles must be possible for us, but also hold that our compliance requires the fortification of our natural psychological resources by grace. This is, as far as I can tell, a consistent form of constructivism.[27]

There is another response open to the constructivist toward which I can only gesture but which is suggested by some recent work on Kant's *Religion*.

The constructivist could endorse the precepts of the Gospel while holding onto the feasibility condition by rethinking what is required to satisfy that condition. She might be led to rethink what is required to satisfy it by thinking again about why that condition is imposed. I believe constructivists think that if complying with moral principles is seen to be impossible, we will not even try to honor them. Thus, the rationale for requiring that principles be feasible is that belief in the feasibility of morality is necessary to sustain our interest in it. As we have seen, Rawls interprets the feasibility condition as requiring principles of justice to be such that human beings can generally honor them, at least in the favorable circumstances of a just society. But the constructivist could maintain that Rawls's interpretation of the condition is too strong, for what we need to sustain our commitment to justice is not the belief that human beings are generally capable of honoring the principles. All we need to believe is that honoring them is not beyond the capacities of human nature. The fact that Christ possessed a fully human, as well as a fully divine, nature and perfectly satisfied the precepts is enough to show that.[28] And so the feasibility condition does not itself stand in the way of adopting precepts as demanding as we like.

This response depends on assumptions in moral psychology that I cannot examine here, and is probably most plausible when combined with some

---

26. See Romans 7:7: "What shall we say then? *Is* the law sin? God forbid. Nay, I had not known sin, but by the law: for I had not known lust, except the law had said, Thou shalt not covet."
27. Paul Weithman, "Relational Equality, Inherent Stability and the Reach of Contractualism," *Social Philosophy and Policy* 31, no. 2 (2015): 92–113, 111–13.
28. See Barbara Herman, "Religion and the Highest Good: Speaking to the Heart of Even the Best of Us" (unpublished typescript on file with author).

version of the previous response about the availability of grace. But this avenue strikes me as one that is at least worthy of exploration.

As we saw, the feasibility condition, somehow understood, is a consequence of taking morality to have a social role. This brings me to the last objection I consider, one that queries the desirability of the social form in which constructivists think moral principles play their role.

As I noted earlier, the constructivist metaphor comes into its own with the identification of valid moral principles. For the constructivist thinks that we can use those principles to construct an object of practical reason which we are to try to realize in our action. That object is a conception of our social world as it might be, and as it would be if everyone complied with the principles. This ideal social world is one whose members share and, insofar as it is possible, promote one another's ends, for that is what some of the principles require.

If the world were one in which members had the end of loving and serving God, the Christian ethicist might agree that that world is indeed an ideal. But instead, it is a world in which—as Rawls says of his well-ordered society—"deliberative rationality has free play."[29] Constructivists assume that the free play of deliberative rationality leads people to adopt a variety of ends. Some of those ends may involve the worship of God The principles governing that world require members to respect one another's free choice of ends.[30] And so whatever "respect" means, the ideal social world of the constructivist is not one in which all members help one another on their journey of faith and lead one another to God. Rather, the social world valorized by constructivism is a social world marked by pluralism. But, the Christian ethicist may say, that is not the appropriate object of our striving. Moreover, by presenting the Kingdom of Ends as an ultimate end, constructivism may mislead us into mistaking it for the Kingdom it really is our vocation to bring about.

I myself find the idea of a tolerant, morally pluralistic community very attractive. In part this is because I value pluralism. In part it is because the conditions of liberty that allow for pluralism are the conditions under which faith is freely developed. And so I would not hastily dismiss either the claim that the constructed object of the cooperation game is a realm of end-setting beings who honor the principles of right or the claim that realizing that object would be a very great good. But another response, more palatable to the Christian ethicist, would be to say that constructivism provides a useful way of conceptualizing a fragment of morality: the morality of distributive justice under modern conditions, given citizens' shared commitment to living as free equals. There is much more to morality than that, and certainly much more to Christian ethics than that. A full philosophical treatment of

---

29. Rawls, *A Theory of Justice*, 496.
30. Korsgaard, *Creating the Kingdom of Ends*, 192–3, 196.

Christian ethics would, for example, have to treat of the moral excellence of the saints and ascetics of the Christian tradition.

Here I have been concerned with the consistency of Christian ethics and the constructivist account of distributive justice and have tried to address some objections that purport to show that the two are inconsistent. The constructivist account of political morality would have to be shown consistent with the fuller philosophical treatment Christian ethics requires. I shall not ask here how that might be shown. For now, I shall simply note that if consistency can be shown, we might think of a society that satisfies constructivist principles as providing us at least a faint and delicate foretaste of that Kingdom which is the object of Christian ethics.

Bibliography

Aristotle. *Politics*. Edited by Carnes Lord. Chicago: University of Chicago Press, 1985.

Friedman, Michael. "Kant's Theory of Geometry." *The Philosophical Review* 94, no. 4 (1985): 455–506.

Herman, Barbara. "Religion and the Highest Good: Speaking to the Heart of Even the Best of Us." (unpublished typescript on file with author).

Hobbes, Thomas. *Leviathan*. Edited by Richard Tuck. Cambridge: Cambridge University Press, 1991.

Kant, Immanuel. "On the Common Saying 'This May Be True in Theory, But It Does Not Apply in Practice.'" In *Kant: Political Writings*, edited by Hans Siegbert Reiss. Cambridge: Cambridge University Press, 1970.

———. *Groundwork of the Metaphysics of Morals*. Edited by Mary McGregor. Cambridge: Cambridge University Press, 2011.

Korsgaard, Christine. *Creating the Kingdom of Ends*. Cambridge: Cambridge University Press, 1996.

———. *Sources of Normativity*. Cambridge: Cambridge University Press, 1996.

———. "Realism and Constructivism in Twentieth-Century Moral Philosophy." In *Philosophy in America at the Turn of the Century*, 99–122. Charlottesville: The Philosophy Documentation Center, 2003.

Locke, John. *Second Treatise of Government*. Edited by C. B. Macpherson. Indianapolis: Hackett Publishing, 1980.

Murray, SJ, John Courtney. "The Problem of Mr. Rawls's Problem." Accessed April 7, 2017. http://woodstock.georgetown.edu/library/Murray/1964d.htm.

Nagel, Thomas. "Moral Conflict and Political Legitimacy." *Philosophy and Public Affairs* 16, no. 3 (1987): 215–40.

Rawls, John. *Political Liberalism*. New York: Columbia University Press, 1995.

———. *Lectures on the History of Moral Philosophy*. Edited by Barbara Herman. Cambridge: Harvard University Press, 2000.

———. "Kantian Constructivism in Moral Theory." *The Journal of Philosophy* 77, no. 9 (September 1980): 516–72. The lectures are reprinted in Rawls, John. *Collected Papers*, edited by Samuel Freeman, 303–58. Cambridge: Harvard University Press, 2001.

———. "The Best of All Games." Accessed April 12, 2017. http://bostonreview.net/rawls- the- best-of-all-games.

Scanlon, T. M. "Contractualism and Utilitarianism." In *Utilitarianism and Beyond*, edited by Amartya Sen and Bernard Williams, 103–26. Cambridge: Cambridge University Press, 1982.

———. "The Appeal and Limits of Constructivism." In *Constructivism in Practical Philosophy*, edited by James Lenman and Yonatan Shemmer, 226–42. New York: Oxford University Press, 2012.

Weithman, Paul. "Augustine and Aquinas on Original Sin and the Function of Political Authority." *The Journal of the History of Philosophy* 30, no. 3 (1992): 353–76.

———. *Why Political Liberalism? On John Rawls's Political Turn*. New York: Oxford University Press, 2010.

———. "Relational Equality, Inherent Stability and the Reach of Contractualism." *Social Philosophy and Policy* 31, no. 2 (2015): 92–113.

———. "Autonomy and Disagreement About Justice in *Political Liberalism*." *Ethics* 128 (October 2017): 95–122.

2 A Humean Account of What Wrongness Amounts To

Kevin Kinghorn

In this chapter I want to argue that there are no facts about the *wrongness* of any action, beyond those facts associated with a Humean-type constructivism. And I want to suggest that the Christian theist should not worry about such an antirealist conclusion but should instead focus on how theism provides insight into natural facts about the goodness and badness of our actions.

I. Wrongness versus Badness

An important starting point for this discussion is to note that the claim "this action is right (or wrong)" is quite different than the claim "this action is good (or bad)." The twin concepts right/wrong are connected to a number of further moral concepts. If I have done something wrong, it seems I am *guilty* of something. I become a candidate for *blame*, and there now exists some basis for *punishing* me. Furthermore, I will seemingly have failed to meet some *obligation* toward someone, and that person will be entitled to press some claim against me.

None of these moral concepts are necessarily connected to a *bad* action I might perform. Perhaps my act of watching a sitcom marathon is a relatively bad action, as compared to how I might otherwise spend my time. But if this action is a part of my genuine leisure time and I have violated no obligation or infringed on anyone's rights, then my action will not be a *wrong* action. The point about my sitcom viewing being a "relatively bad" action also raises a further feature of the twin concepts good/bad, namely, that goodness and badness come in degrees. One action of mine can be better—that is, more good—than another action of mine, as when my action of helping two neighbors is better than my action of helping only one neighbor. By contrast, it seems mistaken to suggest that some action of mine could be "more wrong" than another action of mine. Admittedly, an action might violate multiple laws and fail to meet multiple obligations—as opposed to an action which breaches only a single law or obligation. But the concept of wrongness itself does not admit to degrees in the way that goodness does.

Having briefly sketched some of the differences between the concepts right/wrong and the concepts good/bad, let me emphasize that I would *not* wish to defend a constructivist analysis of the nature of goodness. I think that facts about the noninstrumental goodness, or final value, of certain states of affairs can be established pretty straightforwardly. For sentient creatures (or beings) with a mental life who can experience their lives as going well or not well for them, pleasurable mental states are experienced *as* better than unpleasurable ones. These pleasurable mental states are valuable for the ones who experience them. This point is enough to draw the axiological conclusion that certain mental states have more value—they are better—than others.[1]

This point would also be the beginning of a fuller argument I myself would want to defend about the range of things that have final, or noninstrumental, value. To put my cards on the table, I am a welfarist about the good (i.e., something is only good if it is good *for* someone), and I am a mental statist about welfare (i.e., one's positive mental states are the only things that noninstrumentally contribute to one's welfare). While I will not defend these positions here,[2] the broader point I again want to establish is that there are facts about the goodness of certain states of affairs: specifically, facts about what makes people's lives go well for them.

Although I again think people's lives go well or poorly for them in virtue of their mental states, this claim should not be mistaken for the constructivist claim about how we, as valuing human beings, confer value on things. The constructivist view is that there are "no moral facts independent of the finding that a certain hypothetical procedure would have such and such an upshot."[3] Or, following Sharon Street, the constructivist view can be seen as one in which moral facts are derived from what does or does not follow from some "practical point of view": an evaluative standpoint of some creature or creatures "who take at least some things in the world to be good or bad, better or worse, required or optional, worthy or worthless."[4] But experiencing mental states *as* pleasurable, *as* making one's life go better rather than worse for her, does not involve any procedure. It does not require an evaluative standpoint—other than the trivial point that someone who can experience a pleasurable or unpleasurable mental state is, of course, someone who can value these things.

---

1. Cf. Richard Kraut, *What Is Good and Why* (Cambridge: Harvard University Press, 2007), 73: "One can say that it is bad that people feel pain, and then support that claim by saying that it is bad for them."
2. My extended defense of these claims about final value is found in Kevin Kinghorn, *A Framework for the Good* (Notre Dame: University of Notre Dame Press, 2016), chap. 2.
3. Stephen Darwall, Allan Gibbard, and Peter Railton, "Toward *Fin de Siecle* Ethics: Some Trends," *The Philosophical Review* 101, no. 1 (January 1992): 140.
4. Sharon Street, "What Is Constructivism in Ethics and Metaethics?" *Philosophy Compass* 5 (2010): 366.

Admittedly, mental statism does share with constructivism the view that facts about goodness depend in *some* way on the subjective perspective of individuals. But I again will view facts about (noninstrumental) goodness as facts about the intrinsic qualities of the experiences that sentient creatures or beings have. And since these facts are neither the outcome of some procedure nor a fleshing out through practical reasoning of what follows from some evaluative point of view the thesis of mental statism is pretty far removed from constructivist theories.

Mental statism, and welfarism more generally, offers a formal account of goodness. A state of affairs is good if it makes someone's life go better, rather than worse, for her. And what strictly speaking makes someone's life go well for her are her mental experiences. As to *substantive* questions about what does lead to pleasurable mental states for humans or other creatures, particularly in the long term, these questions seem to me key points of ethical inquiry, and I will say a bit more about these questions in the final section. My takeaway point from this section is that there are truths about the goodness or badness of states of affairs—specifically, truths about what makes the lives of sentient creatures or beings go well for them. Accordingly, I think constructivists are mistaken about the nature of these kinds of normative truths. Yet, when we turn to normative questions about *rightness* or *wrongness*, matters are very different.

II. Our Ideas of Right and Wrong

I noted earlier that facts about the wrongness of some action seem to be necessarily tied to a cluster of other normative facts about whether the actor violated an obligation, infringed on someone else's rights, and stands as a candidate for blame and punishment. If I have committed some wrong action, then I have shirked an obligation toward someone, I have infringed on her rights, and I can properly be blamed and punished. But what exactly is the ontology of an obligation or a right?

Perhaps the moral realist will say, "Whatever their ontology, obligations, and rights are certainly not things we merely *confer* on others. Rather, we recognize that others *have* certain rights, that they *own* certain things. Maybe we will disagree about *how* we recognize such things, but surely we all agree that others do have rights and do own things. And we would be violating an obligation toward them if we made an improper claim to those things which others own, or have a right to. That is, we would be doing something wrong."

To deny this realist line of thought might be thought to be wildly counterintuitive. Nevertheless, I think the realist position about rightness and wrongness is incorrect. The intuitions to which the realist appeals can be best explained without positing non-natural facts about an action's "wrongness." Perhaps the best way to begin this discussion is by asking how we humans arrived at the concept of "wrong."

On this question I want to follow J. S. Mill's basic insight into how matters of "expediency" (i.e., matters of how we can flourish as we live together) can easily become matters of moral "necessity." As we assess threats to our well-being and the well-being of others about whom we care, we identify both severe threats to our security and less severe threats. Our negative attitudes toward the most severe of threats lead us to declare that they are not to be done, no matter what might be said in their favor:

> Our notion, therefore, of the claim we have on our fellow creatures to join in making safe for us the very groundwork of our existence, gathers feelings round it so much more intense than those concerned in any of the more common cases of utility, that the difference in degree . . . becomes a real difference in kind. The claim assumes that character of absoluteness, that apparent infinity, and incommensurability with all other considerations, which constitute the distinction between the feeling of right and wrong and that or ordinary expediency and inexpediency.[5]

As we reflect on, and make decisions about, how we should live together, it is, of course, natural and practically wise to focus especially on those actions that most significantly undermine the things we value (most notably, our well-being). We must settle these matters first before we debate the pros and cons of those actions that affect more peripherally the things we value.

When an action is viewed as a significant enough[6] threat to those things we most value, we agree to sanction those people who perform that action. We convey the idea that this action is not to be done, no matter what might be said for it. Even though, as Mill says, our proscriptions ultimately stem from considerations of "expediency," the language we use takes on a "character of absoluteness." Hence, unlike the incremental language of goodness/badness (in which one action can be said to be better—i.e., more good—than another action), the language of rightness/wrongness is binary, with any action considered either as being wrong or as being right (i.e., permissible, or not wrong).

So, from pragmatic considerations of what is good for us and others, we conclude that some actions are not to be done, period. And this is a good beginning point in exploring what people *mean* when they say that "action X is wrong."

III. The Meaning of *Wrong*

I think it is pretty clear that what most people mean when they say, "That action is wrong," is typically something like "That action is not to be done,

---

5. Jeremy Bentham and John Stuart Mill, *Utilitarianism and Other Essays*, ed. Alan Ryan (London: Penguin Books, 1987), chap. 5, 327–8.
6. Decisions about when an agreed-upon bad action (e.g., marijuana or cigarette smoking) is bad enough to sanction is, of course, a frequent public discussion.

period." Robert Adams, in his early writings, suggested that, for many Christian theists, the meaning of *wrong* is tied to the idea of what is commanded by a loving God.[7] That is, for some people the idea that an action might "violate the commands of a loving God" plays a role in their understanding that some actions can be "wrong." The very meaning of the term "wrong" is grasped (at least in part) by understanding what it would be to violate the commands of God.

I think Adams is probably correct in what some theists mean to convey when they say that some action is wrong. And broadly speaking, the meaning of the term *wrong* may indeed have differing associations within different communities. Still, the central concept that gives the term its common meaning is that a wrong action is an action that is not to be done, period. This point remains so even in cases where we recognize that someone is facing a moral dilemma in not being able to avoid a wrong action. For example, we may say, "It would be wrong to break your promise to have lunch with Fred today, and it would also would be wrong to leave the office anytime today during the current crisis at work." This is why these kinds of moral dilemmas are, after all, dilemmas. No matter what one does, a prima facie case can be made that that action is simply not to be done.

In acknowledging the absolutist character of what people commonly mean to convey when they declare an action "wrong," I acknowledge a potential challenge to the antirealist account of the nature of wrongness I will go on to offer. Sometimes the plausibility of antirealism is challenged on the grounds that most people seem clearly to assume that the realist's facts exist about wrongness. This assumption is shown in the absolutist nature of their statements about wrongness. (The assumption is also shown by, e.g., people's attestation that actions like human enslavement would still be wrong, even if they and everyone else had been brought up to think differently.) The challenge is thus that the antirealist ends up dismissing most everyone's shared intuitions that some actions are wrong, independent of anyone's perspective. And this is then thought to place the plausibility of antirealism into question.

In response, I again state that I am not an antirealist about the nature of *goodness*. In section I, I outlined why I think there are facts to be discovered—not merely constructed—about the goodness of certain states of affairs. But I do want to defend the position that, on matters of *wrongness*, the realist's facts do not exist. And so I will side with J. L. Mackie when it comes to statements about wrongness. At the risk of presumptuousness,

---

7. See Robert Adams, "A Modified Divine Command Theory of Ethical Wrongness," in *Religion and Morality: A Collection of Essays*, ed. Gene H. Outka and John P. Reeder, Jr. (Garden City: Anchor Press, 1973). For Adams's later shift submitting that "contrariness to the commands of a loving God" is best seen as a property that explains the *nature* of wrongness, as a matter of metaphysical necessity, see Robert Adams, "Divine Command Metaethics Modified Again," *Journal of Religious Ethics* 7, no. 1 (Spring 1979): 66–79.

I am committed to the following: inasmuch as people assume the realist's facts about some actions having a property of wrongness when they assert that "action X is wrong," people are simply in error.

In offering an explanation for this widespread error, I would focus on the way in which our moral language often really must be absolutist, even if our considerations are ultimately ones of expediency. In order to build consensus that some actions are not to be done, no matter what might be said in their favor, people in communities agree to use absolutist language when referring to them. Societies cannot function without rules and laws which are thought of in binary terms: one either follows them or violates them. For pragmatic reasons, people cannot constantly perform cost–benefit analyses as they navigate daily life in communities. We all need rules we can simply follow, laws we all agree to keep. And we need to depend on others to do the same.

Importantly, we use absolutist language in the education of our children. With respect to the behavior we deem of crucial importance, we do not want to leave wiggle room. We do not want to invite our children to perform cost–benefit analyses, calculating whether some frowned-upon action "might not really be that bad" or "might actually be worth the cost." The language of good and bad invites these kinds of comparisons of value. But the language of right and wrong (and obligations, rights, and so on) helps us settle things, helps ensure that our children develop habits of good behavior, and, in general, is useful in educating the next generation and building consensus among us all.

So we readily adopt the absolutist language of right and wrong, even while our ultimate concerns—as well as the ultimate justification of our proscriptions—are expedient matters of what is good or valuable. Do the realist's facts exist about some actions having the property of wrongness? I will go on to argue against this view. But it is really not that surprising that there should be the widespread assumption—even if typically an uncritical assumption—among those who use the language of "right and wrong" that some actions *really are wrong*. This is what we have been told since childhood, and perhaps our moral educators were wise to do so. Nevertheless, this itself does not provide good evidence for the realist position on the nature of wrongness. A plausible, antirealist story can be told about why people are in widespread error in thinking that the realist's facts about wrongness exist.

In this section I have been exploring the *meaning* of *wrong*, as that term is typically used. In going on in the next section to analyze the *nature* of wrongness, we will be looking for the formal conditions under which an action would qualify as a wrong one. (There is also the substantive question of which actions occurring in the world meet these conditions.) Put another way, we are looking for the kinds of facts that would make the statement "X is wrong" a true (or false) one. The meanings of descriptive terms can often serve as clues as to the nature of the things being described. But this is not always the case. A descriptive claim like "that dress is blue" does not give us insight into some property of blueness the dress has; rather, it turns out that the existing facts about the dress itself include only properties having to do with the absorption and reflection of various light waves.

I have acknowledged that, when people make the claim "X is wrong," they generally mean that "X is not to be done, period." But my claim is that, in the case of our analysis of wrongness, the meaning of the term can mislead us about the nature of wrongness. The common meaning can suggest that there are stance-independent facts about some actions: they have the property of "wrongness," which humans might discover (and which are not the result of any human construction.) But I want to argue that there is no good reason to suppose that there are such facts—and that the facts that *do* exist about wrongness are something like Humean constructivist facts.

IV. The Nature of Wrongness

My central claim about the nature of wrongness involves the idea of sanction. I do not mean "sanction" in the positive sense in which a licensing board authorizes or gives permission for some event. Rather, I mean *sanction* in the negative sense of punishment or penalty, as when the United Nations imposes sanctions on some rogue nation.

Admittedly, the line between permissible actions (with no intent to sanction) and punishable actions can at times become fuzzy. Suppose a parent has encouraged his children to spend their free time reading rather than watching television. But suppose also that the children have been given an afternoon of leisure time, with the parent agreeing that the children have the final say in what activities they may pursue. In making this agreement, the parent, of course, conveys the intent not to hold it against the children if their actions are not as good as the parent might like. If the children in our example frequently choose to watch sitcom marathons over reading during their leisure time, the parent may inevitably then relate to the children as individuals who do not generally use their leisure time in the wisest manner. And this might at some point blur the line between (merely) frowning upon a bad action and sanctioning the children for their action.

As another example, merely frowning upon cigarette smoking is not the same as prohibiting it by law (with accompanying threat of punishment). However, if cigarette smoking remains legal, but is accompanied by a growing list of disincentives (exorbitant taxes on purchases, an exemption for insurers from having to cover smokers, and so on), then the public policy line becomes blurred between viewing smoking as a bad act and viewing it as a wrong act with accompanying punitive sanctions. Nevertheless, the distinction itself between permission and prohibition is clear enough, even if in some cases it becomes difficult to say when permission ends and aspects (like punishment) of prohibition begin.

My central claim is that facts about the wrongness of some action are reducible to facts about some individual's or group's intent to sanction those who perform that action. I use *intent* here in the sense of intending to do something in the future, rather than in the sense of performing an intentional action. Following Mill's basic insight of how matters of "expediency" can take on the "character of absoluteness" when they are judged to be of utmost importance, individuals or groups may declare that some action which crucially undermines something they value is "not to be done, period." That is, they may declare that that action is "wrong."

When a person or group of people conclude that some action is "not to be done, period" they are not merely forming a belief about some fact—in this case, a fact about the way in which an action undermines something they value. They are taking up a particular normative stance toward those who perform this action. Specifically, they are forming an intention to sanction those who perform the action. A parent may comment that watching a sitcom marathon during the entire stretch of his child's leisure time really "ought not to be done" (in the sense of being a bad action). But if he were to put his child on notice that watching will amount not only to a bad action but also to a *wrong* action, it is the threat of sanction that would introduce this new kind of normative force.

What other language might we use to convey the absoluteness of our position that an action is not to be done, on the threat of sanction? There is, of course, the language of an action being *wrong*. We also use the language of *ownership*. We say that someone "owns her house." And we use the language of *rights*. We say that a homeowner is one who alone "has the right" to use the home as she sees fit. Are there facts, as affirmed by the realist, about the homeowner and her relationship to the house, which onlookers merely recognize? I think it much more plausible to say that any facts about "ownership" or "rights" are reducible to facts about who stands ready to sanction those who would interfere with a person having the final say in how that house is used.

Suppose a stranger shows up at the house in which I currently live. He claims that he is going to turn the house into a wax museum. I object and insist that it is *my* house. I am the one who owns it. I have a right, which the stranger does not have, to decide how the house is used. But how do I defend my claim against the stranger? Well, I produce a government-issued deed to the house. What does this deed represent exactly?

One answer would be that the government recognizes some non-natural property I have: the property of "having a right" to the house. Or perhaps it is a relational property, one of "ownership," that exists between the house and me. This realist story would also include a non-natural property of "wrongness" being attached to the action of interfering with my exercise of my right to the house. On this story, the government deed is (at least largely) a recognition of these facts.

But my contention is that, when a person or group of people conclude that some action is "not to be done," they are not in the first instance forming a belief about some deontic fact. They are taking up a particular normative stance toward those who perform this action. Specifically, they are forming an intention to sanction those who perform the action. A government-issued deed to a house represents the government's intent to sanction those who interfere with the deed holder's use of the house (based on the government's consideration of expediency). When I confront the stranger who wants to turn the house into a wax museum, I show him my deed as a way of saying, "The enforcement arm of the governing body who gave me this deed stands ready to sanction—including forcibly stopping and punishing with fines or jail time—anyone who interferes with my use of this house. And I am going to appeal to them if you persist in challenging my use of it."

The ultimate warning I issue to the stranger is thus that it will be *bad for* him if he persists in challenging my use of the house. And in general, I would want to make the case that the normative force we feel when confronted with an action we think we "ought not to do" can always be spelled out in terms of a desire to avoid missing out on some valuable state of affairs.[8] Contra Kant, categorical imperatives always turn out to be hypothetical imperatives. While I do not have space to defend this claim, what I want to draw attention to at present is that I do not ultimately challenge the stranger by reminding him that the government holds the same belief I do that I "own" the house or that using the house against my wishes would be "wrong." I remind the stranger of the publicly declared intent of the government—revealed in laws and enforcement penalties—to sanction anyone who uses the house against my wishes.

Is there something *beyond* these facts about others' intent to sanction? Are governing bodies recognizing some non-natural facts about rights and ownership and wrongness—and then announcing their intent to sanction as a response to these facts? Perhaps it will be suggested that what the government is recognizing is simply the (natural) fact that I have signed a contract to repay some person or some bank, and *this* is what gives me the non-natural property of having a right to use the house. My response is that it is fine to maintain that the government's intent to sanction is in response to my signing a certain contract. I would simply add that the ultimate explanation of the government's intent to sanction is that, by doing so, something crucially good is preserved: namely, an agreed-upon process for any family to be able to have the same roof over their heads for present and future purposes they may have. But what I would argue is unnecessary is the claim that my signing a contract generates any non-natural properties—such as "wrongness" or "rights" or "obligations." Such properties are superfluous

---

8. My fuller defense of this claim can be found in Kinghorn, *A Framework for the Good*, chap. 3.

An Account of What Wrongness Amounts To 49

to a story of how I can come to have a deed to a house, as well as what role this deed plays in a disagreement about how the house is used.

Admittedly, it is common to talk in terms of my "right" to the house and of my "owning" a house and of it being "wrong" of someone to use my house against my wishes. But as we saw in the previous section, Mill has offered a plausible explanation of this kind of deontic language. As we seek jointly to adhere to (and to communicate to our children that they should adhere to) certain practices that are crucial to our living well together, it is useful to employ language that communicates absoluteness. Although the ultimate explanation of our language lies in considerations of "expediency," the language of *good/bad* invites comparisons of value. It invites negotiation. ("Yes, others have told me that this action is bad, but is it really *that* bad? Perhaps, for me, *not* doing the action would be even worse.") So, in order to settle decisively the matters crucial to our well-being, we adopt the language of rightness/wrongness (and other deontic terms), which is absolutist in nature. This is our way of settling matters and building consensus. "That action is simply not to be done, no matter what might be said in its favor."

My claim is not that we should remove deontic language from public policy discussions. I think such language is very useful, particularly the language of "rights." In advocating practices I believe we should all agree to (for reasons of expediency) concerning how to live well together, I may well take a public position that people have a right to various freedoms, that they have a right to a living wage, and so forth. Mill's explanation of our deontic language need not be taken as an indictment that moral philosophers who side with him are insincere in continuing to use this language in public policy discussions. But in terms of the nature of wrongness—the moral facts that would make the statement "this action is wrong" true and not merely useful—I will stand by my reductionist account that the facts available to us are facts about some person's or group's intent to sanction those who perform this action.

There are at least two main advantages to this reductionist account of what moral wrongness amounts to. First, it preserves the conceptual connection that wrongness has to the cluster of other concepts mentioned at the beginning of section II. If we say that someone has committed a wrong action, we think of them as having violated some *obligation* toward someone, as having infringed on her *rights*. On my account, all these deontic terms simply express that, according to someone, the action is not to be done, on the threat of sanction. As to the connections to blame and punishment, there is no mystery at all why a "wrong" action is necessarily tied to the idea that the one who performs it is subject to blame and punishment. To say that someone acted wrongly simply *is* to take up the normative stance that we (and/or others) stand ready to sanction the person through such measures of blaming and punishing.

In addition to preserving the conceptual connections between wrongness, obligations, rights, punishment, and so forth, my account of wrongness also has the obvious benefit of ontological parsimony. A realist account of some non-natural property—wrongness—is ontologically extravagant by comparison. Later, I address the objection that we do need to suppose such a non-natural property if we are to make sense of our shared moral intuitions. But for now, I note that, if my account survives this kind of objection (and I think it will), then ontological parsimony is a significant advantage.

V. Constructivist Facts about Wrongness

So is the account of wrongness I have offered a kind of constructivist account? In some sense I think it is, though it will very much be a Humean version of constructivism. It is Humean in that the evaluative standpoint from which a person forms an intent to sanction is the standpoint of that individual. Of course, it may be the case that others also stand willing to sanction those who perform some action. So there can be an agreed-upon *social* sanction. And there may be reason to suppose that, because of our shared human nature, we should expect there to be widespread agreement about the kinds of things which individuals will proscribe. But the similarities that may exist among individuals' evaluative starting points, as well as among the circumstances that affect their decisions to sanction or not, are contingent ones. A person's intent to sanction is not the result of any supposedly ideal evaluative standpoint nor the result of any hypothetical procedure. An intent to sanction stems from an individual's own particular standpoint, her own particular evaluation that some action is so bad that she stands ready to sanction those who perform it.

While this view is obviously very Humean in its emphasis on individual standpoints, the account of wrongness I have offered is not a matter of equating a person's statement "action X is wrong" simply with a *desire* the person has that this action not be performed. There is inevitably a *process* of some kind—a procedure, if you will—in moving from a desire to an intent to sanction. Typically, this process will involve weighing the anticipated gains and costs in terms of value. After all, sanctioning others who perform some action comes at a cost. Certain valuable outcomes are compromised. Most obviously, there are the resources and time expended administering punishments, as well as the fractured relationships between ourselves and those we sanction. Yet, in proscribing some action, we judge the costs of *not* proscribing the action to be even greater. (Again, all this can occur at a societal level or an individual level, though I will continue to focus on the way it occurs at an individual level.)

I say all this is *typically* what happens because there may be times when a person proscribes some action without giving much reflective consideration to valued goals or opportunity costs. A person might feel outraged on hearing of some human exploitation practice and resolve at once to stand

An Account of What Wrongness Amounts To 51

against, with threat of sanction, anyone who would perform such an action. But we must be careful here to distinguish (1) forming a quick and minimally reflective intent to sanction a person who performs some action and, more broadly, (2) reacting to a person because of a negative attitude toward the person or action she performs. The second scenario is consistent with an impulsive lashing out at a stranger who accidentally steps on one's toes while jostling for position on a crowded subway platform.

But this second scenario would not amount to forming an intent to sanction. *Some* kind of minimal, reflective process is involved in forming an intent to sanction others. In the previous section I stressed the distinction between (merely) thinking some action *bad* and taking the additional step of proscribing that action on the threat of sanction. Getting from the former to the latter inevitably involves some process of deliberation, even if a very quick judgment about competing values. As mentioned earlier in this section, there is always some cost—some value lost—in proscribing an action and in following through on sanctions. But, of course, the reason we consider proscribing some action is that we feel there is some *other* valuable state of affairs that is in danger of being lost if we do *not* take up this normative stance against that action. Thus, in forming an intent to sanction those who perform some action, there is a process in which one makes comparisons of value and arrives at a judgment about which value(s) to pursue.

What all this points to is that an analysis of the nature of wrongness cannot be reduced merely to an examination of the *desires* a person has. We will need to look at the process which led to the person taking the particular normative stance of intending to sanction. Is this enough to make the account of wrongness I have offered a constructivist account?

I will understand the constructivist as providing a particular kind of answer to the question, "Is this moral statement correct?" And on this question there will *sometimes* be constructivist facts that make people's statements about wrongness correct. One may wonder how the account of wrongness I have offered might possibly leave room for statements capable of being *true*. After all, I have stressed that, in calling an action "wrong," we are fundamentally taking up a particular kind of normative stance: we are forming an intent to sanction those who perform that action. And an *intent* to sanction does not seem to be the kind of thing that could have a truth value.

Yet, in my discussion of wrongness I have noted that there *is* practical judgment involved in moving from (1) a negative attitude toward some action to (2) proscribing that action—and correspondingly in moving from (1) having a negative view of others who perform that action to (2) intending to sanction others who perform it. In fact, it turns out that there are quite a number of judgments that will typically be made. As a starting point, one will need to be an individual who already values things, judging that some things are better (i.e., more good) than others. From that evaluative starting point, one will need to make the judgment that some action crucially undermines something that is of significant value. One will need to judge that the badness of that action is actually so significant that, in the effort to preserve this value, one should commit to sanctioning those who perform that action. In making this judgment, one will also need to have judged that the inevitable cost (i.e., the inevitable loss of something of value) of sanctioning others is not significant enough to override the anticipated value of proscribing the action on the threat of sanction.

So there are a number of judgments here of which we can ask: Are these judgments entailed by the person's evaluative standpoint? Do they follow from the person's practical point of view? Sometimes there will be correct answers to these questions. And it will be constructivist-type facts that make the answers correct.

I think that in *some* cases there will be no single correct answer. For example, in some cases the cost of sanctioning others (with this cost coming in the form of fractured relationships, large expenditures of resources, and so on) might add up to a loss of very significant value. Perhaps it then becomes a difficult judgment whether the cost of sanctioning is worth the anticipated gain. And perhaps there simply is no correct answer to this matter, no judgment that necessarily follows from the person's evaluative point of view. It would be wildly implausible to claim that there is some single formula that allows us all to make comparisons of value in any and all cases—for example, by using a hedonic scale on which all pleasures and pains can be compared and by assuming that pleasure and pain are the only things of value. Comparisons of value will not necessarily yield a single "correct" answer. Thus, a person might reasonably reach a judgment one day about which state of affairs is more valuable—and then reach an opposite conclusion a minute later. There is nothing necessarily irrational about that, no way of saying that one or the other judgment was entailed by the person's evaluative standpoint. So, in *some* cases a person's evaluative standpoint does not necessarily entail a particular judgment as to whether she should proscribe some action on the threat of sanction.

However, in *other* cases such a judgment would indeed seem to follow from her evaluative point of view. As a general point, although comparisons of value are not always clear cut from a particular point of view, sometimes they are. For example, a parent may want to enroll her daughter in a ballet school. There may be a terrific school one hour away and a mediocre school five minutes away. Is it worth the daily two-hour commute? We suppose that going to the better school will make possible several valuable goals the parent has for her child. Yet, the long daily commute will come at the expense of *other* valuable goals the parent has for her child. In making an all-things-considered judgment about comparative value, the parent's cost–benefit analysis may not yield an obvious result.

But what if we suppose that the terrific school is five minutes away and that the mediocre school is one hour away? In this case, given the parent's system of values, a judgment becomes easy. In fact, it would be irrational for the parent to choose the mediocre school, given the system of values we suppose she has. She does make a comparison of value as she considers the option of the mediocre ballet school. But there is only one conclusion she could reach that is consistent with the proper use of practical reasoning. The conclusion that she should enroll her child in the better ballet school is entailed by, it necessarily follows from, the evaluative standpoint we suppose her to have.

Regarding the judgment that a particular action is not to be done, on the threat of sanction, in many cases it may be that this normative stance really is entailed by a person's evaluative standpoint. The cost of sanctioning is perceived as minimal, and the perceived value in ensuring that the action is deterred is huge. In these cases it seems right to speak in terms of whether a person's normative stance of intending to sanction is a *correct* one—where correctness is again a matter of being entailed by the person's evaluative standpoint. Given the account of the nature of wrongness I have offered, my statement, "that action is wrong," can never be true in virtue of some realist fact. But in making this statement I am taking up a normative stance of intending to sanction those who perform that action. And this normative stance may (in some cases) be entailed by my evaluative standpoint.

In sum, constructivist-type facts may sometimes be available in assessing the correctness of a person's judgment that an action is not to be done, on the threat of sanction. Given that an action's property of "wrongness" amounts simply to the property of having been proscribed by some individual(s) on the threat of sanction, there are no stance-independent facts about wrongness that could make a person's claim that "action X is wrong" a correct judgment. But there are certainly constructivist-type facts about what follows from the evaluative standpoint of that individual(s). So my conclusion from this section is that the facts available to us, as we analyze the nature of wrongness, are facts associated with a Humean-type constructivism.

VI. What Is at Stake for the Christian Theist?

Given that the collection of essays containing this one focuses on constructivism in relation to religious ethics, I want to turn to some of the implications my account of wrongness has for the theist. I will engage with Christian theists, though most of the discussion could be adapted to other forms of theism.

To put my own cards on the table: I am a Christian moral philosopher. And from my own discussions over the years, I am quite aware that my anti-realist conclusions about wrongness will not sit easily—at least initially—with most Christian moral philosophers. There is a prominent strand of Christian apologetics that starts with the purportedly obvious existence of objective moral facts and moves to the conclusion that only God can account for the existence of such facts.[9] As I discuss in section VII, I think

---

9. For a good, recent presentation of this moral argument for God's existence, see David Baggett and Jerry Walls, *Good God* (New York: Oxford University Press, 2011).

Christian apologists can point to stance-independent facts about *goodness/badness*, which provide evidential support for the Christian description of God. Yet, if the claims of the previous two sections are correct, there simply are no stance-independent facts about *wrongness* to which the Christian theist might point as part of a framework of objective morality.

In this section I want to consider a broad kind of objection to the constructivist-type account of wrongness I have offered—particularly because it is an objection many Christian theists will no doubt want to raise in defending certain themes they have wanted to emphasize. Before considering this broad objection, I want to remind the reader of the two significant advantages of my account of the nature of wrongness. First, my account of wrongness preserves the necessary connection that exists between wrongness and other concepts such as blame and punishment. If a community proscribes some action with the intent to sanction those who perform it, then violators of that proscription will automatically acquire a social standing within the community: they will stand as guilty within the community, worthy of blame and punishment. No explanation is needed as to why a recognition of (stance-independent) facts about wrongness should move us all to want to blame or punish others who perform a wrong action. Our agreement that an action is wrong simply *is* our taking up a normative stance of intending to sanction (in such forms as blame and punishment) toward those who perform that action.

Second, my account of wrongness makes no appeal to non-natural properties. Other things being equal, ontological parsimony counts in favor of a theory, in comparison with other theories. If we have no compelling reason to affirm a non-natural property of "wrongness," then our fallback position should be to suppose that such a property does not exist. Gilbert Harman has pointed out that, in scientific observations and judgments, presumed facts (e.g., the existence of protons) do help us explain a scientist's observations (e.g., of a vapor trail). But as Harman then noted, we do not need to appeal to some (stance-independent) fact about the "wrongness" of an action in order to explain our reaction to, for example, a cat being set on fire and our subsequent judgment that this action ought not to be done.[10] A purported property of wrongness becomes superfluous in explaining why it is that people proscribe certain actions.

Why have some moral philosophers concluded that stance-independent facts about wrongness do exist? Typically, the claim is that, contra Harman, our reaction to certain states of affairs *cannot*, in fact, plausibly be explained without appealing to some property of wrongness that we recognize. Sometimes thought experiments are offered in support of this claim, and I consider a standard one later in this section. But the claim is often defended by insisting that it should just be intuitively obvious to anyone

---

10. See Gilbert Harman, *The Nature of Morality* (New York: Oxford University Press, 1977), 6–7.

that such facts exist. Consider the way in which David Baggett and Jerry Walls contend for facts about the wrongness of certain actions: "It's wrong, for example, to torture innocent children for fun, and we plainly recognize it.... Reflection yields legitimately difficult questions in ethics, yes, but a great many ethical truths remain obvious."[11] But is it really obvious that an act like torturing a child for fun has some realist property of "wrongness"? I do not at all see how this point is supposed to be obvious.

Let me quickly add that, of course, I find such an act reprehensible and repulsive. I for one will volunteer my intention to sanction anyone who would do such a thing. (And we should keep in mind that *sanction* need not refer to refined chastisement; severe forms of punishment and retribution fall under the umbrella of "sanction.") I am also reassured to note that our society stands ready to sanction—and sanction severely—anyone who would perform such an act. And I think it easy to construct a case, from the Christian perspective, that God stands ready to sanction anyone who would perform such an act. Surely these declarations are sufficient to convey that I take the horrifically bad act of child torture as seriously as anyone else. What is added if I declare, "Also, such an act is just plain wrong!"? Perhaps people may commonly expect to hear such a declaration from anyone who views child torture with the utmost seriousness. And a person's reluctance to make this public declaration may, for some people, signal that the person somehow feels ambiguous about the topic—as though there exists a "gray area" in which child torture might not in all contexts be intolerable. But this is decidedly *not* my reason for resisting the declaration. (At least, I would resist the declaration in the context of offering a philosophical analysis of wrongness; I may agree with the declaration in public policy discussions, as a way of building consensus.) My reason, again, is that there are no (stance-independent) facts that would make such a declaration true.

Baggett and Walls follow C. S. Lewis, William Lane Craig, and other Christian apologists in insisting that humans share a sense of fairness, of justice, of right and wrong that is not reducible to the kinds of considerations of "expediency" that Mill suggested. Lewis noted the way we commonly phrase our arguments: "How'd you like it if anyone did the same to you?"; "That's my seat, I was there first"; "Give me a bit of your orange, I gave you a bit of mine"; "Come on, you promised." He insisted that the appeals here are "to some kind of standard of behaviour which he expects the other man to know about."[12] Indeed, the act of quarrelling itself "means trying to show that the other man is in the wrong. And there would be no sense in trying to do that unless you and he had some sort of agreement as to what Right and Wrong are."[13]

---

11. Baggett and Walls, *Good God*, 9.
12. C. S. Lewis, *Mere Christianity*, revised ed. (New York: Harper San Francisco, 2001), 3.
13. Ibid., 4.

Lewis's favorite example involves the sense of *fairness* all people (ex hypothesi) seem to have, even young children:

> Whenever you find a man who says he does not believe in a real Right and Wrong, you will find the same man going back on this a moment later. He may break his promise to you, but if you try breaking one to him he will be complaining "It's not fair" before you can say Jack Robinson.[14]

Lewis submitted that cultures from around the world understand the binding force of the "laws of human nature." The reason they are considered *laws*, Lewis reasoned, is "because people thought that every one knew it by nature and did not need to be taught it."[15]

Before assessing Lewis's claims, let me note what is at stake in the current discussion. The premise that people share an intuitive sense of right and wrong does not, of course, establish that stance-independent facts about right and wrong exist. But a shared sense of right and wrong might be taken as evidence for these facts. So now my assessment of the claim that people share this intuitive sense: I think that further reflection on the research of social scientists casts doubt on this presumption that people do have the kind of shared sense of justice and of right and wrong that Lewis thought obvious.

Admittedly, as Kristján Kristjánsson notes, a common conclusion that social scientists have often sought to draw from their research is that there exists among humans a "universal sense of (or for) justice."[16] Such a conclusion would certainly support Lewis's line of argument. Yet, conclusions about humans possessing a sense of justice cannot be drawn without normative import from the social scientists conducting their studies. Kristjánsson explains, "There is no non-evaluative royal road to understanding what justice means, be it for children or for adults. . . . [No] empirical theory of justice can avoid resting on a normative premise."[17]

Kristjánsson discusses several leading theories of social scientists about how humans develop their sense of justice.[18] He observes how, inevitably,

> normative considerations steer the design and interpretation of empirical research into the development of justice conceptions by providing assumptions both about what counts as a conception of justice in the

---

14. Ibid., 6.
15. Ibid., 5.
16. Kristján Kristjánsson, *Justice and Desert-Based Emotions* (Aldershot: Ashgate, 2006), 111.
17. Ibid., 117.
18. Especially William Damon, Martin Hoffman, and Melvin Lerner. See Kristjánsson, *Justice*, chap. 4.

An Account of What Wrongness Amounts To   57

first place (and what does not), and about what counts as a better (or worse) conception of justice.[19]

Seemingly, social scientists who have charted the moral sensibilities and development of humans from childhood through adulthood "have normally gone about their business in the conviction that they are merely trading in empirically discernible facts about human growth."[20] The problem, as David Carr has also convincingly shown, is that "any such facts are entirely fictions."[21] Social scientists do not record purely descriptive facts about people's development of a sense of justice and fair play. They construct questions and interpret answers through preexisting lenses of normative terms and concepts.

Thus, for example, when assessing William Damon's stage theory of the development of justice conceptions in children, Kristjánsson observes,

> What we notice at once is the primacy-of-justice thesis: all conceptions of resource allocation must be justice conceptions; all distributive principles just be justice principles (or as Damon would put it, principles of 'positive justice'). But why presume that other moral concerns, such as pity, benevolence or utility, cannot play a role here also, or even non-moral ones, such as pure self-interest?[22]

So how could social researchers on a project reach conclusions about people's moral sensibilities, drawing merely from the empirical data of people's responses to, for example, resource allocation? Such a project would have to avoid privileging any particular framework of ethical concepts, and it would have to avoid presupposing a theory about human motivation. Such a project seems quite a daunting task.

A purely empirical fact which, I think, probably *can* be established is that people from an early age have an understanding of *proportion*. If an adult gives a form of preferential treatment to one child over another, the slighted child will be quick to pick up on this fact and will typically feel un-affirmed, marginalized, and indeed very hurt. More generally, children from the earliest age are deeply affected—positively or negatively—by relationships that are harmonious or strained. As they grow out of infancy, children seem to have a keen sense that certain practices (e.g., refusals to share; refusals to reciprocate acts of kindness proportionally; refusals to consider others' well-being) fracture a healthy group dynamic and, in general, undermine

---

19. Ibid., 112.
20. Ibid., 15.
21. Ibid., 116–17. See David Carr, "Moral Education and the Perils of Developmentalism," *Journal of Moral Education* 31, no. 1 (2002): 5–19.
22. Kristjánsson, *Justice*, 117.

the well-being of themselves and/or others.[23] And, of course, children will, in general, react strongly to anything they perceive as undermining their own well-being and the well-being of others toward whom they have affection. These facts about children's needs and desires seem a plausible basis for explanations about children's reactions to the kinds of behavior Lewis mentions. If so, then this explanation is preferable to the more complex (in terms of metaphysical types) explanation Lewis offers involving a non-natural "moral law" that children and adults recognize.

When Christian theists (and others) point to our purportedly shared recognition that many things are "right or wrong," they actually seem very often to be pointing to our shared recognition that many things are "good or bad." We react negatively to stories of abuse, torture, injustice, and oppression—often declaring, as Walls and Baggett indicate, that such things are "clearly wrong." We judge that they should not be done, period. But instead of reacting to some property of "wrongness," it seems that we are reacting to the extreme badness of such events. We recognize their extremely harmful effects on individuals and communities. We view them as *so* bad that they are not to be done in any context; the matter is not up for debate. But again what we are actually recognizing is the way in which they are *bad* for individuals and communities.

One standard objection to my explanation of our intuitions here is that there are some cases in which a person would not necessarily be *harmed* by some action, even though we recognize that action as clearly wrong. The critic here will appeal to thought experiments of the following kind: "Consider a doctor who places a patient under general anesthetic and molests her in her unconscious state. Suppose she remains unaware of what has happened, so that she does not experience harm of any kind. Though the abuse was therefore not *bad* for her, we are still morally outraged and recognize that the doctor's action was clearly *wrong*." The particulars of this thought experiment might be changed in various ways by the critic, but the general strategy is to find cases in which we view an action as wrong but not necessarily as bad for anyone. And this, of course, would undercut the view I have defended that we view an action as wrong because we view it as extremely bad for us and for others.

My general response is that our intuitive reactions to the kinds of cases the critic raises are not reliable guides in reaching the conclusion the critic wants to reach. The thought experiments suppose that we can set aside considerations of goodness and badness. But I am very pessimistic that we can do this in the manner the critic envisions. In the preceding example, we react strongly against the doctor's action because we recognize how harmful such actions of abuse are. We are aware of how childhood abuse, even if one's

---

23. Children unfortunately are sometimes *too* keen to identify such practices with competitive attitudes sometimes emerging in desires, not simply for proportionality but, instead, for *more* than others receive.

memories are repressed or forgotten, can continue to have terribly damaging long-term effects on a person's emotional state, ability to form trusting relationships, and so forth. We immediately think of an abused person as one who has unquestionably been demeaned and degraded. I would suggest it is very difficult—probably impossible—genuinely to set aside all our considerations of how the abused patient might be negatively affected, so as to imagine for the sake of the example that she is "not harmed" in any way.

Anyone who considers the critic's example will agree that the patient's dignity and worth have not been protected. The question is how to spell out this point. The critic's interpretation amounts to the suggestion that our outrage stems from our recognition that the doctor's actions have some non-natural property, wrongness. But it seems at least as plausible to suggest that our outrage stems from our inability to shake the feeling that damage was inevitably done to the patient, that some of her strongest desires and hopes about how she wants to bond physically and emotionally with other people have been permanently undermined. If this is at all right, then again ontological parsimony should lead us to reject a non-natural property of wrongness as part of the simplest, best explanation of our moral intuitions.

Without the appeal to the realist's facts about wrongness, Christian theists will not be able to generate certain kinds of moral arguments for God's existence. Nevertheless, the Christian theist can still offer distinctive insights into what I take to be the most interesting kinds of moral questions. These questions involve the dual concerns: What does the good life consist in? and How do we attain it?

VII. Nonconstructivist Facts about the Good Life

I do not want to suggest that questions about what God has proscribed are *un*interesting ones. Yet, I think they should only serve as pointers to what the *most* interesting questions are. I recognize that the ethical frameworks proposed by Christian moral philosophers often assign a central role to what God has commanded (or, conversely, proscribed). However, I would suggest that such questions are interesting mainly because they are, in a sense, derivative of the questions I am claiming to be the most interesting ones.

Divine commands seemingly serve three broad purposes. First, God's commands help us identify good states of affairs and how to attain them (as well as bad states of affairs and how to avoid them). Here divine commands serve much the same role that J. S. Mill ascribed to societal laws: they indicate what is viewed as crucial for people's well-being. To ensure that people's lives are going well for them, we must, of course, do more than merely refrain from murdering, cheating, lying to, and exploiting others. But these are a few good starting points. And God's general commands about such matters point us to essential ways we must relate to one another if we are to live well together.

Second, divine commands help reveal to us the shape which our relationships with God are to take, along with the points at which breaks in the relationship will emerge such that steps will need to be taken to repair the relationship. There may be scope for creative give and take within the relationship into which God invites us—a relationship where we can be co-creators with God as we join him in his ongoing work. Still, divine commands establish the parameters of the kind of relationship into which he invites us. If we respond in ways outside the parameters of this relationship—that is, if we do that which God has proscribed—then some cost will have to be absorbed. (Such is the nature of any broken relationship.) God will need to forgive the refusal (or, at least, the failure) to relate to him on the terms he has invited people to relate to him. And someone will need to provide a means of reparation, if it is needed to restore the relationship. This is not to say that, by obeying all of God's commands, we immediately establish fully mature relationships with God and others. Participation in such relationships may require growth over time. It is just that, if no commands of God are broken, there will be no need of reparation and forgiveness along the way.

Third, God's commands reveal the kinds of measures he intends to take as he draws us into maturing relationships with himself and with others. The various ways in which God draws us into these relationships may fall under the broad categories of "positive" encouragement and "negative" chastening. God's proscriptions, accompanied, of course, by the intent to sanction, give us an indication of the kind of "negative" prompting that is in store for us if we perform what God has proscribed, as God continues his broader goal of prompting us to turn to him.

In outlining these three roles played by divine commands, I assume the theological starting point that God's ultimate goal in relating to us is to draw us into perfected relationships with him and with others. It is through these relationships that we attain our highest flourishing as humans. God's commands, like all else God does in relation to us, are thus aimed at drawing us into this good life God wants for us. *These* are the questions—about what the good life consists in and how we can attain it—that are of utmost importance. And divine commands again serve as one means God has to point us to answers to these questions about the shape of the good.

My contention is that Christian theists who are concerned about "objective morality" should focus on facts about how all humans flourish. Neuroscience and other disciplines can certainly help in this endeavor. But Christian theology offers what I think are penetrating insights into how we humans can and cannot flourish in the long run. Christian theology offers a beautiful vision of the kind of life—marked by perfected relationships—God makes possible for all people. There are broad paradoxes that must be unpacked, for example, about the way in which we must "lose" our lives in order to "find" the much richer lives God makes possible for us. Wisdom is needed to discern which of life's pleasures have diminishing returns and which have ever-increasing returns, leading to our highest flourishing. Christian theology has much insight to offer into these facts about the human condition, about what the good life consists in, and about how we can attain it with God's help.

A Christian account of the good life will have perfectionist elements to it. There are particular ways in which all humans, as divine image bearers, will flourish in the long run. The Christian picture of heaven, where our perfected, ever-deepening relationships with God and with others will continue for eternity, depicts this ideal. As a very general (and perfectionist) rule, our lives will be going well for us inasmuch as they approach this ideal. Christian theists might point to everyday observations—such as the irreplaceable role that loving, mutually self-giving relationships play in our mental health—as evidence that the Christian depiction of perfected relationships does, in fact, align with our highest long-term flourishing.

Christian theology also makes claims about the definite way in which this ideal can be achieved—a path which involves a commitment to benevolent pursuits and a submission to God's coordinating control. Again, the Christian theist can point to everyday examples as evidence for these claims. We all experience the need for, and power of, forgiveness. And even while we are attracted to a picture of perfected, loving relationships, where life-diminishing experiences of resentment and distrust and alienation can gain no foothold, our experiences show us all too well that we cannot hope to attain this ideal if left to our own resources.

While I have suggested that the Christian theist has much to say about the shared human condition, I should also acknowledge the differing ways in which people do flourish, depending on their particular gifts and callings. Indeed, the Christian saints are known as much for their idiosyncrasies as for what they have in common. Still, whether facts about all humans or about a particular human, there are facts about goodness to be discovered (and not merely constructed): facts about what the good life consists of and how it can be attained.

These questions about the good are the ones I have suggested as the most interesting for Christian theists (and for everyone else). Perhaps by acknowledging that constructive facts about *wrongness* are the only facts available to us, the Christian theist can more readily focus on an articulation of those truths about the good life that do not admit to any human construction.

Bibliography

Adams, Robert. "A Modified Divine Command Theory of Ethical Wrongness." In *Religion and Morality: A Collection of Essays*, edited by Gene H. Outka and John P. Reeder, Jr. Garden City: Anchor Press, 1973.
———. "Divine Command Metaethics Modified Again." *Journal of Religious Ethics* 7, no. 1 (Spring 1979): 66–79.
Baggett, David, and Jerry Walls. *Good God*. New York: Oxford University Press, 2011.

Bentham, Jeremy, and John Stuart Mill. *Utilitarianism and Other Essays*. Edited by Alan Ryan. London: Penguin Books, 1987.

Carr, David. "Moral Education and the Perils of Developmentalism." *Journal of Moral Education* 31, no. 1 (2002): 5–19.

Darwall, Stephen, Alan Gibbard, and Peter Railton. "Toward *Fin de Siecle* Ethics: Some Trends." *The Philosophical Review* 101, no. 1 (January 1992): 115–89.

Harman, Gilbert. *The Nature of Morality*. New York: Oxford University Press, 1977.

Kinghorn, Kevin. *A Framework for the Good*. Notre Dame: University of Notre Dame Press, 2016.

Kraut, Richard. *What Is Good and Why*. Cambridge: Harvard University Press, 2007.

Kristjánsson, Kristján. *Justice and Desert-Based Emotions*. Aldershot: Ashgate, 2006.

Lewis, C. S. *Mere Christianity*, revised ed. New York: Harper San Francisco, 2001.

Street, Sharon. "What Is Constructivism in Ethics and Metaethics?" *Philosophy Compass* 5 (2010): 363–84.

3 Constructivism in Ethics
A View from Hegelian Semantics[1]

Molly Farneth

One may hold that any one of several things related to morality and ethics is constructed, among them: normative truth itself, entitlement to one's commitments to normative principles and judgments, and their semantic content. Metaethical constructivism, as it has been debated in moral philosophy, is largely concerned with the first of these. It is an account of the construction of truth. Although there is no universally agreed-on definition of the position, we might begin with Carla Bagnoli's definition of metaethical constructivism as "the view that insofar as there are normative truths, they are not fixed by normative facts that are independent of what rational agents would agree to under some specified conditions of choice."[2]

This way of defining the position bears the marks of John Rawls's influential account of Kantian constructivism.[3] In his 1980 John Dewey lectures, published as "Kantian Constructivism in Moral Theory," Rawls argues that the "first principles of justice" that citizens ought to endorse are those that would result from a reasonable procedure of construction under ideal or hypothetical conditions. He specifies these conditions in his idea of the original position, in which "free and equal moral persons" stand behind a veil of ignorance, unaware of their social statuses, abilities and dispositions, and conceptions of the good.[4] What makes Rawls's view of constructivism

---

1. I presented earlier versions of this chapter at a session organized by the Moral Theory interest group at the Society of Christian Ethics in January 2016 and at a workshop at Wake Forest University in September 2016. I am grateful to the organizers and participants at those two sessions for their thoughtful engagement. I am especially grateful to Kevin Jung and Jeffrey Stout for their comments and provocations on an earlier draft of this chapter.
2. Carla Bagnoli, "Constructivism in Metaethics," in *The Stanford Encyclopedia of Philosophy*, Fall 2017 ed., ed. Edward N. Zalta, accessed August 15, 2017, https://plato.stanford.edu/archives/fall2017/entries/constructivism-metaethics/.
3. John Rawls, "Kantian Constructivism in Moral Theory," *The Journal of Philosophy* 77, no. 9 (1980): 515–72. The details of Rawls's position evolved over time; here I can offer only a general outline. For a critical reading of Rawls's Kantianism, see Onora O'Neill, "Constructivism in Rawls and Kant," in *The Cambridge Companion to Rawls* (Cambridge: Cambridge University Press, 2006), 347–67.
4. See Rawls, "Kantian Constructivism," 522–4, and *A Theory of Justice* (Cambridge: Harvard University Press, 1971), especially 17–21.

specifically Kantian, he suggests, is its view of the persons engaged in this procedure of construction as rational subjects and its suggestion that the principles that emerge through this procedure are those that could be agreed upon by such subjects. Rawls writes,

> What distinguishes the Kantian form of constructivism is essentially this: it specifies a particular conception of the person as an element in a reasonable procedure of construction, the outcome of which determines the content of the first principles of justice. Expressed another way: this kind of view sets up a certain procedure of construction which answers to certain reasonable requirements, and within this procedure persons characterized as rational agents of construction specify, through their agreements, the first principles of justice.[5]

Rawls's Kantian constructivism explains moral truth in terms of what rational agents would legislate or endorse under idealized conditions. In this view, the truth or correctness of principles concerning justice is determined by their rational acceptability under the conditions specified in the original position.

Rawls's Kantian constructivism, therefore, involves an account of moral truth and an account of rational entitlement in that domain. It does not, however, involve an explicit semantics—that is to say, it does not give an account of the content of its candidates for truth or falsity. In this respect, Rawls's Kantian constructivism is not unusual among accounts of constructivism. As Bagnoli notes, many metaethical constructivists regard semantics as irrelevant to their concerns about truth and normativity. She writes that, for them, "the philosophical issue worth thinking about is normativity, and this is not something that we can explain solely via semantics. For Kantians, explaining normativity requires philosophers to engage in philosophical investigations into the ideas of autonomy, agency, and practical rationality."[6] To explain truth and/or normativity, it is supposed, one need not account for the content or meaning of normative principles and judgments.

---

5. Rawls, "Kantian Constructivism," 516.
6. Bagnoli. Kantian constructivists are not alone in downplaying the relevance of semantics to metaethical constructivism. The Humean constructivist Sharon Street, for instance, writes that "constructivists appear to some . . . to be oddly nonchalant about the semantic task of explaining the meaning of normative terms. It is because the constructivist thinks that the debate about mind-dependence . . . is where the most important philosophical action is. This isn't to say that the semantic task should be ignored. But it is to say that we won't understand the nature of value until we settle the debate between realism and metaethical constructivism, and that we won't understand whether morality is objective until we settle the debate between Kantian and Humean metaethical constructivism" (Street, "What Is Constructivism in Ethics and Metaethics?" *Philosophy Compass* 5, no. 5 (2010): 280.) My aim in this chapter is to show that semantics—and, in particular, Hegel's semantics—has something important to add to these debates.

Contrast this view with Robert Brandom's claim that G. W. F. Hegel's semantics underlies his account of normativity, authority, and truth. Brandom's massive work in progress, *A Spirit of Trust: A Semantic Reading of Hegel's Phenomenology*, is an attempt to make good on this claim.[7] Brandom contends that the "punchline" of Hegel's most influential work, the *Phenomenology of Spirit*, is that "semantic self-consciousness—awareness of the transcendental conditions of the intelligibility of determinately contentful attitudes, of thinking, believing, meaning, or intending anything—consists in explicitly acknowledging an always-already implicit commitment to adopt generous recognitive attitudes of reciprocal confession and recollective forgiveness."[8] In other words, Brandom contends that the story that Hegel tells in the *Phenomenology of Spirit* is the story of consciousness gradually coming to recognize that its commitments are generated and acquire whatever meaning they have through ongoing social practices (including confession and forgiveness, practices to which I return at the end of this chapter). Even if one rejects the suggestion that the *Phenomenology of Spirit* is *primarily* a project in semantics, one may be convinced (as I am) that an adequate, socially, and temporally attuned semantics is among the concerns and contributions of Hegel's work.

While Hegel has been a relatively marginal figure in debates about constructivism, a Hegelian constructivism that builds on the insights of Hegel's ethical theory—including those laid out in Brandom's semantic reading of Hegel—may be emerging. Various articulations of Hegelian constructivism share a view of Hegel as building on constructivist elements of Kant's moral philosophy, particularly Kant's view of rational agents as loci of authority, while locating these agents in actual social and historical processes that make the process of construction possible.[9] Brandom's reading of Hegel,

---

7. Robert B. Brandom, *A Spirit of Trust: A Semantic Reading of Hegel's Phenomenology* (draft chapters available at www.pitt.edu/~brandom/spirit_of_trust_2014.html). My understanding of Hegel's semantics in indebted to Brandom as well as to Jeffrey Stout. Brandom's philosophy of language is detailed in *Making It Explicit: Reasoning, Representing & Discursive Commitment* (Cambridge: Harvard University Press, 1994). Jeffrey Stout's work draws on both Hegel's philosophy and Brandom's (Hegelian) semantics and has clarified the implications of these for thinking about religious and democratic ethics. See Stout, *Ethics After Babel: The Languages of Morals and Their Discontents* (Princeton: Princeton University Press, 1989), and *Democracy and Tradition* (Princeton: Princeton University Press, 2004), especially 270–86.
8. Brandom, *Making It Explicit*, mss.
9. Arto Laitinen identifies several distinctive strands of constructivism in recent Hegel scholarship. What these strands have in common is a view of Hegel's continuity with, and extension of, Kant's critical philosophy. An assessment of Laitinen's typology is beyond our scope here, but it is worth noting that he groups Robert Pippin, Terry Pinkard, and Robert Brandom together as proponents of what he calls "the standard story" of Hegelian constructivism. The present essay is particularly rooted in these three scholars' interpretive work on Hegel. See Laitinen, "Hegelian Constructivism in Ethical Theory?" in *"I That Is We and We That Is I." Perspectives on Contemporary Hegel: Social Ontology, Recognition, Naturalism, and*

in particular, foregrounds the semantics that is downplayed or ignored in many accounts of constructivism, including most Kantian varieties.

By calling attention to Hegel's semantics, I aim to bring out the possible significance of a "Hegelian constructivism" for contemporary metaethics. In what follows, I outline Hegel's account of the construction of the content or meaning of candidates for normative truth or falsity and suggest what follows from that account in terms of normativity, authority, and truth. This, then, sets the stage for a conversation with Kantian constructivists about what might be missing from that account and what the implications of an explicit semantics might be.

I. The Construction of (Semantic) Content

At the end of chapter 5 ("Reason") of the *Phenomenology of Spirit*, Hegel discusses a position in modern moral philosophy that he refers to as "reason as law-giver," which posits that reason can construct the moral law.[10] Hegel offers two examples of such laws, "pronouncements knowingly made by the rationality of common sense" (§422). The first of these is that "everyone ought to speak the truth" (§423). Hegel's discussion of this principle aims to show that, while its form appears universal, its content is indeterminate and contingent. It depends on one knowing the truth, being convinced of the truth, and so forth. Hegel writes,

> This contingency of content has universality merely in the form of the proposition in which it is expressed; but as an ethical proposition, it promises a universal and necessary content, and it thus contradicts itself by virtue of the contingency of its content.
>
> (§423)

The second pronouncement that he considers is to "love thy neighbor as thyself" (§424). Once again, Hegel suggests that the form of the proposition is universal, but its content is contingent. One must know how to love one's neighbor "intelligently," and it is not self-evident from the principle

---

the *Critique of Kantian Constructivism*, ed. Italo Testa and Luigi Ruggiu (Leiden: Brill, 2016), 127–46. For additional perspectives on Hegelian constructivism, see Tom Rockmore, *German Idealism as Constructivism* (Chicago: University of Chicago Press, 2016); Kenneth R. Westphal, "Normative Constructivism: Hegel's Radical Social Philosophy," *Sats* 8, no. 2 (2007): 7–41; "Hegel's Natural Law Constructivism: Progress in Principle and in Practice," in *Hegel's Political Philosophy: On the Normative Significance of Method and System*, ed. Thom Brooks and Sebastian Stein (Oxford: Oxford University Press, 2017); and "Hegel, Natural Law & Moral Constructivism," *The Owl of Minerva* 47, no. 1 (2018), http://dx.doi.org/10.5840/owl201752719.

10. G. W. F. Hegel, *Phenomenology of Spirit*, trans. Terry Pinkard, accessed November 24, 2017, www.academia.edu/16699140/Translation_of_Phenomenology_of_Spirit. In-text citations list the paragraph number in Pinkard's translation.

itself what that might mean. He writes that "this law thereby has no more universal content than did the first law which was considered and it does not express anything that exists in and for itself, which, as an absolute ethical law, it is supposed to do" (§424).

With both of these examples, Hegel's discussion is brief and his reasoning more implicit than explicit. Although the target of his criticism seems to be something like Kant's categorical imperative, Kant is not referenced, and Hegel's examples align only rather awkwardly with Kant's various formulations of the categorical imperative. If we assume that Hegel is a reasonably astute reader of Kant, and thus aware that Kant's position is more complicated than the overly simplistic charge of formalism would suggest, we must ask, "What is he trying to get at here?"

The key to answering this question comes only later, as Hegel sets up the transition from chapter 5 to chapter 6 of the *Phenomenology of Spirit*—that is, from Hegel's consideration of "reason" to his consideration of "spirit," which is his name for socially and historically embedded normativity. It initially appears that "neither determinate laws nor a knowledge of these determinate laws is able to come about" on the basis of formal reason (§431). But that's not the whole story. Hegel writes

> that both law-giving and law-testing have shown themselves to be in vain means that both, *when taken individually and in isolation*, are merely moments of the ethical consciousness which never ceases to be in movement; and the movement in which they come on the scene has a formal sense, namely, that as a result the ethical substance exhibits itself as consciousness.
>
> (§431, emphasis added)[11]

Hegel's point is not that reason cannot give the moral law but, rather, that reason's law-giving depends on the social practices in which those laws are made determinate. As he writes in the introduction to chapter 6,

> all the previous shapes of consciousness are abstractions from [spirit]. They are just this, that spirit analyses itself, distinguishes its moments, and lingers at each individual moment. This activity of isolating such moments has as its *presupposition* and its *durable existence*, that is, this activity of isolating only exists in the spirit which is existence.
>
> (§439)

Formal reason is abstracted from an account of practical *reasoning*, understood as an ongoing social practice. Spirit is always already its context and the source of its content.

---

11. I discuss "law-testing" (as distinct from "law-giving") in more detail in the following section.

The features of moral philosophy that Hegel thematizes and criticizes in this section of the *Phenomenology of Spirit* presuppose that we can arrive at an account of moral truth by first providing an account of practical rationality but without providing an account of how candidates for moral truth and falsity acquire determinate content. That is to say, they assume that we can have an account of the construction of moral truths without an explicit semantics. Hegel is abstracting from the complications of Kant's moral philosophy by positing something worth calling formal reason and asking whether this can account for the determinate content of a command or moral principle. His ensuing discussion is supposed to support the conclusion that an account of reason as a lawgiver is incomplete without an explicit semantics.

If Brandom's reading of Hegel is correct, then Hegel's advance on Kant's moral philosophy is to offer such a semantics.[12] It goes like this: the meaning of a moral principle depends on at least three things. First, it depends on the concepts employed by the principle having been applied to cases; second, it depends on the relevant practical inferences about the relations among those concepts having been made; and third, it depends on people holding one another accountable for these acts of concept-use and inference-making. Hegel takes the content of a normative principle to be a function of our applications of the relevant concepts to cases and the inferences we make from the concept applications that we regard as proper. These are practices that we engage in with one another, over time, in a process that involves undertaking commitments and being held accountable for one's commitments by others.

In order to commit myself to the moral principle "*Love thy neighbor as thyself*," for example, I need to know who counts as a *neighbor*. I also need to know what actions count as acts of *love*. The meaning of those concepts is shaped by their application to cases. The concepts of *love* and *neighbor* mean what they do because of the ways that people have used those concepts over time.[13] This is an ongoing process. We are born into

---

12. Brandom writes, "Hegel thinks that Kant has been insufficiently critical regarding two important, intimately related issues. First, he has not enquired deeply enough into the conditions of the possibility of the determinateness of the rules that specify the contents of ordinary empirical concepts. Second, Kant is virtually silent on the issue of their origins." See Brandom, "Some Pragmatist Themes in Hegel's Idealism: Negotiation and Administration in Hegel's Account of the Content and Structure of Conceptual Norms," *European Journal of Philosophy* 7, no. 2 (1999): 165.

13. Following Wittgenstein, Brandom characterizes this as a meaning-as-use view of semantic content, for instance, in the conclusion of *Making It Explicit*, where he writes that "the irreducibly normative pragmatics (theory of social practice) presented here is elaborated in terms of the basic deontic statuses of *commitment* and *entitlement* to commitments, and the essentially perspectival scorekeeping attitudes of attributing and acknowledging those deontic statuses. The semantics, or theory of the sorts of conceptual content that can be conferred by such deontic scorekeeping practices, take the form of an account of the *inferential*, *substitutional*, and *anaphoric* articulation that distinguishes specifically *discursive*

communities in which concepts are used in particular ways. We learn how to use those concepts in ways that are likely to be recognized by others as carrying on in the same pattern of use. Past usage guides and constrains our concept-use, but innovations are always possible as we apply existing concepts to new situations. For instance, I might apply the concept *neighbor* to the migrant farmworker in California who picked the strawberries that are sitting on my kitchen counter in Pennsylvania. In the context of a globalized economy, I might argue, the farmworker and I are bound together by economic, political, and social conditions that echo those of physical neighbors. In this example, I apply a concept to an actual case, drawing on my sense of the content of the concept as it has been applied to cases in the past.

Second, the inference from a person being my neighbor to my being obligated to treat that person lovingly must be made. A person who commits herself to the moral principle expressed in the command "*Love thy neighbor as thyself*" is, in fact, committing herself to the propriety of the inference from a person being my neighbor to my obligation to treat her lovingly.[14] If the migrant farmworker is indeed my neighbor—if that is a proper application of the concept *neighbor*—then I am obligated to treat her lovingly. This is a practical inference insofar as it entails an intention to act in a particular way (e.g., "*I shall act lovingly toward N.*"). It is also a material inference insofar as it concerns the non-logical content of the concepts. The inference from a person N being my neighbor to my being obligated to treat N lovingly depends on extra-logical relations among the relevant concepts.

Thus, it is in the context of evolving social practices that the content of any particular principle is determined. The meaning of the principle expressed in the command "*Love thy neighbor as thyself*," therefore, depends on actual practices of concept application, inference, and discursive accountability. People apply the concepts *love* and *neighbor* to particular cases, make the inference from someone being one's neighbor to one being obligated to act lovingly toward them, and hold one another accountable for these concept applications and inferences.

---

commitments. The result is a use theory of meaning—a specification of the social-functional roles that doxastic and practical commitments and the speech acts that express them must play in order to qualify as semantically contentful" (649, emphasis in original).

14. We can distinguish between this Hegelian form of expressivism and the emotivist and neo-Kantian prescriptivist ones. Each of these theories holds that moral principles play an expressive role, but they take different things to be expressed by the person who is committed to the principle. Emotivism holds that what is expressed is a pro-attitude toward (in this case) neighbor-love. Neo-Kantian prescriptivism holds that what is expressed is a prescription of neighbor-love to all addressees and a commitment to the universalization of that prescription. The Hegelian form of expressivism, by contrast, holds that what is expressed is a commitment to the propriety of the inference from N being one's neighbor to treating N lovingly. It is therefore a move in a process of practical, dialectical reasoning that is being endorsed or licensed.

When Mr. Rogers sang, "Won't you be my neighbor?" he was inviting the children watching *Mister Rogers' Neighborhood* to apply the concept *neighbor* to themselves, even though they may have lived far from the Pittsburgh neighborhood that was Mr. Rogers's television home. Let's assume, given that he was a Presbyterian minister, that Mr. Rogers was indeed committed to the moral principle expressed in the command "*Love thy neighbor as thyself.*" If that's right, then Mr. Rogers was also making the material practical inference from calling these children *neighbors* to acting lovingly toward them. Finally, his application of the concept *neighbor* and any inferences related to that application were acts that others—not least the children watching the program—could track and hold Mr. Rogers accountable for ("*What is he talking about? I'm not his neighbor!*" Or, "*He says I'm his neighbor, so he ought to respond kindly to my letters should I write to him in a kindly way.*")

The upshot of Hegel's semantics is that moral principles cannot mean much unless or until they are connected to practices of concept application, inference, commitment tracking, and accountability. A person cannot conjure a determinate moral principle in complete abstraction from whatever social practices and forms of community she participates in. She must be a member of communities or traditions in which people think, talk, act, and judge one another in accordance with a shared or partially shared history of concept applications and inferences. In this way, people in a community or tradition teach one another what their moral principles mean. The determinate content of the moral principles of people who share a community or tradition emerges in the course of their shared life.

If Brandom's reading of Hegel is correct, an account of the construction of normative truth cannot do without an account of the content or meaning of candidates for normative truth. The examples that Hegel considers in the *Phenomenology of Spirit* are not intended to be decisive arguments against Kant's categorical imperative. Rather, they are meant to draw attention to a topic that Kant is not thinking about, namely, the question of what gives us a contentful candidate for truth in the first place. If this question is best answered in terms of a socially and historically attuned semantics—if, to put it in Hegelian terms, *Moralität* is premised on *Sittlichkeit*—then the social practices that generate determinate content are already available to us when we return to the topic of rational entitlement.

II. The Construction of Rational Entitlement

The same social practices that determine the content of candidates for moral truth and falsity also determine who is rationally entitled to endorse or accept which commitments. Once we have an account of the former, a dialectical account of the latter is not too far behind. Immediately following his discussion of "reason as law-giver," Hegel turns to what he calls "reason as testing laws" (§428–30). The position being investigated here admits that the determinate content of concepts and principles is not generated by formal reason alone, but it holds that contentful concepts and principles must pass certain tests of universalizability and non-contradiction in order for people to be rationally entitled to their commitment to them. It is reason—conceived as a static faculty that is wholly independent of social practices—that conducts these tests. Hegel's example in this section is expressed in the question, "[O]ught it to be a law in and for itself that there should be property?" (§429). Hegel's discussion is intended to show that although the affirmative answer to that question passes the tests of universalizability and non-contradiction, the negative answer to that question does as well. He writes,

> When each of these determinatenesses *is represented* simply as property or nonproperty *without any further development*, one is as simple as the other, i.e., is not self-contradictory. The standard of the law which reason possesses in itself therefore fits every case equally well and is thus in fact no criterion at all.
>
> (§430, emphasis added)

Here, Hegel suggests that there is nothing irrational about the institution of property *per se*, but insists that formal rationality alone cannot recommend it over against nonproperty. Entitlement to the commitment that "it ought to be a law in and for itself that there ought to be property" presupposes a contentful concept of property along with its associated rights and institutions.

Once again, here, I suspect that Hegel is less interested in presenting a decisive argument against Kant's moral philosophy than in drawing his readers' attention to what is already in place when such questions are being posed—namely, the determinate content of concepts and the inferential relations among them. When we answer the question about property, we already have in place the contentful concept of property, one that is inferentially related to other concepts in our discourse (rights, ownership, etc.). Conceptual content and inferential patterns, moreover, are licensed and endorsed through ongoing social practices. To represent property or nonproperty "*without any further development*," as Hegel puts it, is once again to abstract from these practices in ways that obscure the social-practical basis of entitlement and authority.

My concept applications and inferences mean what they do, in part, because other people have applied the same concepts and made similar inferences in the past and, in part, because other people may one day find one or more of my concepts or inferences wanting. In using a concept, I am undertaking a commitment—a commitment to the propriety of using the concept in the way that I am using it. I may or may not be entitled to this commitment. I am, in any case, responsible for my commitment, commitments being essentially the sorts of things for which one bears responsibility before others. We track the commitments of those with whom we interact, in our effort to make sense of what they say and do.

Once we see that the determinate content in and inferential relations concerning a moral principle or ethical norm emerge from social practices, it becomes clear that our account of whether we are entitled to our commitment to that principle or norm must be dialectical. If I seek to use the principle or norm in new ways, I must be prepared to give an account of the propriety of my usage that connects it to the strengths and weaknesses of various past and present alternatives. That propriety is then recognized, or rejected, by other concept-users. Once again, this view shifts our attention from formal reason to reasoning, understood as a set of practices. These practices include making and evaluating claims, citing examples, engaging in immanent critique, and holding oneself and others responsible.[15] It is through these practices that we might be said to determine which principles and norms we ought to, and are entitled to, endorse.

Despite this rather formal and abstract description of concept-use, inference, and discursive accountability, this is an informal, concrete, everyday process. We are all engaged in it, all the time, as we go about thinking, talking, acting, and making judgments about the way things are with the world. This process is the source of the determinate content of our concepts and our entitlement to our commitments. Moreover, this process takes place in all of our communities, not least in religious ones.

While accounts of constructivism—whether what is constructed is taken to be content or meaning, rational entitlement, or truth itself—are often rejected by Christians, such views are not foreign to religious and theological ethics. We find views similar to Hegel's in Christian theological works such as George Lindbeck's *The Nature of Doctrine*, Bruce Marshall's *Trinity and Truth*, and, more recently, Kevin Hector's *Theology without Metaphysics*.[16] Hector is interested in the relationship between the claims that Christians make about God—God-talk—and the truth of the Gospel. His way of characterizing this relationship emphasizes the social-practical basis of content and entitlement. Hector argues that Christians' God-talk draws on past uses of relevant concepts and makes judgments about how those past uses apply to new situations. Members of Christian communities pay attention to one another's concept-use and inferences, and they judge the

---

15. Practices of reasoning are not limited to inferential moves; they also include non-inferential moves, although these are to be understood within the context of broader patterns of inference. A constructivist account of normativity therefore can accept that there are non-inferential judgments, including moral intuitions, while it rejects the view that such judgments are somehow pre-conceptual and/or infallible. For a detailed account of non-inferential judgments, see Stout, *Democracy and Tradition*, 217–24.
16. See George Lindbeck, *The Nature of Doctrine* (Louisville: Westminster John Knox Press, 1984); Bruce Marshall, *Trinity and Truth* (Cambridge: Cambridge University Press, 2004); and Kevin Hector, *Theology Without Metaphysics: God, Language, and the Spirit of Recognition* (Chicago: University of Chicago Press, 2011).

legitimacy of those uses. That legitimacy, Hector argues, is judged in terms of its "conformity to Christ" and to the tradition that follows from Christ.[17]

While judgment in terms of "conformity to Christ" initially sounds like an appeal to an epistemic standard that lies outside of Christians' relationships and social practices, it turns out to be embedded in the practices through which people judge one another's concept applications and inferences. Hector writes that

> Christ taught his disciples how to follow him, he recognized them as competent to recognize other persons as doing so; the disciples, in turn, recognized still others as competent recognizers, and so on; in this way, the Spirit implicit in Christ's own normative assessments was passed along from person to person.[18]

The standard that is used to judge one another's entitlement to concepts, principles, norms, doctrines, deeds, and other commitments—their conformity to Christ—is always already mediated through relationships and practices: Christ's relationship with his disciples, the relationships among Christ's followers, the Spirit's ongoing relationship with the church.

III. The Construction of Truth?

Hegel's semantics is connected to a social-historical account of rational entitlement that appears to be an alternative to the relatively abstract account on which Kantian constructivism builds its account of moral truth. But Hegel's semantics and epistemology leave open the question of what Hegel has to say about the construction of normative truth itself. This being at the center of contemporary debates about metaethical constructivism, let me suggest what might be ruled in or out by Hegel's views on the matters already discussed.

In the introduction to the *Phenomenology of Spirit*, Hegel warns readers not to begin their philosophical inquiry with a one-sidedly objectivist model of truth. As Hegel writes,

> [such a model] above all presupposes that the absolute stands *on one side of a divide* and *cognition on the other*, and that cognition exists on its own, that it is separated from the absolute but is still something real. That is, it presupposes that since such a cognition is external to the absolute, it is also indeed external to the truth, but that it is nonetheless itself truthful.
>
> (§74)

Such a model, in other words, presumes that the absolute is independent of cognition, where independence is conceived in terms of a subject–object

---

17. Hector, *Theology Without Metaphysics*, 234.
18. Ibid., 38–9.

divide. In this view, the absolute stands on one side of this divide; cognition stands on the other side. By contrast, Hegel's view is that the concepts that people use in cognition are bound up with both the people who use them and the actual things that they are about. People apply concepts to cases—real-life situations—which means that these cases play a role in shaping them. Normative principles and judgments employ concepts that acquire significance by being applied to such cases. A principle acquires authority insofar as it helps the community handle such cases without generating rational dissatisfaction with the community's form of life or some features thereof. A principle loses authority insofar as it generates alienation from or reveals inadequacies within that form of life. In these instances, people revise, reformulate, or reject the principle—or the form of life.

An adequate semantics and epistemology must, Hegel thinks, set aside a subject–object dichotomy. The concepts that subjects have at hand are not merely subjective in the sense of being confined to the subject's side of a gap between subjects and objects. Concepts acquire their content through repeated application by multiple subjects to the world in the context of social practices that essentially involve reference to actual persons and things. They are shaped by the needs of human beings, as well as by the dissatisfaction that arises when human beings and nonhuman objects are described or treated in ways that dominate those human beings or alienate them from the form of life they inhabit. The dialectical process in which we interact with other human beings and with nonhuman objects in the world shapes the concepts that we have available to us.

Hegel's semantics and epistemology appear to have further implications for how we think about truth. The collection of subjects, objects, norms, and norm-generating practices that hold these things in relation are, together, what Hegel calls spirit. There is a sense, then, in which it is *spirit* that determines which commitments and assertions are true, as well as what semantic content they have and which ones people are rationally entitled to hold or make in a given social and historical context. Hegel says something like this in the preface to the *Phenomenology of Spirit*, where he writes that "the truth is the whole" (§20)—although it is not self-evident whether his claim here is about the epistemic standard of truth or about truth itself. It is clearer which accounts of truth Hegel wants to rule out—namely, any such accounts that locate or fix truth on one side or the other of a subject–object divide.

One account of truth with which Hegel's view might initially be confused—but that he actually appears to rule out—is conventionalism. Conventionalism, as I use the term here, is the view that conformity to the norms actually accepted by some community is enough to make those norms correct or true. This position is one more often attributed to others than claimed as one's own—a kind of philosophical name-calling.[19] But, in any case, Hegel's

---

19. I have heard the term applied not only to Hegel's position but also to those of contemporary philosophers who follow Hegel on matters of semantics and epistemology, including Richard Rorty and Robert Brandom.

semantics and epistemology ought not be taken as underwriting the view that normative truth is a matter of agreement or convention.

In fact, Hegel's view, which aims to avoid subject–object dualism by recognizing the ways that subjects and objects are bound together through social practices in which people apply concepts to cases and then hold one another accountable for such concept-use on the basis of others' judgments about their adequacy, enables a response to the charge of conventionalism. In a conventionalist view, normative truths are the result of social convention or agreement and, thus, the principles that ought to be endorsed are those that the community as a whole endorses. A conventionalist would share Hegel's emphasis on the social practices by which content and entitlement are constructed but would lack Hegel's rejection of subject–object dualism. For the conventionalist, the standard of truth lies *solely* in subjects.

In describing the conventionalist view, I have used the phrase "standard of truth" to equivocate between two things—the standard by which one's entitlement to a commitment is to be judged and the standard that makes a commitment true. The former, one might suggest, is an epistemological standard, the latter an ontological one. But these are not unrelated. Conventionalism posits a standard of truth that accounts for both normative truth and rational entitlement. (Recall that the Kantian view with which we began posits a standard of truth that accounts for both moral truth and rational entitlement.) This stands in contrast to a minimalist (or deflationary) account that abandons the task of discovering or naming the standard that *makes* a commitment true. I return to the minimalist account of truth in a moment.

Conventionalism depends on what Brandom has called an I–we construal of social practices. In such an account, the community is taken to have a privileged or God's-eye view of the truth of the matter—a view against which individuals' claims and commitments are judged. Brandom writes that

> [I–we] construals fund a distinction between what particular individuals *treat* or *take* to be a correct application of a concept, on the one hand, and what *is* a correct application, on the other, by contrasting individual takings with communal ones.[20]

In a conventionalist view, there is no way to assess the rightness or wrongness of the community as a whole, because there is no gap between what "we" (the community) take to be the case and what is actually the case. In other words, I–we construals of social practices cannot account for the distinction between how concepts are applied by communities and how they *ought* to be applied—that is, what would be a correct application of the concept. In the conventionalist view, truth becomes

> defined as how things are according to a discursive perspective that meets certain conditions; it is settled in advance that any perspective

---

20. Brandom, *Making It Explicit*, 593.

from which a distinction appears between how things seem from such a privileged point of view and how things in fact are is itself without any authority at all.[21]

Conventionalist uses of the concept *true*, therefore, stand at odds with our ordinary use of that concept, which typically indicates not simply what we as a group believe to be the case, but, rather, what *is* the case. When I say that "X is true," I take myself to be making this stronger claim: not that I am justified at that moment in believing X or that I'm going to go ahead and act as though X, but, rather, that X is the case. As Jeffrey Stout writes,

> what we have agreed to do, in effect, is treat truth in practice as something that cannot be settled by communal agreement. It is this underlying social agreement on the use of certain words in the process of self-criticism that gives the term "true" its non-relative sense.[22]

Stout's view honors this ordinary use of the concept *true* not by searching for or naming a standard of truth that resides in objects (conceived as wholly independent of subjects, in a way premised on a subject–object dichotomy) but by recognizing that the distinction between what a person or group *believes* to be true and what *is* true is a distinction that is present in our social practices of concept-use and judgment. What neo-pragmatist accounts of truth such as Brandom's and Stout's have in common is their refusal to back up this ordinary language distinction with a metaphysical explanation of a property in which truth is supposed to consist. Such accounts are sometimes called minimalist or deflationary accounts of truth because they are disinclined to search for or identify some ontological entity that "truth" is supposed to name. When pressed for a definition of what truth *is* on such an account, minimalists will counter that further definitions are not actually explanatory—and, if pressed too far, are likely to fall back on the subject–object dichotomy that Hegel warns against.

To be clear, I am not claiming that this is Hegel's own account of truth. As mentioned earlier, it is easier to see what Hegel rules out than what positive account, if any, he offers us. What I am suggesting, however, is that those who follow Hegel on semantics and epistemology might well find themselves sympathetic to a minimalist account of truth such as those proposed by

---

21. Ibid., 600.
22. Stout, *Democracy and Tradition*, 277. Contrast Stout's rejection of the view of objectivity as a matter of communal agreement with Rawls's claim that "Kantian constructivism holds that moral objectivity is to be understood in terms of a suitably constructed social point of view that *all can accept*" ("Kantian Constructivism," 519, emphasis added). In this description of the position, Rawls risks casting Kantian constructivism as a form of conventionalism that has an I–we construal of social practices as opposed to a more clearly agonistic I–thou construal.

contemporary neo-pragmatists. Such an account of truth requires an I-thou construal of social practices. On such an account, there is no perspective that is privileged in advance—including the settled consensus of a group. People stand in relationships of reciprocal recognition, each recognizing the other as a locus of authority and responsibility for their claims and commitments. Brandom argues,

> [This] social metaphysics of claim-making settles what it means for a claim to be true by settling what one is doing in *taking* it to be true. It does not settle which claims *are* true—that is, are *correctly* taken to be true. That issue is adjudicated differently from different points of view, and although they are not of equal worth, there is no bird's-eye view above the fray of competing claims from which those that deserve to prevail can be identified, nor from which even necessary and sufficient conditions for such deserts can be formulated.[23]

An I–thou model of sociality insists that there is no privileged position, including that of the community itself, in this process of using concepts, making inferences and claims, and holding one another responsible for them.

An entire community can be wrong about a normative principle or judgment. We all can surely think of examples from our own communities. The community thought that X was true, but we recognize, in retrospect, that the community was wrong. Robert Pippin gives an example that illustrates this point well:

> If we want to understand why [the] gender-based division of labor became so much less credible a norm in the last third of the twentieth century, and exclusively in the technologically advanced commercial republics of the West, one begins to become a 'Hegelian' with the simple realization of how implausible it would be to insist that the injustice of such a basis for a division of labor, the reasons for rejecting such a practice, were always in principle available from the beginning of human attempts to justify their practices, and were 'discovered' sometime in the early nineteen-seventies. And yet our commitment to such a rejection is far stronger than a 'new development in how we go on.'[24]

Pippin's example shows the Hegelian view of normativity in action. Here we have a case of a widespread social norm—the gender-based division of labor—that is now rejected by many of the members of post-industrial Western societies. Problems in that form of life revealed something about the inadequacy of the norm to the people and about the things that it purported

---

23. Brandom, *Making It Explicit*, 601.
24. Robert Pippin, "Back to Hegel?" *Mediations* 26, no. 2 (Summer 2012): 1–22.

to be about. It generated alienation and rational dissatisfaction. As a result of these developments, we now take ourselves to be in a position to say that such norms are unjust because they deprive some or all of the people who have lived in accordance with them their due. This is a normative judgment. In committing myself to it, I am saying, in effect, that the gender-based division of labor is wrong. But, on the Hegelian view, I also recognize that the reasons by which I justify my judgment about the gender-based division of labor came to light only in response to ideas, practices, and forms of life that have appeared before.

So, why does Pippin argue that it is implausible to insist that the reasons that I might offer for rejecting the gender-based division of labor were always available *out there*, waiting to be discovered? For one thing, such reasons are themselves historically indexed. Concepts such as equal protection under the law have their own history of emergence and use. And the relationships, practices, and institutions in which such concepts are actualized or contested—including families, businesses, political institutions, and religious communities—also have a history. Women's suffrage, the birth control pill, the need for female workers in World War II, and second-wave feminism, to take only a few examples, introduced the possibility of new relationships, practices, and institutions that licensed new uses of concepts and inferential patterns. If it is the case that in the course of the twentieth century, increasing numbers of people came to see the gender-based division of labor as unjust, it is not because they finally unearthed reasons that had always in principle been available to them but, rather, because the inadequacies of that way of organizing a community were attended to and overcome in light of the alternatives that emerged through new ways of thinking about and organizing the other norms, relationships, practices, and institutions that they care about.

Conventionalism recognizes the importance of sociality in the institution of norms, but it fails to get at the truth of ethical life. If the conventionalist view were correct, then there could be no grounds for rational dissatisfaction with any actual form of ethical life. We know, for empirical reasons as well as philosophical ones, that there *are* such grounds. Widespread moral principles, ethical norms, and, indeed, entire ways of organizing societies have left people unhappy, alienated, and dominated, generating rational dissatisfaction. Sometimes, such principles, norms, and societies have been challenged and changed. Hegelian constructivism offers a way of understanding the grounds for such dissatisfaction and change while rejecting the view that consensus about such matters is the measure of their goodness, rightness, or truth.

IV. Conclusion

Late in the *Phenomenology of Spirit*, Hegel describes two characters who come into conflict but manage to reconcile with one another by confessing to and forgiving each other (§665–670). Their reconciliation is premised on their achievement of reciprocal recognition, a form of relationship in which each treats the other *as it would treat itself*, as one authorized to make claims and take action and as one who is fit to be held responsible for those claims and actions.[25]

It is at this point in the *Phenomenology of Spirit* that what Hegel calls "absolute spirit" emerges. Absolute spirit is the "standard of truth"—although, as we have seen, the meaning of that claim remains elusive in Hegel's own work. His work does, however, suggest that whatever is self-sufficient and authoritative (i.e., absolute) emerges amid ongoing social practices and relationships. Unlike the account of formal rationality that he offers earlier in the *Phenomenology of Spirit*, the account of absolute spirit does not abstract from these practices and relationships but acknowledges them. Contrast the practices of confession and forgiveness—through which reconciliation is actualized and absolute spirit makes its appearance—with the law that one ought to "love thy neighbor as thyself" conceived as abstracted from any such practices. "Such laws," Hegel writes, "stay fixed at the '*ought*,' and they have no *actuality*; they are not *laws*, they are merely *commands*" (§424). Hegel thinks that such laws, *conceived in isolation*, cannot tell us how or why we ought to act in a particular way. It is through practices of making claims, taking action, and holding one another accountable that people contribute to the construction of normative principles. Through their confession and forgiveness, the two parties to the conflict demonstrate how the principle contained in the command to love thy neighbor as thyself becomes a contentful commitment to which a person might be entitled, through social practices and relationships.

To return to the claim with which I began this chapter: one might be a constructivist about a number of matters related to morality and ethics, including content, entitlement, and truth. Hegel, I have argued, is a constructivist about content and entitlement. His views on these matters are clearer than his views on truth, although I have tried to show that following Hegel on matters of content and rationality does make a difference for how we think about the various options when it comes to an account of normativity and truth. And so, to conclude, I want to suggest that Hegel's semantics and his account of rational entitlement ought to reopen the conversation about the relevance of semantics to metaethical constructivism, not least to its Kantian varieties. Does metaethical constructivism need an explicit semantics, as Hegel's discussion of "reason as lawgiver" seems to suggest? If it does, is the best option one in which the meaning of concepts depends on their use? Must this use be understood in social and historical terms, as practices (including practices of concept use, inference, and discursive

---

25. I analyze this section of the *Phenomenology of Spirit* at length in *Hegel's Social Ethics: Religion, Conflict, and Rituals of Reconciliation* (Princeton: Princeton University Press, 2017), 65–80.

accountability) that take place among people, over time, as Hegel suggests? Once we have such a semantics in hand, can rational entitlement to a principle or judgment still be described in the relatively abstract terms specified by an ideal or hypothetical decision-making procedure? What about truth? Is the result here a supplement or an alternative to Kantian constructivism? Such questions—the answers to which are far from settled—may be the opening to a potentially fruitful conversation between the traditions of Kantian and Hegelian ethics.

Bibliography

Bagnoli, Carla. "Constructivism in Metaethics." In *The Stanford Encyclopedia of Philosophy*, Fall 2017 ed., edited by Edward N. Zalta. Accessed August 15, 2017. https://plato.stanford.edu/archives/fall2017/entries/constructivism-metaethics/.

Brandom, Robert B. *Making It Explicit: Reasoning, Representing, and Discursive Commitment*. Cambridge: Harvard University Press, 1994.

———. "Some Pragmatist Themes in Hegel's Idealism: Negotiation and Administration in Hegel's Account of the Structure and Content of Conceptual Norms." *European Journal of Philosophy* 7, no. 2 (1999): 164–89.

———. *Articulating Reasons: An Introduction to Inferentialism*. Cambridge: Harvard University Press, 2001.

———. *A Spirit of Trust: A Semantic Reading of Hegel's Phenomenology*. Draft chapters available at www.pitt.edu/~brandom/spirit_of_trust_2014.html.

Farneth, Molly. *Hegel's Social Ethics: Religion, Conflict, and Rituals of Reconciliation*. Princeton: Princeton University Press, 2017.

Hector, Kevin. *Theology Without Metaphysics: God, Language, and the Spirit of Recognition*. Chicago: University of Chicago Press, 2011.

Hegel, G. W. F. *Phenomenology of Spirit*. Translated by Terry Pinkard. Accessed November 24, 2017. www.academia.edu/16699140/Translation_of_Phenomenology_of_Spirit.

Laitinen, Arto. "Hegelian Constructivism in Ethical Theory?" In *"I That Is We and We That Is I" Perspectives on Contemporary Hegel: Social Ontology, Recognition, Naturalism, and the Critique of Kantian Constructivism*, edited by Italo Testa and Luigi Ruggiu, 127–46. Leiden: Brill, 2016.

Lindbeck, George. *The Nature of Doctrine*. Louisville: Westminster John Knox Press, 1984.

Marshall, Bruce. *Trinity and Truth*. Cambridge: Cambridge University Press, 2004.

O'Neill, Onora. "Constructivism in Rawls and Kant." In *The Cambridge Companion to Rawls*, 347–67. Cambridge: Cambridge University Press, 2006.

Pinkard, Terry. *Hegel's Phenomenology: The Sociality of Reason*. Cambridge: Cambridge University Press, 1996.

Pippin, Robert. "Back to Hegel?" *Mediations* 26, no. 2 (Summer 2012): 1–22.

Rawls, John. *A Theory of Justice*. Cambridge: Harvard University Press, 1971.

———. "Kantian Constructivism in Moral Theory." *The Journal of Philosophy* 77, no. 9 (September 1980): 515–72.

Rockmore, Tom. *German Idealism as Constructivism*. Chicago: University of Chicago Press, 2016.

Stout, Jeffrey. *Ethics After Babel: The Languages of Morals and Their Discontents*. Princeton: Princeton University Press, 1988.

———. *Democracy and Tradition*. Princeton: Princeton University Press, 2004.
Street, Sharon. "What Is Constructivism in Ethics and Metaethics?" *Philosophy Compass* 5, no. 5 (2010): 363–84.
Westphal, Kenneth R. "Normative Constructivism: Hegel's Radical Social Philosophy." *Sats* 8, no. 2 (2007): 7–41.
———. "Hegel's Natural Law Constructivism: Progress in Principle and in Practice." In *Hegel's Political Philosophy: On the Normative Significance of Method and System*, edited by Thom Brooks and Sebastian Stein, 253–79. Oxford: Oxford University Press, 2017.
———. "Hegel, Natural Law & Moral Constructivism." *The Owl of Minerva* 47, no. 1 (2018). http://dx.doi.org/10.5840/owl201752719.

4 What Should Theists Say about Constructivist Positions in Metaethics?

Christian B. Miller

Constructivist positions in metaethics are on the rise in recent years, thanks to the work of philosophers such as John Rawls, Christine Korsgaard, Tim Scanlon, and Sharon Street, among many others. Similarly, there has been a flurry of activity among theistic philosophers examining the relationship between God and normative facts, including important contributions by John Hare, C. Stephen Evans, Mark Murphy, Robert Adams, and Philip Quinn. But so far as I am aware, the literature of these positions have almost never intersected with each other. Constructivists have said very little about God, and theists working on religious ethics have said very little about constructivist views in metaethics. In this chapter, I draw some connections between the literature of each and hopefully will inspire others to continue to investigate this sadly neglected area.

My main conclusion is that theists should be hesitant about accepting any of the leading versions of constructivism in the contemporary metaethics literature. However, toward the end of the paper, I suggest that they should be open to forms of constructivism wherein God is the metaphysical basis for some of the moral properties.

The chapter proceeds in four parts. First, I clarify what *theism* and *constructivism* will mean for the purposes of this chapter. This will help clarify the project of the chapter by the end of section 1. Then, in section 2, I offer two general arguments for why theists should be hesitant about accepting at least secular forms of constructivism. The third section illustrates these arguments in more detail by applying them to three actual constructivist positions in the literature: Firth's ideal-observer theory, Tiberius's wisdom-based theory, and Street's Humean theory. Finally, in section 4, I turn to constructivist views wherein God is the one who is responsible for constructing morality.

I. Preliminaries

I do not intend anything complicated by 'theism.' A theistic religion, as I will understand it, is one that holds at least that:

1. God exists.
2. God is omniscient and omnipotent.

3. God is omnibenevolent, which includes being perfectly good, loving, and virtuous.
4. God created the universe and is still actively involved in the universe after creating it.

Leading examples of theistic religions are Judaism, Christianity, and Islam. Of course, there is much more to how these religions think about God, and there are some important differences in their thinking as well. But for the purposes of this chapter we do not need to get into those details.

Sadly, there is little consensus in the metaethics literature about what makes for a constructivist position. I won't take the time here to work through all the leading proposals and try to sort out which is the most promising. Instead, I will just offer a very broad and inclusive characterization. If, as I argue in the subsequent sections, it turns out that 'constructivism' so understood is implausible from a theistic perspective in most of its forms, then using a very broad characterization will only make my conclusion that much more interesting and important.

Here is the characterization I will be working from:

(CON) X is [normative term] if and only if (and because) X tends to elicit [response] from [respondents] in [circumstance].[1]

---

[1]. This formulation of what is known as the basic equation has been influenced by Shope 1978, Wright 1988, 1992, Johnston 1989, 1993, Pettit 1991, and De Clercq 2002, who also raise problems for it as well.

This formulation is intended to encompass a commonly used proceduralist characterization of constructivism, such as the following:

> The constructivist is a hypothetical proceduralist. He endorses some hypothetical procedure as determining which principles constitute valid standards of morality ... there are no moral facts independent of the finding that a certain hypothetical procedure would have such and such an upshot.
>
> (Darwall, Gibbard, and Railton 1992: 13)

Similarly David Copp writes,

> In brief, a constructivist theory defines a hypothetical procedure that could in principle be followed, where the outcome of the procedure is a set of standards that the theory holds to be true *because* they are yielded by the procedure.
>
> (Copp 2013: 116, emphasis his)

(CON) includes this hypothetical proceduralist position, but is broader as well. For it includes views which appeal not to hypothetical procedures but rather to the responses of actual people, whether those be ordinary human beings or (for theists) the divine person. These options will be developed more in what follows. For relevant discussion of proceduralist characterizations of constructivism, see Street (2010) and Copp (2013, especially 126).

(CON) is also broad in scope such that certain views which are sometimes taken to be forms of naturalist realism, like Railton (1986) and Smith (1994), could count as constructivist positions. I have no problems with this, and indeed have argued elsewhere that this is how they should be classified (Miller 2009a; see also Hussain 2012: 184). But I acknowledge this is a controversial matter. Fortunately, as noted in the main text, I am just stipulatively adopting a broad characterization for the purposes of this chapter. If my arguments apply to

As an example to make this less abstract, here is one way of understanding John Rawls's version of constructivism with respect only to principles of justice:

> (RAW) P is a principle of justice if and only if (and because) P is what free and rational persons concerned to further their own interests would accept in an initial position of equality as defining the fundamental terms of their association.[2]

The normative term is a principle of justice, the response is acceptance, the respondents are free and rational persons, and the circumstance is an initial position of equality.

Two quick observations at this point are worth making before delving into further details about (CON). First, as the Rawls example shows, one could be a constructivist just about *certain* normative facts without being a constructivist about *all* normative facts. In the literature, this gets expressed using different terminology, but here I use the labels of *restricted* versus *unrestricted* versions of constructivism.[3] Note that unrestricted constructivists don't just stop at moral facts—they take constructivism to be the correct approach with respect to all *normative* facts whatsoever (which includes the epistemic, prudential, aesthetic, and other realms of the normative).

Second, it is important that the dependence relation in constructivist positions is always right to left. In other words, it is *because* of the particular responses of these respondents that certain normative facts obtain. In the case of Rawls, it is *because* of what these free and rational persons accept that there exist certain principles of justice.

This helps to clarify the main rival to constructivism, which is normative realism. As I will understand the two views, both constructivists and normative realists believe in the existence of normative facts. What they disagree about is their metaphysical nature. Constructivists hold that these facts are mind-dependent. They exist and are the way they are because of the responses of the relevant respondents. As Sharon Street writes, "[t]here are no standards of correctness determining whether an agent's values are correct or incorrect except those set by her own further values."[4]

---

views like Railton's and Smith's as well, then so much the better, regardless of how at the end of the day we choose to characterize them.
2. Rawls 1971: chapter one.
3. Sharon Street uses restricted versus thoroughgoing or metaethical constructivism (2008: 208, 2010: 367). Yonathan Shemmer uses local versus global constructivism (2012: 161).
4. Street 2008: 223. Similarly, she describes 'attitude-dependent conceptions' as holding that "there are *no* facts about how an agent has most normative reason to live that hold independently of that agent's evaluative attitudes and what follows from within the standpoint constituted by them; instead, an agent's normative reasons are always ultimately a function of that agent's own evaluative attitudes and what is logically or instrumentally entailed by

Normative realists, on the other hand, hold that the normative facts are mind-independent. The existence and nature of these facts are unaffected by changes in the responses of people towards them. So, for instance, a normative realist might say that what the Nazis did would still be wrong even if (somehow!) the relevant respondents specified by constructivists endorsed Nazism.[5]

With these observations out to the way, let me return to (CON) and clarify who some of the different 'respondents' might be whose responses fix the normative facts. Here it is worth distinguishing (at least) four different constructivist approaches to thinking about these respondents:

a. *Actual Human Being(s)*. If a constructivist tries to ground normative facts on the responses of actual human beings, this will usually wind up being some form of normative relativism. Here are two examples of very simple relativist positions which illustrate this:

> (NR1) X is a reason for a person to do Y if and only if, and because, the person judges X to be a reason for him or her to do Y.
> (NR2) X is a reason for a person to do Y if and only if, and because, the person's culture considers X to be a reason to do Y.

The first version is an example of individual normative relativism. The second is an example of cultural normative relativism. Both fit within the broad parameters of constructivism outlined in (CON).

b. *Hypothetical Human Being(s)*. Few constructivists in philosophy these days are tempted to make the respondents actual human beings (and for good reason, I might add). Instead, the leading approach is to look to the relevant responses of hypothetical versions of human beings. Often it is just *one* hypothetical human being, namely a version of the person in question (such as myself), where some refinements have been made to the person's psychology such that her responses have been appropriately filtered or screened in some way.

Here are some examples of this approach to help make things less abstract. The first is from David Lewis:

> (LEW) X is a value if and only if, and because, we would be disposed to value X under conditions of the fullest imaginative acquaintance with X.[6]

---

those attitudes in combination with the non-normative facts" (2009: 274, emphasis hers). See also Shafer-Landau 2003: 14–16 and Street 2010: 367, 371, 2012: 41.
5. For my attempt to spell out what mind-independence amounts to and how it can be used to distinguished realist from antirealist positions in metaethics and in other areas of philosophy more generally, see Miller 2007, 2009a. For a different approach, see Copp 2013.
6. Lewis 1989.

The second is from Michael Smith:

> (SMI) S has a normative reason to do action X in circumstances C if and only if, and because, S's fully rational counterpart would desire S to do X in C.[7]

Both of these are restricted versions of constructivism—one for value and one for normative reasons—but they both share the approach of looking to the responses of some suitably improved human beings.

c. *Hypothetical Non-Human Being(s)*. While hypothetical human beings are all the rage in the constructivist literature, a particularly famous example focuses instead on a hypothetical being who is more god-like than human:

> (FIR) X is [moral term F] if and only if, and because, any ideal observer would respond in the relevant way in the relevant circumstance to X.[8]

I won't unpack this view here, as we will return to it in some detail in section 3.

d. *Actual Divine Being(s)*. Note that (CON) is broad enough that even a theistic God could count as the respondent. For instance, on a traditional divine command theory about moral obligations:

> (DC) Action A is morally obligatory for person S to do in some set of circumstances if and only if (and because) S's doing A in those circumstances is commanded by God.

There are other approaches besides this one to thinking about how God might ground normative properties; in section 4 we will take them up in more detail.[9]

Naturally, there is much more to be said in clarifying what constructivism amounts to and the various versions it might take. By way of ending this section, though, we are now in a much better position to clarify what the main project of this chapter is going to be.

In what follows, I will assume (just for the sake of argument) that theism is true and a theistic God does exist. Clearly the first three kinds of constructivism just outlined are secular approaches to metaethics. They do not depend in any way on the existence of God. The fourth approach naturally does.

---

7. Smith 1994: chapter five. S's 'fully rational counterpart' just means the fully rational version of S.
8. Firth 1952: 229.
9. In principle, one could even appeal to actual non-human beings that are not divine beings. But I don't have any idea what such a view would look like.

The goal of the chapter is to make progress in answering this question:

> *Main Question:* From a theistic perspective, how plausible are the secular types of constructivism as accounts of the metaphysical basis of normative facts?

My answer, to anticipate, is going to be that they are very implausible. A secondary question that arises in section 4 is:

> *Secondary Question:* From a theistic perspective, how plausible are the theistic types of constructivism as accounts of the metaphysical basis of normative facts?

Here my answer is going to be that they are also implausible for the most part, with one exception.

Note that the discussion will proceed from the truth of theism to an assessment of versions of constructivism. This is a very different discussion from what one finds in the literature on moral arguments for the existence of God. There philosophers argue from claims in metaethics *to* the conclusion that God exists.[10] For instance, they might argue that the best explanation for the existence of moral facts is that God put them into place. This is an important discussion as well, needless to say, but it is not the discussion found hereafter.

It might seem that the answer to the main question is obviously negative. After all, why would theists think any *secular* approach to moral facts is plausible? But we shouldn't simply jump to that conclusion, for at least three reasons. First, theists have said very little about secular constructivists views, at least from a theistic perspective, so this is unexplored territory. Second, merely being a theistic (as opposed to a secular) version of constructivism doesn't thereby automatically make constructivism any more plausible. In fact, I argue in section 4 that most forms of theistic constructivism are *just as* implausible as their secular counterparts, even from a theistic perspective. And finally, theists should not discount a metaethical position merely because it is secular, since the leading position among theistic philosophers about the metaphysics of normative facts is some version of *secular normative realism*. Here normative facts exist in a response-independent way, which includes being independent even of God's responses. God is not the source of these facts and cannot change them. God's normative standing—whether God is good, for instance, or just—is determined by what these independent normative facts say about God, just like those facts determine whether I am a good or a just person.

But there might be some good reasons, whether on secular or theistic grounds, to challenge this normative realist position. Secular constructivist

---

10. For a helpful overview of such arguments, see Evans 2016.

views might have more to offer than secular normative realist positions. At least we should not close the door on this possibility without giving some thought to the matter.

Hence, I think that we should take the main question quite seriously. So let's now turn to it directly.

II. Two Arguments against Secular Constructivism Given Theism

In the previous section, we saw that constructivist positions could be divided into four main types depending on who the class of respondents is supposed to be: actual human beings, hypothetical human beings, hypothetical non-human beings, and actual divine beings. We will save the last kind until section 4. What should theists make of the three secular options?

They should quickly jettison the first. Moral relativist positions, which tie moral facts to the responses of actual individuals or cultures, are already fraught with numerous problems just on philosophical grounds.[11] But from a theistic perspective they seem completely untenable. For it is hard to think that God would leave it up to individuals or cultures to decide whatever they like about moral matters. This is especially apparent when we turn to actual theistic religions. Time and again we see in the Bible and the Koran how God morally condemns human behavior on the basis of invoking a higher morality that clearly seems to have more authority than whatever the people in question are thinking.

Versions of constructivism which appeal to hypothetical beings, however, cannot be so easily dismissed by theists. I do think, however, that there are two compelling arguments that should lead theists away from them. I call them the *comparison argument* and the *divine normative properties argument*.

The comparison argument, as its name suggests, undertakes a comparative assessment of *hypothetical constructivism* (as I will call constructivist views that appeal to either hypothetical human beings or non-human beings) with *theistic constructivism* (as I will call constructivist views where an actually existing theistic God is the relevant respondent). It claims that, comparatively speaking, there are good reasons to favor theistic over hypothetical constructivism and no good reasons (or at least not as good reasons) to do the reverse.

One such reason is as follows. For theists, God actually exists, and he has various responses towards what human agents do in the world (acceptance, condemnation, celebration, and so forth). Without getting into the details of theistic constructivism yet, the view would take certain of God's responses as in some way serving as the basis for constructing moral facts.

---

11. See, for example, Shafer-Landau 2004.

For instance, God's condemnation of torture could make torture morally wrong.

To accept hypothetical constructivism, however, a theist would need to not only accept that God has these responses toward human behavior but also hold that they play no metaphysical role whatsoever in grounding the normative facts. Instead, the responses of purely hypothetical beings serve as the ground instead. And this seems implausible, comparatively speaking. What is it about the responses of hypothetical beings which make them so much better suited to serve as the basis for normativity? After all, God is all-knowing, all-powerful, and all-loving, and furthermore, he actually exists and cares deeply about this world (according to theists). Why think that this being's responses are less well suited to ground the normative than those of a being or beings which exist only in remote possible worlds and not in the actual world?

A second reason to favor theistic constructivism is epistemological. On this approach, when God forms the relevant responses, they ground the normative facts, and so God's being able to know what is normatively the case ends up being a trivial matter. He just makes it that way. But compare what happens from God's perspective when it comes to hypothetical constructivism. When reacting to human behavior, God first determines what the responses would be of certain hypothetical human or non-human beings. This strikes me as odd. It seems odd, in other words, to think that God has to consult the hypothetical reactions of, say, my full rational self, or those of the ideal observer, in forming his own reactions to how well I am behaving.

The third reason is also epistemic, but in this case it has to do with how we human beings are supposed to determine what the normative facts are. There are clear epistemic obstacles to figuring out the responses of my hypothetical self, or the ideal observer. There are also clear epistemic obstacles to figuring out what a theistic God's responses are. However, comparatively speaking, the obstacles in the latter case do not seem to be as pronounced. Why? Because at least a theistic God, given his actual existence, could communicate those reactions with human beings—whether through sacred texts, prophets, inspiration, conscience, or the like. And all the theistic religions claim that he has, in fact, done this. Merely hypothetical beings, on the other hand, cannot do any of these things.

But, it might be objected, when God is communicating to human beings about normative matters, it could be that he is just relaying to us what the responses are of the hypothetical beings which ground the normative facts. In other words, he is giving us a hand in figuring out what these beings are thinking.

What should we make of this objection? I think we should grant that this *could* be what is happening. Yet—and here is the fourth and final reason in the comparison argument—it does not *seem like* that is what is actually happening. When we turn to the details of actual theistic religions and their sacred texts, it seems instead that God himself has the authority to decide what is morally right and wrong, for instance.[12] At no point do we get any indication that he is consulting with hypothetical beings in order to arrive at an answer.

So to sum up, the comparison argument is not a knockdown argument in favor of theistic constructivism. But it does offer a variety of considerations which tip the balance in its favor and against hypothetical constructivism.

Let me turn much more briefly to what I call the divine normative properties argument. So far, our focus has been on the normative facts that pertain to human beings. But God himself is said to be perfectly good and to have virtues like wisdom and justice. Hypothetical constructivism seems like it would have a hard time accounting for those properties.

Consider hypothetical human beings first. The basic idea would be that God is good because of the relevant responses of one or more improved human beings. But clearly no theist could accept an approach like this. God's own goodness does not depend in any way on what human beings (real or hypothetical) think.

Now consider hypothetical non-human beings. God is good, the claim would be, only because of how one of these beings responds to God's existence. But again, this seems deeply implausible, especially the more the being differs from God, say, by being disinterested. God doesn't derive his goodness from what other beings think. And if (perhaps counterpossibly) these other beings thought that God was *not* good, that wouldn't change the fact that he is.

One last point about this argument. As noted in the previous section, most hypothetical constructivists start with a given human being and then ground normative facts in the relevant responses of an improved version of that person. Whatever the merits of that approach might be in the human case, it fails dramatically in the divine case. For there are no improvements to make to God. God, for theists, is already a perfect being. And if we look to his responses to ground the moral facts, then we have thereby abandoned hypothetical constructivism for theistic constructivism.

Before ending, it is important to address a potential response to both of these arguments. One thing hypothetical constructivists might do at this point is to not only say that they are willing to grant the arguments but also highlight how there are famous problems for theistic constructivism with the Euthyphro dilemma. These problems can tip the overall balance of considerations back in favor of a hypothetical constructivist approach.

One of these well-known problems for theistic constructivism is the "arbitrariness" objection. Either God's relevant responses are based on reasons or they are not. If they are based on reasons, then those reasons will appeal to objective norms outside of God, and so the view ceases to be a form of constructivism. It collapses into realism. Or the responses are not based on

---

12. For a good development of this point, see Quinn 2000.

reasons, in which case they are arbitrary and render God less than perfectly rational, which is an unacceptable consequence for theists.[13]

Now I don't think the theistic constructivist actually has much to worry about from this objection.[14] But let's grant for the moment that it is a serious objection. Unfortunately for the hypothetical constructivist, invoking the arbitrariness objection would end up backfiring. For the very same objection can be leveled against her view as well. Either the responses of the hypothetical being will be based on reasons or they will not be, and the same problematic consequences would follow—if they do at all—in her case as well.

Or consider the "anything goes" objection to theistic constructivism. If God's responses can construct the normative facts, then we would find statements like the following turning out to be true:

> If God commands me to torture an innocent child, then it is morally obligatory for me to torture an innocent child.

But, of course, it is absurd to think that I am morally required to torture an innocent child.

Again, I think the theistic constructivist has plausible responses to make to this objection as well.[15] The point here, though, is that the anything-goes objection, if wielded by a hypothetical constructivist, would backfire too. Consider statements like the following:

> If my fully rational self wants my actual self to torture an innocent child, then it is morally obligatory for me to torture an innocent child.
>
> If the ideal observer wants my actual self to torture an innocent child, then it is morally obligatory for me to torture an innocent child.

These, too, are absurd in precisely the same way.

The upshot of this section, then, is that from a theistic perspective there seem to be some serious problems with accepting hypothetical versions of constructivism. Plus, whatever prominent objections there are to theistic constructivism carry over to the hypothetical version too.

III. A Quick Look at Some Actual Versions of Hypothetical Constructivism

The previous section tried to evaluate the plausibility of hypothetical constructivism at a high level of abstraction. The hope is that the two arguments raised there—the comparison argument and the divine normative properties

---

13. For more on this objection, see Miller 2013.
14. For a response, see Miller 2013.
15. See Miller 2013.

92 *Christian B. Miller*

argument—are suitably general to apply to all hypothetical constructivist positions as such, thereby allowing us to bypass the tedious task of having to reconstruct and assess them all one by one.

Still, it is worth reviewing at least a few of the leading versions today, if for no other reason than to reiterate the same concerns again with a more concrete and focused target in mind. I start with a version of hypothetical constructivism that appeals to a non-human being and then follow that up with two versions that invoke hypothetical human beings.

III.1. *Firth's Ideal Observer Theory*

In his classic paper "Ethical Absolutism and the Ideal Observer," Roderick Firth offered the account of moral facts we saw earlier:

> (FIR) X is [moral term F] if and only if, and because, any ideal observer would respond in the relevant way in the relevant circumstance to X.[16]

What is it to be an ideal observer? On Firth's account, it includes the following:

1. Being omniscient about non-ethical facts
2. Being omnipercipient
3. Being disinterested
4. Being dispassionate
5. Being consistent

Firth admits that "any plausible description of an ideal observer will be a partial description of God, if God is conceived to be an infallible moral judge."[17] But it is clear that there are also significant differences between this being and a theistic God. For instance, the ideal observer is not omnipotent, and also does not possess the virtues of love and compassion.[18]

Should a theist be tempted to adopt this position? I do not see a reason why she would be, *qua* theist. Both the comparison and divine normative properties arguments can help to spell out some of the theist's reservations. First, on metaphysical, epistemological, and scriptural grounds, theistic constructivism seems preferable to Firth's view for the reasons outlined in the previous section. Second, it is not at all clear how the view would plausibly

---

16. See Firth 1952: 229. Actually, his account was proposed at the semantic rather than the metaphysical level. Thus, he offered an analysis of the meaning of X's being F (1952: 229). I have recast his proposal in metaphysical terms simply to make it consistent with the rest of the accounts in this chapter. Also, note that his proposal is for moral facts, rather than all normative facts, but nothing will hinge on this in the preceding.
17. Firth 1952: 237.
18. Firth 1952: 237, 243.

account for God's own normative properties. Thus, using God's goodness as the test case, we would get:

> God is good if and only if, and because, any ideal observer would respond in the relevant way in the relevant circumstance to God.

But this seems to get things precisely backward. It isn't this hypothetical being that makes it the case that God is good. Rather, it is because God is good in the first place that the observer subsequently reacts the way that it does. Finally, it should be clear that analogs of the arbitrariness and anything goes objections to theistic constructivism would apply to the ideal observer approach as well.

III.2. Tiberius's Wise Judgment Constructivism

Valerie Tiberius's version of constructivism, as outlined in her paper "Constructivism and Wise Judgment," is much more limited in scope. She offers a version of what we earlier called restricted constructivism, which is only aimed at giving an account of one aspect of the normative, rather than all normative facts. That aspect is what a person has all-things-considered reason to do. Given that there often are competing considerations in real-world decision-making, we form such judgments as best we can to attempt to discern what the considerations collectively lead us to do.

Here is her account, which she calls wise judgment constructivism:

> (TIB) X is all-things-considered best if and only if, and because, X is what I would judge myself to have reason to do if I were to judge wisely.[19]

Wise judgment, in turn, is "just judgment in accordance with the norms of excellent judgment."[20] Note that Tiberius's account is explicitly non-reductive. She appeals to all kinds of other normative notions in spelling out what wisdom and excellent judgment involve.[21]

As stated, the view invokes my hypothetical self, and so is a version of constructivism grounded in hypothetical human beings.[22] It should be clear enough at this point how the two arguments from the previous section

---

19. Tiberius 2012: 210.
20. Tiberius 2012: 196.
21. Tiberius 2012: 204.
22. This is the way she officially put the view on page 210. But earlier she noted that it could be stated in terms of the judgments of a perfectly wise person who, in my case, is not Christian Miller. According to Tiberius, if we keep in mind a few qualifications, then the difference between these two approaches is "relatively inconsequential" (207). I assume this perfectly wise person would be a human being, and so for my purposes it doesn't really matter, either, which version we go with.

94 Christian B. Miller

would apply here as well. For the comparison argument, it is not obvious why a theist would opt for the judgments of a wise hypothetical human being when she can ground all-things-considered judgments in a perfectly wise God who actually exists. Consider, for instance, this description that Tiberius gives of the wise person:

> The wise person identifies the relevant considerations by making sure that her judgments conform to all the norms of good judgment in the best possible way. She puts these reasons together to form a justification for her judgment about what one has best all-in reason to do in the circumstances.[23]

But a theist would chime in and say that she actually knows of someone who does exactly this: God.

Plus, Tiberius acknowledges that if we invoke hypothetical human beings, there is going to be room left for error.[24] And she admits that different wise human beings might arrive at different all-things-consider judgments in the same circumstances, opening the door for a limited form of relativism.[25] Both of these features of Tiberius's account are drawbacks in my mind, and both of them do not arise when the wise person is a theistic being.

The divine normative properties argument can also be mentioned briefly. Since Tiberius is only proposing a restricted form of constructivism, the argument would not apply to, say, God's goodness or virtues. But it would apply to God's all-things-considered judgments. And since God is already perfectly wise, it looks like the view—at least with respect to God's own judgments—would collapse into theistic constructivism.

III.3. Street's Formalist Constructivism

In a number of recent papers, Sharon Street has helpfully clarified what a constructivist approach in metaethics involves, as well as developed an important version of her own.[26] Street's view is an unrestricted form of constructivism, which aims to ground all normative facts in general by invoking the responses of hypothetical human beings. Here is how the view is formally characterized:

> (STR) X is a reason for a person to do Y if and only if, and because, the judgment that X is a reason for the person to Y withstands scrutiny from the standpoint of the person's other judgments about reasons.[27]

---

23. Tiberius 2012: 201.
24. Tiberius 2012: 210.
25. Tiberius 2012: 208.
26. See Street 2008, 2009, 2010, 2012.
27. Street 2008: 223. See also Street 2010: 369.

Theists and Constructivist Positions 95

While Street talks in terms of 'reasons,' she is clear that this is just a label for any normative notion, such as goodness or obligation.[28] The key idea is that there needs to be a kind of coherence between any particular normative judgment and the other judgments the person holds.

This is not, as it might initially seem, a relativist view basing normative facts in whatever a person happens to judge at the moment. For my actual set of normative judgments is likely inconsistent in all kinds of ways.[29] To see this, let's unpack a bit more what Street means by "withstands scrutiny."

According to Street, whenever we make a normative judgment, there are standards involved by which our reasoning can be judged (whether we consciously recognize this or not). A nice example she gives involves the instrumental principle. She writes that:

> simply by judging yourself to have reason to Y, you're *thereby*—as a constitutive matter—also judging yourself to have reason to take the means to Y, whatever those may be. So even if you don't know that Z is a means to Y, and think you have no reason whatsoever to Z, you *do* have a reason to Z—*according to you*. Your very own normative judgment says so; *it* sets the standard according to which you are making a mistake if you think you have no reason to Z.[30]

According to Street, then, for a normative judgment to withstand scrutiny is "for that judgment not to be mistaken as determined by the standards of correctness that are constitutively set by those other normative judgments in combination with the non-normative facts."[31]

What normative judgments we happen to have now are not likely going to all withstand scrutiny in Street's sense. Rather, it is only the hypothetical set of a person's normative judgments that have been appropriately filtered and purged that Street thinks is the basis for the normative facts that pertain to that person.

Note that Street's restrictions on what goes into this hypothetical set are only formal. No substantive criteria, such as a principle of morality, are involved. Nor does she think that the result of the filtering process will be one or more values that everyone must have. As she writes:

> [i]f you had entered the world taking entirely different things to be reasons, on my view, you would have *had* entirely different reasons. You might even have had reason to throw yourself under an oncoming boulder, or to die for the sake of eating a particular bowl of chili, or indeed to prefer the destruction of the world to the scratching of your finger.[32]

---

28. Street 2008: 209 fn. 5, 2009: 274 fn. 7.
29. Street 2009: 281.
30. Street 2008: 229, emphasis hers.
31. Street 2008: 230.
32. Street 2008: 244, emphasis hers. See also Street 2009, 2010: 369–70, 2012: 41.

Hence, a fully consistent Caligula, bent on the destruction of other people, is a possibility in her view.[33]

I don't think I need to elaborate very much on what theists are likely going to say about Street's view. Using the comparison argument, theistic constructivism is going to come out much more favorably, I suspect. Theists are not likely to accept that there can be a rational Caligula with normative reasons that permit (and perhaps even require) his behavior. And they are likely going to maintain that there are substantive normative considerations that apply to all people, regardless of whether their hypothetical set includes them or not. One example might include that all human beings have dignity and worth in virtue of being created in the image of God.

Similarly, with respect to God's own normative properties, they won't be dependent on hypothetical human judgments. Nor will they be dependent on some improved version of God's judgments, since there is no such improved version. Theistic constructivism looms.

In this section, we have briefly looked in more detail at three leading versions of hypothetical constructivism. In each case, the comparison and divine normative properties arguments seem to apply straightforwardly. If these arguments do indeed raise valid concerns, theists should be reticent to adopt any of these positions.

However, examining three versions is not the same as examining all the versions of constructivism in the literature. And I have to leave open the possibility that some of the other versions might do a better job at avoiding the challenges that have been raised.[34]

For now, though, let's turn to theistic constructivism directly in the remainder of the chapter.

IV. Assessing Theistic Constructivism

Constructivism based on the responses of actual human beings wasn't even entertained. Hypothetical human and non-human constructivism seemed like they would raise red flags for theists and would end up being comparatively less plausible than theistic constructivism. So that means that theists should therefore accept theistic constructivism?

Not so fast. For one thing, there is the alternative of jettisoning constructivism altogether and accepting a realist position, whereby the normative facts exist in a mind-independent manner even with respect to God's mind.

---

33. See Street (2009, 2010: 371). As she writes, "[i]f Caligula is aware of all the non-normative facts and has recognized every normative conclusion that follows from his own values in combination with those facts, then there is nothing he is failing to see" (2010: 371).
34. In particular, Kantian versions of constructivism, such as the one developed by Christine Korsgaard (1996), would need to be carefully examined. Given how complex these views tend to be, I couldn't do them justice in this chapter but hope to discuss them in future work.

For another thing, theistic constructivism—in most of its forms—is simply implausible. Let's start with unrestricted theistic constructivism, which holds that God's relevant responses are the metaphysical basis for all the normative properties there are.

This view won't work, for it fails with respect to God's own normative properties. The simplest example is the one we have already used throughout the chapter, which is God's goodness. If we adopt this version of constructivism, God's goodness is not fundamental but derivative from his own responses:

> God is good if and only if (and because) God tends to elicit [response] from God in [circumstance].

But this clearly has things backward. God doesn't make himself good by judging or in some other way responding to himself that way. Rather, he is already good, metaphysically speaking, prior to making any particular judgments.

Once theists reject constructivism about God's goodness, though, it is natural to reject constructivism for, say, goodness across the board in the human as well as the divine case. And that is what many theistic philosophers have, in fact, done. For instance, according to arguably the leading contemporary account of goodness from a theistic perspective, things in this world are good to the extent to which they resemble God's goodness in such a way as to give God a reason for loving them. This is Robert Adams's influential proposal in his book *Finite and Infinite Goods*.[35] The point is not to recommend Adams's view here but only to use it as an example of how most theistic philosophers not only reject constructivism about God's goodness but also about axiology in general.

Let's next consider God's character. Theists think that God is perfectly loving, just, forgiving, and merciful, for instance. These are all normative properties God has, namely, virtues. But God's responses don't make him have these normative properties. He already *is* virtuous to begin with, and his responses follow necessarily and derivatively *from* his character.

Or consider God's rationality, reasonableness, and wisdom. Again, these are normative properties God has necessarily. Yet God does not bootstrap himself into having these properties simply by responding in his mind that he does. Again, that is to get matters metaphysically backward.

Suddenly the prospects for theistic constructivism are starting to look rather bleak. It seems that when it comes to God, the view is a bad fit for one kind of normativity after another.

But not so fast. Where the view stands the best chance is with respect to normative properties that (1) don't apply to God himself but (2) do apply to

---

35. Adams 1999: 36.

98 Christian B. Miller

other beings apart from God, such as human beings. What properties might these be, if any?

The best candidates are deontological moral obligations and the related properties of the morally forbidden and the morally optional.[36] Theists are typically inclined to think that such obligations exist and are closely related to God, with the Ten Commandments serving as the best illustration. At the same time, many theists are hesitant to think that God is under any moral obligations himself. God might be in the business of requiring us to do certain things, such as loving our neighbors. But he is not morally required to do that himself; he just does it naturally as part of his nature. Obligations seem like an odd thing to invoke in the case of God.[37]

So where we have arrived in this chapter is that, of all the forms of constructivism in metaethics, the one that is likely going to be most appealing to theists is a form of theistic constructivism which is restricted just to deontological moral properties.[38] With respect to all the other normative properties, theists seem to be wise to opt for a realist approach instead. And while the deontological properties might be the best bet for constructivists, it *still* could turn out that the constructivist approach is less plausible at the end of the day than is the realist alternative.

Let's suppose, though, that theistic constructivism just about the deontic really is the best game in town. In the remainder of the chapter, I want to spell out some of the issues that need to be addressed if a theist wants to develop the view in more detail. I won't pretend to try to settle any of those issues here. My only goal in the space remaining is to put them on the table.

Philip Quinn has helpfully provided the following schema for thinking about what needs to be clarified if someone wants to maintain that some part of the normative could depend on God:

Normative status M stands in dependence relation D to divine act A.[39]

We have already specified M as the morally obligatory and related deontic notions. Let's turn then to divine act A. Here are the four leading options in the recent literature for thinking about what that action is:

36. Perhaps the same is true of non-moral deontological properties, such as our epistemic obligations, but I won't consider this issue here.
37. For helpful discussion of this point see Alston (1989).
38. It might be tempting to call this view a form of divine subjectivism about deontic properties. However, 'subjectivism' is often used as a label for a specific kind of approach in metaethics, whereby normative properties are grounded in reports of a person's mental attitudes rather than expressions of them. This is definitely not the kind of view at issue here, and so to avoid any misleading associations I have not used the terminology of 'subjectivism' in this chapter. Thanks to Kevin Jung for encouraging me to clarify this.
39. Quinn 2000: 53. I have changed "moral status" in Quinn's schema to "normative status" to reflect the broader focus of this chapter. See also the excellent discussion of this schema in Murphy (2012).

Divine Command Theory: An act A is morally obligatory for S to perform if and only if (and because) God commands A to perform S.[40]

Divine Virtue Theory: An act A is morally obligatory for S to perform if and only if (and because) God's virtues require A to perform S.

Divine Intention Theory: An act A is morally obligatory for S to perform if and only if (and because) God intends for A to perform S.

Divine Desire Theory: An act A is morally obligatory for S to perform if and only if (and because) God desires for A to perform S.

I have discussed these views at length elsewhere, as have others. Let me say only a brief word about each of them here.[41]

For divine command theory, in bringing about a moral obligation God must actively do something communicative by issuing a command. Hence, this view stands in contrast with the other three, which all have to do with God's will that exists independently of whether God does anything to communicate it.[42] As Robert Adams has written, God's commands "must have been issued, promulgated, or somehow revealed."[43] But the divine command theorist is happy to understand this revelation broadly so that it does not just include not only what is found in sacred texts like the Bible or the Koran but also, for instance, what might be found in a person's conscience.[44]

Divine virtue theory is a relatively new version of theistic constructivism, developed in great detail by Linda Zagzebski in her book *Divine Motivation Theory*. As its name suggests, the theory starts with God's virtues and, in particular, their motivational component. For Zagzebski, a divine virtue is "the combination of a perfect motive with perfect success in bringing about the end, if any, of the motive."[45] Morally obligatory actions, in turn, are grounded in what is required by the virtues of God.

For divine intention theory, when God intends for us to act freely in a certain way, that action becomes obligatory for us to do. So if my donating to charity is obligatory, that is because (and only because) God has intended that I make the donation. More precisely, these will be God's *antecedent* intentions. As a general matter, if God intends for something to happen, then it is going to happen. But then intentions would seem to be a bad fit for grounding moral obligations, given the obvious empirical fact that people

---

40. For all these options, I present them as involving a specific action and a specific individual moral agent. But, instead, they could involve a type of behavior, such as murder, and moral agents, in general. The views on offer can be easily rephrased to take this into account. I have also omitted the circumstances clause to make things a bit less cumbersome.
41. The next few paragraphs are adapted from Miller forthcoming, with permission of Cambridge University Press.
42. For more on the difference between God's commands and God's will, see Adams 1999: 258–62 and Murphy 1998: 9, 2012 section 2.3.
43. Adams 1979: 140.
44. For more, see Adams 1979: 140, 1999: 263–4.
45. Zagzebski 2004: 205.

routinely do not do what they are morally required to do. God's antecedent intentions, though, have to do with what he intends, *apart from* what the human being(s) will freely choose to do in the circumstances. So, for example, God's antecedent intention that I donate to charity today while I am on the computer would not include anything about what my free choice is concerning whether to donate.[46]

Finally, we come to divine desire theory. The basic idea is that if God, all things considered, wants me to do some particular action, then that makes it the case that I have a moral obligation to do it. And if he wants, all things considered, for me to *not* do another action, then that action is rendered morally forbidden. What grounds the deontic, thus, is precisely what God wants us to do with our lives. This is the view I myself hold about the ground of human moral obligations, and I have developed it in some detail elsewhere.[47]

The project for our restricted theistic constructivist, therefore, becomes one of first deciding which of these four positions she wants to accept or, instead, developing a fifth one. Then she needs to offer arguments for why her choice is to be preferred and answer objections that have been raised against it. This is a serious undertaking, to say the least.

Less important, and only briefly mentioned here, is the task of specifying the dependence relation D. Here are the four leading options, using the divine desire theory only by way of illustration:[48]

Meaning Equivalence:

Taking the injured stranger to the hospital is morally obligatory for me to do *means* that God desires for me to take the injured stranger to the hospital.

Identity:

The fact that taking the injured stranger to the hospital is morally obligatory for me to do is identical to the fact that God desires for me to take the injured stranger to the hospital.

Causal:

The fact that taking the injured stranger to the hospital is morally obligatory for me to do is caused by God's desire for me to take the injured stranger to the hospital.

---

46. For related discussion, see Murphy 1998 and Quinn 2000, 2002.
47. See Miller 2009b, 2009c.
48. For similar surveys, see Wierenga 1983, Quinn 2000: 54–5, and Murphy 2002: chapter four, 2012 section 2.4. These four options are not intended to be exhaustive.

Non-Reductive Constitution:

> The fact that taking the injured stranger to the hospital is morally obligatory for me to do is constituted by but not identical to the fact that God desires for me to take the injured stranger to the hospital.

Sorting out the differences between these relations and trying to determine which is the most plausible candidate are, I admit, matters of rather abstract philosophical discussion. Fortunately, we do not need to go down this path here.

In this section, we have honed in on a restricted form of theistic constructivism as being the most plausible kind of constructivism from a theistic perspective. We have also seen, in a preliminary way, some of the issues that need to be sorted out in order to develop such a view about deontological moral facts. A few contemporary philosophers of religion are contributing actively to this work but, clearly, a lot more needs to be done.

V. Conclusion

The main goal of this chapter has been to make progress in addressing the following:

> *Main Question*: From a theistic perspective, how plausible are the secular types of constructivism as accounts of the metaphysical basis of normative facts?

For now, I think the answer to this question is that they are not very plausible.

But that doesn't mean that theists should be quick to sign up for theistic constructivism either. In fact, most versions of that approach are implausible as well. We did, though, identify what I think is the best constructivist option for the theist to consider, one that is restricted just to deontological moral facts. Whether it ends up being a better option, all things considered, than a moral realist account of those facts remains to be seen.[49]

Bibliography

Adams, Robert. "Divine Command Metaethics Modified Again." *The Journal of Religious Ethics* 7, no. 1 (Spring 1979). Reprinted in *The Virtue of Faith and Other Essays in Philosophical Theology*, 128–44. New York: Oxford University Press, 1987.

---

49. I am very grateful to Kevin Jung for inviting me to be a part of this volume and for his helpful comments. Work on this chapter was supported by a grant from the Templeton Religion Trust. The opinions expressed here are those of the author and do not necessarily reflect the views of the Templeton Religion Trust.

———. *Finite and Infinite Goods: A Framework for Ethics*. New York: Oxford University Press, 1999.

Alston, William. "Some Suggestions for Divine Command Theorists." In *Christian Theism and the Problems of Philosophy*, edited by Michael Beaty, 303–26. Notre Dame: University of Notre Dame Press, 1989. Reprinted in *Divine Nature and Human Language: Essays in Philosophical Theology*, 253–73. Ithaca: Cornell University Press, 1989.

Copp, David. "Is Constructivism an Alternative to Moral Realism?" In *Constructivism in Ethics*, edited by Carla Bagnoli, 108–32. Cambridge: Cambridge University Press, 2013.

Darwall, Stephen, Allan Gibbard, and Peter Railton. "Toward Fin de Siècle Ethics: Some Trends." *The Philosophical Review* 101, no. 1 (January 1992): 115–89. Reprinted in *Moral Discourse and Practice: Some Philosophical Approaches*, edited by Stephen Darwall, Allan Gibbard, and Peter Railton, 3–47. Oxford: Oxford University Press, 1997.

De Clercq, Rafael. "Two Conceptions of Response-Dependence." *Philosophical Studies* 107, no. 2 (January 2002): 159–77.

Evans, C. Stephen. "Moral Arguments for the Existence of God." In *The Stanford Encyclopedia of Philosophy*, Winter 2016 ed., edited by Edward N. Zalta. 2016. Accessed September 1, 2017. https://plato.stanford.edu/entries/moral-arguments-god/.

Firth, Roderick. "Ethical Absolutism and the Ideal Observer." *Philosophy and Phenomenological Research* 12, no. 3 (March 1952): 317–45. Reprinted in *Twentieth Century Ethical Theory*, edited by Steven Cahn and Joram Haber, 225–46. Upper Saddle River: Prentice-Hall, 1995.

Hussain, Nadeem. "A Problem for Ambitious Metanormative Constructivism." In *Constructivism in Practical Philosophy*, edited by James Lenman and Yonatan Shemmer, 180–94. Oxford: Oxford University Press, 2012.

Johnston, Mark. "Dispositional Theories of Value." *Proceedings of the Aristotelian Society, Supplementary Volumes* 63 (1989): 139–74.

———. "Objectivity Refigured: Pragmatism Without Verificationism." In *Reality, Representation, and Projection*, edited by John Haldane and Crispin Wright, 85–130. Oxford: Oxford University Press, 1993.

Korsgaard, Christine. *The Sources of Normativity*. Cambridge: Cambridge University Press, 1996.

Lewis, David. "Dispositional Theories of Value." *The Proceedings of the Aristotelian Society, Supplementary Volumes* 63 (1989): 113–37.

Miller, Christian. "The Conditions of Realism." *The Journal of Philosophical Research* 32 (2007): 95–132.

———. "The Conditions of Moral Realism." *The Journal of Philosophical Research* 34 (2009a): 123–55.

———. "Divine Desire Theory and Obligation." In *New Waves in Philosophy of Religion*, edited by Yujin Nagasawa and Erik J. Wielenberg, 105–24. New York: Palgrave Macmillan, 2009b.

———. "Divine Will Theory: Desires or Intentions?" In *Oxford Studies in Philosophy of Religion*, Vol. 2, 185–207. Oxford: Oxford University Press, 2009c.

———. "The Euthyphro Dilemma." In *The Blackwell International Encyclopedia of Ethics*, 1–7. Oxford: Blackwell Publishing, 2013.

———. "The Naturalistic Fallacy and Theological Ethics." In *The Naturalistic Fallacy*, edited by Neil Sinclair. Cambridge: Cambridge University Press (forthcoming).

Murphy, Mark. "Divine Command, Divine Will, and Moral Obligation." *Faith and Philosophy* 15 (1998): 3–27.

———. *An Essay on Divine Authority*. Ithaca: Cornell University Press, 2002.

———. "Theological Voluntarism." In *The Stanford Encyclopedia of Philosophy*, Winter 2014 ed., edited by Edward N. Zalta. Accessed September 1, 2017. https://plato.stanford.edu/entries/voluntarism-theological/.

Pettit, Philip. "Realism and Response-Dependence." *Mind* 100, no. 1 (October 1991): 587–626. Reprinted in *Rules, Reasons, and Norms: Selected Essays*, 26–48. Oxford: Clarendon Press, 2002.

Quinn, Philip. *Divine Commands and Moral Requirements*. Oxford: Clarendon Press, 1978.

———. "Divine Command Theory." In *The Blackwell Guide to Ethical Theory*, edited by Hugh LaFollette, 53–73. Oxford: Blackwell, 2000.

———. "Obligation, Divine Commands and Abraham's Dilemma." *Philosophy and Phenomenological Research* 64, no. 2 (March 2002): 459–66.

Railton, Peter. "Moral Realism." *Philosophical Review* 95, no. 2 (April 1986): 163–207.

Rawls, John. *A Theory of Justice*. Cambridge: Harvard University Press, 1971.

———. *Whatever Happened to Good and Evil?* Oxford: Oxford University Press, 2004.

Shemmer, Yonatan. "Constructing Coherence." In *Constructivism in Practical Philosophy*, edited by James Lenman and Yonatan Shemmer, 159–79. Oxford: Oxford University Press, 2012.

Shope, Robert. "The Conditional Fallacy in Contemporary Philosophy." *The Journal of Philosophy* 75, no. 8 (August 1978): 397–413.

Smith, Michael. *The Moral Problem*. Oxford: Blackwell, 1994.

Street, Sharon. "Constructivism About Reasons." In *Oxford Studies in Metaethics*, Vol. 3, edited by Russ Shafer-Landau, 207–45. Oxford: Oxford University Press, 2008.

———. "In Defense of Future Tuesday Indifference: Ideally Coherent Eccentrics and the Contingency of What Matters." *Philosophical Issues* 19 (2009): 273–98.

———. "What Is Constructivism in Ethics and Metaethics?" *Philosophy Compass* 5 (2010): 363–84.

———. "Coming to Terms with Contingency: Humean Constructivism About Practical Reason." In *Constructivism in Practical Philosophy*, edited by James Lenman and Yonatan Shemmer, 40–59. Oxford: Oxford University Press, 2012.

Tiberius, Valerie. "Constructivism and Wise Judgment." In *Constructivism in Practical Philosophy*, edited by James Lenman and Yonatan Shemmer, 195–212. Oxford: Oxford University Press, 2012.

Wierenga, Edward. "A Defensible Divine Command Theory." *Nous* 17, no. 3 (1983): 387–407.

Wright, Crispin. "Realism, Antirealism, Irrealism, Quasi-Realism." *Midwest Studies in Philosophy* 12, no. 1 (1988): 25–49. Reprinted in *Metaphysics: An Anthology*, edited by Jaegwon Kim and Ernest Sosa, 649–65. Oxford: Blackwell Publishers, 1999.

———. *Truth and Objectivity*. Cambridge: Harvard University Press, 1992.

Zagzebski, Linda. *Divine Motivation Theory*. Cambridge: Cambridge University Press, 2004.

5 Kantian Constructivism, Autonomy, and Religious Ethics[1]

Charles Lockwood

This chapter aims to assess the relationship between constructivism and religious ethics by focusing specifically on the form of constructivism that has been attributed to Immanuel Kant. Most closely associated with John Rawls, the constructivist reading of Kant involves the claim that moral principles are not traceable to an order of value independent of humanity but must instead be constructed by human beings through an idealized procedure, since our own role in such a procedure is what makes morality autonomous or self-legislated, rather than heteronomous, or imposed from a source outside the self. Rawls and others who follow this reading of Kant assume that constructivism is required to make sense of Kant's commitment to autonomy.

In what follows, my aim is to assess the coherence of this form of constructivism and consider its significance for religious ethics, specifically in terms of its compatibility with theism. I want to suggest that Rawls's constructivist reading of Kant faces challenges in terms of its own coherence and also in terms of its appeal for religious ethics. In addition, I argue that Kant's own account of morality actually differs from Rawls's reading, for while Kant does give significant emphasis to autonomy, he does not claim that morality is a construction or human creation. My overall suggestion is that Kant offers a way of affirming autonomy while also envisioning a moral community that includes both humanity and God.

I. Autonomy in Rawls's Kantian Constructivism

I want to begin here by considering Rawls's own reading of Kant since Rawls is generally considered to be the first interpreter to frame Kant's moral philosophy in constructivist terms. Moreover, Rawls's reading has influenced

---

1. I would like to thank Kevin Jung for his gracious hospitality in hosting the Wake Forest conference where this paper was first presented, and for very helpful comments during the conference and afterward. I would also like to thank the other conference participants—especially Molly Farneth, who served as respondent to the paper, and Paul Weithman, who offered incisive comments in the subsequent discussion.

numerous other recent constructivist interpretations of Kant, especially those of J. B. Schneewind, Onora O'Neill, and Christine Korsgaard.[2] In discussing Rawls, I highlight the role that autonomy plays in his constructivist reading. I also suggest that the constructivism Rawls attributes to Kant seems both incoherent on its own terms and hard to square with theism—or at least the kind of theism that would see God and humanity as members of a shared moral community.

Before I delve into the details of Rawls's reading, I should note that despite the debts to Kant that are evident in *A Theory of Justice* (dating from the early 1970s), Rawls did not develop a comprehensive constructivist reading of Kant until later, as seen in his 1980 Dewey Lectures on "Kantian Constructivism in Moral Theory"[3] and another essay, "Themes in Kant's Moral Philosophy,"[4] from 1989. Yet some of the clearest features of Rawls's interpretation can be found in his Harvard course lectures on the history of modern moral philosophy from the 1980s and 1990s.[5] Given their clarity, I rely mainly on those lectures in what follows.

In his course lectures and across his later writings, Rawls develops an interpretation of Kant's constructivism that emphasizes the significance of a procedure of construction, as well as the role of such a procedure in substantiating Kant's commitment to a morality of autonomy rather than heteronomy. It is helpful to start with how, in his Harvard lectures, Rawls characterizes Kant's understanding of autonomy. To say that we are autonomous is to say, on Rawls's reading of Kant, that "we can be bound only by a law that we can give to ourselves as reasonable and rational, or as free and equal legislative members of a possible realm of ends."[6] For Rawls,

---

2. For Schneewind, see *The Invention of Autonomy: A History of Modern Moral Philosophy* (Cambridge: Cambridge University Press, 1998), and *Essays on the History of Moral Philosophy* (Oxford: Oxford University Press, 2010). For O'Neill, see *Acting on Principle: An Essay on Kantian Ethics* (New York: Columbia University Press, 1975), and *Constructions of Reason: Explorations of Kant's Practical Philosophy* (Cambridge: Cambridge University Press, 1989). For Korsgaard, see *Creating the Kingdom of Ends* (Cambridge: Cambridge University Press, 1996); *The Sources of Normativity* (Cambridge: Cambridge University Press, 1996); *The Constitution of Agency: Essays on Practical Reason and Moral Psychology* (Oxford: Oxford University Press, 2008); and *Self-Constitution: Agency, Identity, and Integrity* (Oxford: Oxford University Press, 2009). For broader recent discussions of constructivism that extend beyond Kant, see *Constructivism in Practical Philosophy*, ed. James Lenman and Yonatan Shemmer (Oxford: Oxford University Press, 2012), and *Constructivism in Ethics*, ed. Carla Bagnoli (Cambridge: Cambridge University Press, 2013).
3. John Rawls, "Kantian Constructivism in Moral Theory," *Journal of Philosophy* 77 (1980): 515–72. Reprinted in John Rawls, *Collected Papers*, ed. Samuel Freeman (Cambridge: Harvard University Press, 1999), 303–58.
4. Ibid., "Themes in Kant's Moral Philosophy," in *Kant's Transcendental Deductions: The Three 'Critiques' and the 'Opus postumum*,' ed. Eckart Förster (Stanford: Stanford University Press, 1989). Reprinted in Rawls, *Collected Papers*, 497–528.
5. Ibid., *Lectures on the History of Moral Philosophy*, ed. Barbara Herman (Cambridge: Harvard University Press, 2000).
6. Ibid., 207.

this understanding of autonomy entails that we generate the content of the moral law, which is further spelled out through specific moral principles, including duties of justice and of virtue. Moreover, autonomy also entails that we are bound by that moral content precisely because we have given it to ourselves. This process of self-legislation occurs through a procedure that is structured, as Rawls indicates, by a conception of ourselves as reasonable and rational, and as free and equal co-legislators in a realm of ends. Rawls refers to this procedure as the categorical imperative procedure, or the "CI-procedure,"[7] on the grounds that for Kant, the moral law involves imperatives or demands that hold categorically—universally and necessarily—rather than merely hypothetically. Because this CI-procedure is one through which the content of specific moral principles is to be constructed, Rawls therefore refers to this combined framework as Kant's "moral constructivism."[8]

Crucial here is the way that Rawls connects autonomy together with Kant's alleged constructivism. For Rawls, the framework of constructivism can be distinguished from approaches that would understand the content of moral principles not as constructed, but as discovered or acknowledged—that is, "as given by a prior and independent moral order determining the fitnesses of things."[9] Thus, to hold that such moral principles are constructed is to reject the claim that they might be located within a moral order that is prior to, or independent of, the procedure of construction. According to Rawls, moreover, Kant's moral framework is to be understood as constructivist precisely because the alternative account of moral first principles—locating them within a prior and independent moral order and hence as things to be merely discovered or acknowledged—would conflict with the demands of Kant's idea of autonomy. As Rawls explains, autonomy for Kant entails that the first principles of morality are tied only to the procedure of construction itself, including the conception of ourselves as free and equal persons that governs the procedure, as well as the more specific content that is generated by that procedure. Thus, "Kant's idea of autonomy requires that there exists no moral order prior to and independent of those conceptions that determine the form of the procedure that specifies the content of the duties of justice and of virtue."[10] If any such prior or independent moral order were to be relied upon, Rawls maintains, it would render morality not autonomous, but heteronomous—since in that case, the content of moral first principles would not be self-legislated through an autonomous procedure of construction.[11]

7. Ibid., 162.
8. Ibid., 165.
9. Ibid., 207.
10. Ibid., 236–7.
11. Alongside this argument that only constructivism is consistent with Kant's idea of autonomy, Rawls also argues that constructivism has a more sophisticated account of the person

Constructivism, Autonomy, and Ethics 107

According to Rawls's reading, then, Kant is a constructivist because constructivism is what his commitment to autonomy requires. If we are to be self-legislators with respect to the moral law, then the content of our moral first principles cannot derive from any order of value beyond us but must instead be tied only to the constructivist procedure and the values it generates. In his Harvard lectures, and in his other writings on Kant's constructivism, Rawls presents himself as largely in agreement with Kant on these points and, to that extent, provides not only an interpretation of Kant but also an endorsement of the constructivist framework.[12]

Yet is the constructivist view that Rawls offers here a coherent one? Drawing on the work of Charles Larmore, I want to suggest that the view Rawls attributes to Kant faces serious difficulties. Larmore acknowledges that the view might initially appear quite appealing, given its rejection of claims about some independent moral order—some order of value that lies beyond humanity itself. Indeed, it is easy to imagine that claims about such a moral order might be greeted with skepticism: "Where exactly are such moral facts to be located in the fabric of reality?"[13] Yet Larmore finds that constructivism must still rely on something akin to moral facts, or some prior moral order, in order to account for the procedure of construction itself. For if, as Rawls argues, Kant's CI-procedure of constructing moral principles involves a commitment to being reasonable and rational, it already involves—even before the procedure begins—a moral understanding of persons as free and equal, and thus, as Larmore observes, it already "embodies an allegiance to what is nothing less than a moral principle in its own right." Thus, Kant's constructivism, in Rawls's depiction, requires "a moral foundation that must already be in place, which is not itself constructed."[14]

---

than the alternative view. If moral first principles are thought to be merely discovered or acknowledged in a prior moral order, this requires "but a sparse conception of the person, based on the idea of the person as knower," for if "the content of first principles is already given . . . persons need only to be able to know that these first principles are and to be moved by this knowledge" (*Lectures*, 237). Moral constructivism, by contrast, involves "a fuller conception of the person, of a kind required to specify the form, structure, and content of a constructivist moral view" (ibid., 238).

12. In his own constructive work—as opposed to his interpretive claims about Kant—Rawls does deviate in some respects from the specific kind of constructivism he attributes to Kant himself. In his Dewey Lectures, Rawls sketches out a "Kantian constructivism," rather than trying to be faithful to all the specific details of Kant's own alleged constructivism, and in Rawls's sketch, he seeks to show how the understanding of justice as fairness that he had developed in *A Theory of Justice* could be framed in constructivist terms. In the 1990s, Rawls also made reference to a "political constructivism," as distinct from Kant's moral constructivism, in *Political Liberalism* (New York: Columbia University Press, 1993). Yet even Rawls's deviations from a strict Kantian moral constructivism preserve an emphasis on the role of some kind of constructivist procedure as a requirement of autonomy.

13. Charles Larmore, *The Autonomy of Morality* (Cambridge: Cambridge University Press, 2008), 83.

14. Ibid., 84.

Rawls himself seems to concede this, even if he does not fully appreciate the significance of that concession for his overall account of Kant's constructivism. For as Rawls acknowledges in his Harvard lectures,

> [t]he idea here is that not everything can be constructed. Every construction has its basis, certain materials, as it were, from which it begins. While the CI-procedure is not . . . constructed but laid out, it does have a basis: the conception of free and equal persons as reasonable and rational, a conception that is mirrored in the procedure.[15]

Larmore notes that passage in his criticism of Rawls, but I should also call attention to another revealing passage that could further complicate Rawls's account. It is Rawls's clarification that "the CI-procedure should not be viewed as an account of an alleged process of reasoning that we are said to be consciously and explicitly going through whenever moral questions arise," since, as he adds,

> I take Kant to hold . . . that our moral reasoning . . . satisfies the requirements of the procedure without being consciously or explicitly guided by it. People in everyday life have no explicit knowledge of these requirements; nor to reason correctly do they need to know of them. Kant's aim is not to teach us what is right and wrong: that we already know. Rather, he sees the value of the philosophical understanding of the moral law as securing more firmly our acceptance of it by revealing to us how it is rooted in our personality as autonomous and as having the moral powers that make us free and equal legislating members of a possible realm of ends.[16]

In both of these passages, Rawls essentially concedes that Kant's constructivism itself requires a moral foundation since the constructivist procedure is itself based on moral commitments about free and equal persons and already presumes knowledge of right and wrong.[17] Rawls might respond that there is still an important difference between the moral commitments that shape the constructivist procedure and the principles that result from that procedure,

---

15. Rawls, *Lectures*, 240.
16. Ibid., 218.
17. By granting that Kant thinks that we already know right from wrong, Rawls seems to undermine the argument that constructivism entails a fuller conception of the person than the alternative view, which would treat the person as a mere knower (*Lectures*, 237–8). Perhaps Rawls means to suggest that constructivism entails a view of the person as a knower and as possessing a further roster of moral attributes, such as being free and equal in a realm of ends. Yet it is not clear why the alternative view, according to which there is a prior and independent moral order that is not constructed by us, could not also affirm that roster of moral attributes. Indeed, it would seem that such attributes would be part of the moral knowledge being presupposed on such a view.

but the basis for that distinction is not clear. If autonomy requires that we construct our moral principles through a constructivist procedure, then why do we not also need to construct the commitments underlying the procedure itself—and yet what, then, would shape that prior process of construction? Why does autonomy, in this understanding, not require construction all the way down? A concern arises here about a regress of constructivist procedures, which Rawls could be trying to avoid by stipulating that the basis for the procedure is not itself constructed. Yet if there is something about that underlying basis that can simply be acknowledged—rather than constructed—without threatening our autonomy, then why does autonomy require any constructivist procedure at all?

I submit that the constructivism Rawls sets out here suffers from incoherence. On one hand, it is framed as rejecting any reliance on a prior, independent moral order—that is, an order that would supposedly undermine our autonomy. On the other hand, however, the basis for its own procedure of construction rests on an undeniably moral foundation involving a certain conception of ourselves as free and equal persons. Larmore is right, I think, to suggest that Rawls's own reliance on such a moral foundation suggests that constructivism cannot be consistently maintained and that moral principles cannot be a merely human creation. Rather, as Larmore claims, they must instead "be understood as having an authority independent of our own devising."[18]

In addition to concerns about incoherence, this model of Kantian constructivism is also hard to reconcile with forms of theism that would understand God to share in any kind of moral community with human beings. Although Rawls does not explicitly reject the possibility that God could play a role within the constructivist procedure that he envisions among free and equal co-legislators in a realm of ends, his discussion implies that such a realm consists only of human persons, especially since his talk of equality would seem to rule out any sense of a divine being who stands within some kind of hierarchical relationship toward human beings. Moreover, in framing autonomy in terms of a rejection of any prior or independent order of value—on the grounds that such an order would, again, conflict with autonomy—Rawls makes it hard to see how this constructivist view of autonomy could be compatible with forms of theism that understand morality to extend beyond humanity and to involve some kind of order of value that connects human beings with a deity that they do not create themselves.[19]

---

18. Larmore, *The Autonomy of Morality*, 84.
19. As Kevin Jung has helpfully pointed out to me, there may be forms of theism—such as those developed in process theology—that might be more compatible with constructivism than I am suggesting here. However, I think more would need to be said about how those forms of theism could characterize the divine role in the moral community in terms that are not in a significant sense reducible to the role played by human beings.

II. Kant's View of Autonomy: An Alternative Interpretation

Turning now to Kant himself, my aim is to show that while he has a strong commitment to autonomy, that commitment does not entail a constructivist view of morality. Indeed, I argue that while Kant shares with constructivists an emphasis on autonomy, he does so without falling into the problems of incoherence that plague Rawls's constructivist account and that Kant's own approach is also much more amenable to theism than is Rawls's view. Whereas Rawls sees Kant arguing *from* autonomy to constructivism, I instead find that Kant argues *to* autonomy based on a prior understanding of morality itself. For Rawls, the demands of autonomy create the need for a constructivist procedure in order to generate moral content, but for Kant himself, by contrast, the appeal to autonomy is much more rooted in concerns about moral motivation, and these concerns arise only against the background of a prior understanding of what kind of substantive content morality involves. For Kant, then, autonomy is fully compatible with the claim that morality is not simply constructed by us. Rather than requiring the construction or creation of moral principles, autonomy instead involves acknowledging the binding authority of such principles and legislating them for ourselves by endorsing them as our own.[20]

I focus here on Kant's *Groundwork for the Metaphysics of Morals* (1785) since it is the work in which Kant first develops an extended account of a morality of autonomy and the work most often cited by constructivist interpreters of Kant. In his preface to the *Groundwork*, Kant lays out the central aim of the work and also indicates some of the starting assumptions upon which his subsequent argument will rely. An especially important assumption for Kant is that morality cannot be something contingent, holding for some human beings and not for others or under some conditions and not others. Rather, morality must hold universally and necessarily, for, in fact, it binds not just all human beings but all rational beings:

> Everyone must grant that a law, if it is to hold morally, that is, as a ground of an obligation, must carry with it absolute necessity; that,

---

20. In the discussion of Kant that follows, my reading of Kant has some affinities with those offered by Karl Ameriks, John E. Hare, and Robert Stern. For Ameriks, see *Kant and the Fate of Autonomy: Problems in the Appropriation of the Critical Philosophy* (Cambridge: Cambridge University Press, 2000); *Interpreting Kant's Critiques* (Oxford: Clarendon Press, 2003); *Kant and the Historical Turn: Philosophy as Critical Interpretation* (Oxford: Clarendon Press, 2006); and *Kant's Elliptical Path* (Oxford: Clarendon Press, 2012). For Hare, see *The Moral Gap: Kantian Ethics, Human Limits, and God's Assistance* (Oxford: Clarendon Press, 1996); *God's Call: Moral Realism, God's Commands, and Human Autonomy* (Grand Rapids: Eerdmans, 2001); and *God and Morality: A Philosophical History* (Oxford: Blackwell, 2007). For Stern, see *Understanding Moral Obligation: Kant, Hegel, Kierkegaard* (Cambridge: Cambridge University Press, 2012), and *Kantian Ethics: Value, Agency, and Obligation* (Oxford: Oxford University Press, 2015).

for example, the command "thou shalt not lie" does not hold only for human beings, as if other rational beings did not have to heed it, and so with all other moral laws properly so called.

(4:389)[21]

In starting with a view of morality that would hold for all rational beings, not just for human beings, Kant is already gesturing toward a set of considerations that would challenge the constructivist understanding of morality as a human creation. If morality is taken to hold for all rational beings—including, as Kant will suggest, for God—then it is hard to see how Kant's view of moral principles could be adequately accounted for through a merely human procedure or process of construction.

Kant also stresses in the preface that the *Groundwork*'s central aim is to address a specific sort of worry, namely, the likelihood that morality itself will be corrupted unless its basis can be set out unambiguously. The concern is not that we lack knowledge of the content of morality but, rather, that our motivation to follow morality for its own sake could be sapped by competing interests if we lack a clear articulation of what sets morality apart from those other interests. For, Kant worries that

> morals themselves remain subject to all sorts of corruption as long as we are without that clue and supreme norm by which to appraise them correctly. For, in the case of what is to be morally good it is not enough that it *conform* with the moral law but it must also be done *for the sake of the law*; without this, that conformity is only very contingent and precarious, since a ground that is not moral will indeed now and then produce actions in conformity with the law, but it will also often produce actions contrary to the law.

(4:390, original emphasis)

The concern that drives Kant here has to do with moral motivation, rather than the need to provide substantive moral content that would otherwise be lacking. The distinction that he sets out between what merely conforms to law and what is done for the sake of the law is not a distinction between right and wrong action (say, truth-telling versus lying), but between two different kinds of motivation for the same action (on what grounds does one tell the truth?). Given that Kant identifies the aim of the work as one of clarifying moral motivation rather than supplying missing moral content, here, too, a constructivist reading starts to falter, since on such a reading, a constructive process or procedure is needed to help fill in such content.

---

21. References to Kant's works follow the volume:page number method of citation used for the edition of Kant's *Gesammelte Schriften* edited by the Royal Prussian Academy of Sciences. I am using the translation of the *Groundwork* found in Immanuel Kant, *Practical Philosophy*, trans. and ed. Mary J. Gregor (Cambridge: Cambridge University Press, 1996).

Kant ends the preface by explaining that his strategy for addressing this concern about moral motivation is to set out morality's "supreme principle," in order to clarify what sets morality apart from competing interests. He will do so by starting from "common cognition" (4:392), or ordinary moral thinking, and then making explicit the supreme principle he already finds implicit in such thinking. He has already been modeling this strategy in a way in the preface, since he has already set out what he takes to be a common view of morality as something that holds for all rational beings. In his fuller elaboration of this strategy, in the work's subsequent sections, he will also come to show that such a view entails moral autonomy.

Drawing on the remainder of the *Groundwork*, I want to highlight how these themes already found in the preface are more fully developed, in order to show that Kant does not cast his own idea of autonomy in constructivist terms. Before doing so, however, I also want to note a distinction in Kant's treatment of the will that is of central concern for discussing his view of autonomy—namely, the distinction between the German terms *Willkür* and *Wille*, both of which are typically (and confusingly) translated as *will* in English. While Kant does not develop this distinction systematically in the *Groundwork*, it is implicit there and becomes explicitly articulated later, in *Religion within the Boundaries of Mere Reason* (1793) and *The Metaphysics of Morals* (1797). As Henry Allison observes, even in the *Groundwork* Kant already suggests "a certain duality of function within the will."[22] The *Willkür/Wille* distinction captures this duality: *Willkür* refers to the will understood in its executive function, as the power or capacity to choose between different possible laws that could guide action (does the law on which one acts find its determining ground in reason or, rather, in my inclinations?), whereas *Wille* refers to the will understood in its rational legislative function—that is, the will that can give its own law, or a will determined specifically by reason rather than inclination. Thus, as Allison remarks, "this distinction allows us to speak of the will as giving the law to, or even as being the law for, itself, since this is just a matter of *Wille* giving the law to, or being the law for, *Willkür*."[23] As I hope to make clear in what follows, such talk of the will giving the law to itself is what Kant means by autonomy.

As I now turn to consider the remainder of the *Groundwork*, there are two further points that are especially important. The first is that Kant frames morality as holding for all rational beings, while at the same time drawing a distinction between the sort of being that has a wholly rational nature, and those beings—such as human beings—that have a dualistic or divided nature, possessing reason as well as sensible inclinations. Kant asserts that all rational beings possess a will (understood in terms of the executive function just mentioned), which he defines as the use of reason in its capacity to act according to laws. Indeed, he claims that to speak of the will in this

---

22. Henry E. Allison, *Kant's Theory of Freedom* (Cambridge: Cambridge University Press, 1990), 130.
23. Ibid.

sense is to speak of practical reason itself, since reason employed practically is required "for the derivation of actions from laws" (4:412). Yet even if all rational beings possess such a will, not all beings are equipped to exercise their will in the same manner. For a being with a wholly rational nature, "reason infallibly determines the will," and such a will is described as holy, since there are no inclinations that could conflict with reason; for beings with a divided nature, however, "this will is not by its nature necessarily obedient" (4:412–413). For human beings, who have a divided nature, the will is instead subject to imperatives, or commands expressed as statements of what one ought to do, even if one's inclinations might lead one to want to do otherwise. Because God is thought to possess a wholly rational nature, without inclinations that might conflict with reason, "the 'ought' is out of place here" (4:414). Unlike a human will, then, God's holy will is not seen as being subject to imperatives.

The second important point to highlight here concerns a distinction between types of moral motivation for human beings. For the human will, and indeed for the will of any being with a divided nature, imperatives command either hypothetically or categorically; this is, of course, a distinction between a demand that holds merely conditionally, according to this or that contingent circumstance, and one that holds universally and necessarily, irrespective of such contingencies. Yet, in another move that is crucial for his idea of autonomy, Kant explains that a hypothetical imperative refers more specifically to a command involving an action taken "as a means to achieving something else that one wills," whereas the categorical imperative involves the demand for an action one ought to do "of itself, without reference to another end" (4:414). The suggestion here is that a merely hypothetical imperative, unlike the categorical imperative, is built on achieving some end supplied by one's sensible inclinations rather than by reason. For Kant, such inclinations are contingent, for they can vary from one human being to another, and even if some inclinations are invariant across humanity, they are nevertheless specific to humanity, rather than holding for all rational beings. Thus, they are still contingent in a crucial sense.[24]

Given the way that the distinction between hypothetical and categorical imperatives is drawn, it is no surprise that Kant refers to the categorical imperative as "the imperative **of morality**" (4:415, original emphasis). For again, Kant begins with the assumption that morality must hold for all rational beings and, hence, cannot be contingent and variable like merely hypothetical imperatives. Yet it is important to note that both categorical and hypothetical imperatives involve reason since both involve willing some kind of action, and the executive will (*Willkür*) is itself defined as the use of reason in its capacity to derive actions from laws. The important difference

---

24. Echoing a concern he had already raised in the preface, Kant stresses a bit later in the *Groundwork* that morality "must hold not only for human beings but for all *rational beings as such*, not merely under contingent conditions and with exceptions but with *absolute necessity*" (4:408, original emphasis).

is that in the case of a hypothetical imperative, the executive will serves some end supplied by the inclinations, while for the categorical imperative, the executive will acts in accordance with the legislative will (*Wille*) and hence on the basis of reason alone, not the inclinations.

To return to the case of truth-telling and lying that Kant raised back in the preface, there is a difference between a command to tell the truth in order to acquire a good reputation (or to avoid the embarrassment of getting caught in a lie) and the command to tell the truth simply because morality requires it, regardless of what may result from that action. In both cases, reason is involved, because one is acting on the basis of a law, or a principle that guides action. In the first case, reason—that is, the executive will (*Willkür*)—acts in pursuit of some desired object (say, to get a good reputation or to avoid the embarrassment of getting caught lying), and insofar as that desire motivates the action, reason is operating in the service of the inclinations. In the second case, however, reason is acting on a different principle, which takes no account of such desires, and thus what motivates is reason itself—or, the legislative will (*Wille*)—rather than the inclinations. To act morally—or, as Kant has it, in accordance with the categorical imperative rather than some merely hypothetical imperative—is thus to be motivated to act on the basis of reason itself. This, too, should not be surprising, if morality holds for all rational beings.

Drawing on the preceding points, Kant finally turns to autonomy. He does so, he explains, to account for what he calls the failure of "all previous efforts that have ever been made to discover the principle of morality" (4:432). Given my focus on the problems that a constructivist reading of Kant presents, it is worth noting here that Kant speaks here of previous attempts to discover—rather than to construct or generate—the principle of morality. Turning specifically to autonomy, he argues that while previous views of morality have acknowledged the way in which human beings are subject to laws, such views have failed to see that morality involves subjection to a law that is self-legislated, in the sense of being legislated by one's own will. Thus, he claims that the supreme principle of morality is "the principle of the **autonomy** of the will in contrast with every other, which I accordingly count as **heteronomy**" (4:433, original emphasis).

Now it might seem that this contrast between autonomy and heteronomy should be understood, as constructivists suggest, as that between a moral principle whose content is constructed by the self and one whose content has already been given in a prior moral order that stands outside the self. Just a couple of pages before he introduces the autonomy/heteronomy distinction, he remarks that

> the will is not merely subject to the law but subject to it in such a way that it must be viewed as also giving the law to itself and just because of this as first subject of the law (of which it can regard itself as the author).
> (4:431)

Talk of authorship of the law might seem to suggest that the law is actually brought into being, or constructed from scratch, rather than being acknowledged as something that subsists in a prior moral order.

However, in his further explication of the autonomy/heteronomy contrast, Kant makes very clear that this distinction is in fact intended to more fully spell out what is involved in the contrast between the categorical imperative and merely hypothetical imperatives—a contrast that is centrally concerned with moral motivation, rather than with concerns about how to generate the content of morality. Indeed, Kant claims that the problem with all previous accounts of morality, which he considers heteronomous, is that they see human beings as subject only to hypothetical imperatives, and therefore, they fail to recognize that there is such a thing as a categorical imperative. As he puts it, if one saw the human being "only as subject to a law (whatever it may be)," without specifying that it must be a law that holds categorically, or unconditionally, then

> this law had to carry with it some interest by way of attraction or constraint, since it did not as a law arise from *his* will; in order to conform with the law, his will had instead to be constrained by *something else* to act in a certain way.
>
> (4:432–433, original emphasis)

Although Kant could have been a bit more precise here, it is clear enough that he is again relying on the contrast between a categorical imperative that involves a command that the will—which is, again, practical reason—gives to itself, while merely hypothetical imperatives involve putting the will in the service not of itself, as reason, but in the service of inclinations that lie outside the will.

Kant reinforces this point several pages later, when he says that the difference between autonomy and heteronomy lies in whether the will (*Willkür*) gives a law to itself (and hence acts in accordance with *Wille*) or whether it instead is acting in the service of some desired object. Thus, autonomy of the will is "the property of the will by which it is a law to itself (independently of any property of the objects of volition)," while in the case of heteronomy, the will "does not give itself the law; instead the object, by means of its relation to the will, gives the law to it" (4:440–441). To solidify the autonomy/heteronomy distinction even further, Kant returns to the case of truth-telling, which could be taken as a principle of action on the basis of either a hypothetical or categorical imperative. Referring to both kinds of imperatives, he observes that

> the former says: I ought not to lie if I will to keep my reputation; but the latter says: I ought not to lie even though it would not bring me the least discredit. The latter must therefore abstract from all objects to this extent: that they have no *influence* at all on the will, so that practical reason (the will) may not merely administer an interest not belonging

to it, but may simply show its own commanding authority as supreme lawgiving.

(4:441, original emphasis)

A hypothetical imperative is merely heteronomous because the will, understood here again as practical reason, is employed in the service of some desire or interest that is external to the will itself, whereas the categorical imperative, which is not based on such a desire, is autonomous in relying only on the will's own internal dictates. Kant's dualistic account of the human being, divided by reason and the inclinations, is absolutely central here. Indeed, the distinction between autonomy and heteronomy ultimately has to do with moral motivation—more specifically, with which side of our nature provides the motive for moral action.

Since nowhere in Kant's account of the autonomy/heteronomy distinction does he cast that distinction as one pertaining to the origin of moral content—does such content come from us, as a human creation, or from some independent order of value?—I submit that it is a mistake to treat Kantian autonomy, as constructivists do, as requiring the claim that moral content must be entirely constructed by us. Moreover, Kant's discussion of that distinction proceeds in tandem with an account of how all rational beings must be understood as standing together within a shared moral community, which he calls *"a kingdom of ends"* (4:433, original emphasis). Rawls refers to this community as a realm of ends, as already noted. Yet that way of rendering Kant's point does not capture the distinction he draws between the king or sovereign in that community and mere members—a distinction that reinforces the point made earlier in the *Groundwork* that while morality is something that links together God and humanity, God and human beings relate to morality in different ways. The distinction here further challenges constructivist claims that would treat morality as simply a human construction, for again, how could a moral law that is thought to hold even beyond humanity be only a human creation? Kant differentiates the divine and human roles within the moral community—the kingdom of ends—by granting that while every rational being "must always regard himself as lawgiving in a kingdom of ends possible through freedom of the will, whether as a member or as sovereign," a mere member is lawgiving in the kingdom but also subject to those laws, while the sovereign is not subject in the same way, for the sovereign is "a completely independent being, without needs and with unlimited resources adequate to his will" (4:434). Here Kant echoes his earlier remarks about how, for the divine will, there are no imperatives, while for our human wills, imperatives apply because there is always a possible conflict between our reason, on one hand, and the needs rooted in our inclinations, on the other. He also seems to suggest that despite this crucial difference, both the divine will and a human will can be autonomous, albeit not in the same way. For, Kant explains, a will that is necessarily in harmony with "the laws of autonomy" is "a *holy*, absolutely good will," while for a will that is "not absolutely good," in which conflict between reason and inclination always remains possible—a will such as our ours—the relationship to autonomy remains one of "*obligation*" (4:439, original emphasis). For us, then, there remains a sense of what one ought to do, even if it is not what one actually wants to do.

My reading of Kant suggests, then, that his distinction between autonomy and heteronomy is not about whether the source of moral content lies in our own creative activity or in some independent order of value but is, instead, concerned with moral motivation: Is it our reason that motivates our action—or our inclinations? Autonomy requires the former, while heteronomy obtains in the case of the latter. Now Kant would be sure to grant that there may be plenty of times that our reason does and indeed should operate in service of our inclinations since he takes it for granted that we have unavoidable needs on account of our sensible nature.[25] The concern, rather, is whether we prioritize our inclinations over our reason when these source of motivation conflict (when, say, we are tempted to lie but know we should tell the truth) and whether actions that appear moral are actually done for other motives (say, when we tell the truth out of a desire to get a good reputation or to avoid the embarrassment of getting caught in a lie, rather than telling the truth because it is the right thing to do).

The latter cases are of especially great concern for Kant—that is, cases that might appear moral from the outside but are lacking in moral worth from the inside. In the preface, he referred to such cases as ones in which an action is done merely in conformity with the moral law but not for the sake of the law. He returns to this concern in his discussion of autonomy and heteronomy and relates it to the difference between the divine and the human, when he speaks of how "the worth of rational beings" is to be appraised "only by their disinterested conduct," and of how the "essence of things," in terms of moral worth, is not to be construed in terms of mere appearances, since "that which . . . alone constitutes the worth of a human being is that in terms of which he must also be appraised by whoever does it, even by the supreme being" (4:439). Kant claims here not only that the autonomy/heteronomy distinction concerns moral motivation—is my motivation for apparently moral conduct disinterested, or based on my interest or desire for some outcome?—but also that such motivation matters because it is something for which we bear responsibility and are held accountable by God (or as he puts it, "the supreme being"). These sorts of considerations receive much greater attention in Kant's three *Critiques*—the *Critique of*

---

25. Earlier in the *Groundwork*, Kant observes that it is unavoidable for human beings to desire happiness, and while he insists that reason has a role to play beyond merely securing the conditions of happiness, he acknowledges at the same time that the goodness of the will—that is, moral goodness, as distinct from the will's happiness—"need not . . . be the sole and complete good" (4:396). That is to say, Kant acknowledges that there is a good in happiness itself, even if that good cannot override the importance of a morally good will.

Pure Reason (1781), the *Critique of Practical Reason* (1788), and the *Critique of the Power of Judgment* (1790)—as well as in the later *Religion*, but it is important to recognize that they also appear here in the *Groundwork*, which is the work of Kant's that is most often appealed to by those seeking to offer constructivist interpretations.

I have been arguing that Kant's *Groundwork* is an argument on behalf of autonomy, but not constructivism, and at this point two objections may arise. The first concerns why someone like Rawls would so strongly emphasize the importance of a procedure of construction (which he calls the CI-procedure), if Kant is not actually a constructivist. The second objection concerns the coherence of Kant's own view of autonomy.

Turning first to Rawls's emphasis on a procedure of construction, it is important to recall that for Rawls, this CI-procedure (the categorical imperative procedure) is the mechanism for developing the content of specific moral principles. Yet to the extent that Kant does appeal to any such procedure involving the categorical imperative, I find that its purpose is not to generate or construct moral content that would otherwise be lacking, but rather to provide a test for those who already have some sense of morality's demands, so that (and here Kant's concerns in the *Groundwork*'s preface resurface) their moral commitment will not be corrupted by the intrusion of sensible inclinations. Put another way, Kant's references to such a procedure serve as a test of moral motivation, not an attempt to develop moral content from scratch. Rawls's discussion of the CI-procedure draws on the point in the *Groundwork*, where Kant claims that he will enumerate four specific examples of moral duties—including both duties to ourselves and to other human beings and perfect as well as imperfect duties—to show how they can be derived from the categorical imperative.[26] It is crucial to see here, however, that rather than claiming to develop a procedure to generate the content of these duties (as if that content would be otherwise unavailable), Kant is doing something quite different: he is taking these duties as ones with which we are already familiar (even if our commitment to them is not certain) and then trying to clarify their rationale by showing how they reflect an imperative that is categorical and not merely hypothetical in nature. Looking briefly at the duty not to commit suicide (offered as an example of a perfect duty to oneself), Kant imagines a person who, on one hand, "feels sick of life because of a series of troubles that has grown to the point of despair" but, on the other hand, is "still so far in possession of his reason that he can ask himself whether it would not be contrary to his

---

26. For Kant, perfect duties are those that admit of no exception (and often involve absolute prohibitions, which for him include prohibitions against suicide and lying), whereas imperfect duties, such as the duties to develop one's own talents and to help others in need, allow for discretion in how (and the extent to which) they are fulfilled.

duty to himself to take his own life" (4:422).[27] In this example (as in the others he offers, including the duty not to lie and duties to develop one's own talents and to help others in need), Kant presents a person who already has some sense of moral duty—a person who has at least an inkling that a contemplated course of action could be contrary to such duty—but risks not acting on that sense, by letting inclinations corrupt the moral commitment. By showing how the categorical imperative (and not just this or that hypothetical imperative) underlies the specific duties he discusses, Kant aims to show that the duties have their basis in reason alone, not in the inclinations, and thus, he is addressing a concern about moral motivation. Moreover, Kant indicates that the four examples he presents are not meant to enumerate all of our specific moral duties (since it is not until the later *Metaphysics of Morals* that he discusses the whole range of duties in depth) but are instead offered as representative examples of how different categories of already-recognized duties can all be connected to the categorical imperative so that their shared rationale can be clarified and our commitment to them strengthened.

The second objection I want to consider involves whether Kant really cares about autonomy after all. For if Kant is committed to autonomy alongside claims about a rational community that includes both God and humanity and about God as a judge of human moral worth, one might think that this is a strange kind of autonomy, at least to many contemporary readers. In contemporary usage, autonomy is often thought to refer to an unimpeded ability to choose whatever we want. Yet for Kant, it is crucial that our autonomy is the autonomy of reason, since mere choosing could involve following merely hypothetical imperatives (allowing the object of one's desire to provide the motive for one's choice), while for Kant, autonomy involves choosing in accordance with the categorical imperative, which is to say, in accordance with reason's own demands, as opposed to whatever we may happen to desire. Here again Kant's distinction between *Willkür* and *Wille* can prove helpful: according to his distinctive understanding of autonomy, possessing a will in the sense of having one's own power of choice—an executive function (*Willkür*)—does not in itself constitute autonomy, since one's power of choice could still be exercised merely in the service of the inclinations and, hence, in a heteronomous manner. Rather, autonomy lies more specifically in choosing to make the legislative will (*Wille*)—the law of reason alone, not the inclinations—one's own law.

However, even if Kant's distinctive understanding of autonomy is granted, a further concern might arise. If the autonomy I am describing here entails

---

27. Here I am not offering a defense of all the specific duties that Kant is enumerating (such as the duty not to commit suicide) but, rather, making a broader point about the method he is adopting, which I see as contrasting with the constructivist method that Rawls ascribes to Kant.

the subordination of our desires to reason in cases where they come into conflict, then is this still genuine autonomy, in the sense of *self*-legislation, or is it rather submission to something imposed *on the self* from outside? In response, I would suggest that what matters for Kant is that autonomy reflects our distinct status as human beings. On one hand, the moral law does involve a sense of constraint for us (since we do not always want to do what we should do), and the law's demand has binding authority over us, even if it conflicts with what we may desire at a given moment. On the other hand, however, the moral law is not alien to us, because it is the expression of our own reason, and in that sense it is our own law. Hence, the moral law, while involving a sense of constraint, is self-legislated insofar as it is a law with which we ourselves can identify, as a fundamental part of our own nature, rather than being some kind of arbitrary, tyrannical imposition. Karl Ameriks expresses this point when he says that for Kant, the moral principles we rely on are "not external to our *essential nature*, which for Kant is our sheer rationality," and hence, "they in one sense have a significant 'internal' source—they come from something 'in' us."[28] That being said, Kant does not treat these principles as simply human constructions, because they are shared between us and other rational beings, including God. In that sense they are connected with an order of value beyond us—an order of value that we participate in, and endorse, but do not create on our own.

Offering an interpretation with some similarities to that of Ameriks, John Hare has suggested that for Kant, autonomy is related to the moral law in the following manner: "We endorse the law, but we do not bring it into existence."[29] To buttress his claim that we do not create the moral law ourselves, Hare points to a passage from the lectures on ethics that Kant delivered to his students at the University of Königsberg. There Kant claims that the moral law holds with necessity, just like the proposition that a triangle has three angles. Thus, even God does not create the moral law, any more than God creates the proposition that triangles possess three angles.[30] Yet if that is the case, then the moral law is tied to an order of value that is not a human creation—and it is not a divine creation either. While I am hesitant to put too much weight on this claim from Kant's ethics lectures, since it does not come from his own published writings, I think the claim is still fully compatible with what Kant says in the *Groundwork*, since there Kant suggests that human beings and God stand together within a moral community oriented around the moral law, and he seems to take the existence of the law, and our recognition that it possesses substantive content, as a starting point for his argument about autonomy. To be autonomous, then, is to give

---

28. Ameriks, *Kant and the Fate of Autonomy*, 14. Original emphasis.
29. Hare, *God and Morality*, 177.
30. Ibid., 142–3. For the passage in Kant's ethics lectures, see 27:283, found in Kant, *Lectures on Ethics*, ed. Peter Heath and J. B. Schneewind and trans. Peter Heath (Cambridge: Cambridge University Press, 1997).

oneself the moral law, not in the sense of bringing the law into existence, or creating it through a human procedure, but, rather, in the sense of relating to, and endorsing, that law as a feature of our own essential nature.

III. Autonomy and Theism

I have been arguing that a non-constructivist interpretation of Kantian autonomy is not only more accurate as a reading of Kant's own work, but also more clearly compatible with those forms of theism that understand morality in terms of an order of value that links God and humanity.[31] Kant's references to the kingdom of ends in the *Groundwork* suggest that he locates human beings and God within a shared moral community—even if he also distinguishes between God as the kingdom's sovereign and human beings as mere members of the kingdom. But even if Kant envisions a role for God here, are there particular ways of construing the relationship between God and morality that Kant's non-constructivist approach would rule out? Can more be said about the role of theism in Kant's ethics?

It is clear, I think, that Kant's approach cannot be reconciled with strongly voluntarist forms of divine command theory that make morality itself entirely dependent on God's will.[32] If we were to consider Kant's assertion that the moral law is neither a human nor a divine creation (a claim that is made explicit in his ethics lectures and is compatible with his published writings, even if not explicitly stated there), then we would have to conclude that Kant's framework would rule out strongly voluntarist claims about God's will as the source of the moral law itself. If the moral law originated simply from the divine will and had no deep connection to our own wills as human beings, then there would be no basis for our autonomy and for the kind of shared moral community that Kant envisions between God and humanity.

Yet a number of contemporary defenders of divine command theory, including Robert Adams and Stephen Evans, also reject such a strongly

---

31. While I am taking up the question of Kant's relation to theism here, I am not able to address the further issue of whether Kant's views may be compatible with specific Christian claims—an issue that is the subject of ongoing debate. For a helpful introduction to key points in the debate, see the essays in Philip J. Rossi and Michael Wreen, eds., *Kant's Philosophy of Religion Reconsidered* (Bloomington: Indiana University Press, 1991), and Chris L. Firestone and Stephen R. Palmquist, eds., *Kant and the New Philosophy of Religion* (Bloomington: Indiana University Press, 2006). For more sustained treatments, see Hare, *The Moral Gap* and *God and Morality*, along with Gordon E. Michalson, Jr., *Kant and the Problem of God* (Oxford: Blackwell, 1999), and Christopher J. Insole, *Kant and the Creation of Freedom: A Theological Problem* (Oxford: Oxford University Press, 2013).
32. For a helpful, brief overview of this kind of strong voluntarism, see Stern, *Understanding Moral Obligation*, 41–52. Stern specifically identifies Ockham, Luther, and Calvin as examples. For a more detailed treatment of Luther and Calvin, see Schneewind, *The Invention of Autonomy*, 27–36.

voluntarist account of morality, instead arguing that divine commands provide the basis only for what counts as morally obligatory—not for moral value as such.[33] They stress that a theory of moral obligation must be distinguished from a theory of the good, and that while moral obligation is best understood as being rooted in divine commands, claims about what could constitute a divine command (and about God's own moral character) involve presuppositions rooted in a prior theory of the good. For these theorists, then, the morally good is not itself simply a creation of God's will: the divine will (as expressed in commands) is rather what makes something that is already morally good also morally obligatory. Adams articulates the role of a prior theory of the good when he explains that the divine commands that confer moral obligation are those of a specific kind of God: "It is only the commands of a definitively good God, who, for example, is not cruel but loving, that are a good candidate for the role of defining moral obligation."[34] Evans makes a similar point: "Some theory of the good must be presupposed . . . since an important part of what makes God's commands binding is that God is himself essentially good and thus his commands are directed to the good."[35] Moreover, both Adams and Evans also affirm that divine command theory can be upheld alongside a commitment to autonomy, where autonomy is understood as entailing that we assume responsibility for our moral choices and for making at least some determinations about what actually constitutes a divine command. Both also argue that if divine command theory rests on a prior theory of the good, then autonomy would entail sharing with God a sense of that good and working together to pursue it.[36]

These contemporary divine command theorists therefore separate moral value as such from moral obligation and hold that even the divine will is not the source of moral value as such, while also affirming that autonomy is compatible with divine commands. Kant, too, suggests a distinction between moral value and the issue of moral obligation, and so there might be some overlap between his framework and those of contemporary divine command theorists, but does his own account of autonomy make room for divine commands as grounds of obligation? Kant's published writings could be thought to give some justification for considering him a divine command theorist, especially since in both the *Critique of Practical Reason* and *Religion*, Kant defines religion in terms of the recognition that all

33. See Robert Merrihew Adams, *Finite and Infinite Goods: A Framework for Ethics* (Oxford: Oxford University Press, 1999), and C. Stephen Evans, *God and Moral Obligation* (Oxford: Oxford University Press, 2013). See also Stern, *Understanding Moral Obligation*, 41–52, where he identifies Scotus, Suarez, and Culverwell as examples of this kind of divine command theory, as contrasted with the strong voluntarism of Ockham, Luther, and Calvin.
34. Adams, *Finite and Infinite Goods*, 250.
35. Evans, *God and Moral Obligation*, 26.
36. See Adams, *Finite and Infinite Goods*, 270–6, and Evans, *God and Moral Obligation*, 94–8.

duties—all moral obligations—are to be seen as divine commands.[37] Indeed, Hare argues that Kant is a divine command theorist in the following sense: God's commands play a key role in grounding moral obligation, even if those commands are not the source of moral value as such, and this is compatible with a commitment to autonomy. Drawing on Kant's references to the recognition of our duties as divine commands, as well as his discussion in the *Groundwork* of God's role as the sovereign in the kingdom of ends, Hare says of our membership in that kingdom:

> Members . . . make the law and are subject to the law (they are autonomous), but the sovereign, in addition to being a member, has a special role: other members are subject to his will, while he is not subject to the will of any other member.[38]

Hence, on Hare's reading of Kant, God's will serves a distinct role in grounding moral obligation, beyond our own autonomous willing as human beings. Hare also claims that while human beings and God are both "authors of the obligation of the law," neither is the author of "the law itself" (since, again, the moral law is neither a divine nor a human creation).[39]

Yet there are reasons for doubting whether Kant is, in fact, a divine command theorist. Despite his repeated references to the recognition of duties as divine commands, he also argues in the *Groundwork* that theories that would root moral obligation in divine commands should be classified as heteronomous, and hence as conflicting with autonomy. He claims there that such theories would end up making the motivation for obedience to God rest on hope of reward and/or fear of punishment—and hence root such motivation in the inclinations, rather than in reason's own dictates.[40] Hare has argued that this rejection of divine command theory is aimed at a strongly voluntarist version of the theory (specifically the one espoused by Christian August Crusius), rather than at all forms of divine command theory. However, other scholars, such as Robert Stern (and Adams), disagree and maintain that Kant does, in fact, reject the theory as such.[41]

I think Kant's writings are genuinely ambiguous on this point since he does clearly make arguments against divine command theory while also referring to duties in terms of divine commands. Perhaps the wisest position to adopt in this particular debate is to affirm the extent to which Kant's ethics is

---

37. For the passage in the *Critique of Practical Reason*, see 5:129, found in Kant, *Practical Philosophy*, and for the passage in *Religion Within the Boundaries of Mere Reason*, see 6:153, found in Kant, *Religion and Rational Theology*, trans. and ed. Allen W. Wood and George di Giovanni (Cambridge: Cambridge University Press, 1996).
38. Hare, *God and Morality*, 155–6.
39. Ibid., 177.
40. For this discussion in the *Groundwork*, see 4:443, found in Kant, *Practical Philosophy*.
41. See Stern, *Understanding Moral Obligation*, 53–67, and Adams, *Finite and Infinite Goods*, 270–1.

robustly theistic, even if it is not unambiguously a divine command theory of moral obligation, and to note at the same time that divine command theory is itself just one of numerous accounts of the relationship between God and morality. Even in the *Groundwork*—often seen as the work most amenable to a constructivist and non-theistic interpretation—Kant emphasizes God's role as sovereign in the kingdom of ends, and develops at length a contrast between the divine will and merely human wills, such that concerns about duty, or obligation, only arise for the wills of human beings (since what we may want to do can conflict with what we should do) and not for God. Moreover, Kant holds in the *Groundwork*—as well as in all three *Critiques*, and *Religion*, among other writings—that God serves as judge of whether even outwardly moral actions are truly done for their own sake, rather than for one's own advantage. This distinction concerning motivation is also, of course, deeply intertwined with Kant's autonomy/heteronomy distinction.

IV. Conclusion: Beyond Constructivism

In the preceding pages, I have challenged Rawls's constructivist reading of Kant both in terms of its accuracy as an interpretation of Kant and as a coherent position in its own right. While Rawls and other constructivists are correct in emphasizing Kant's commitment to autonomy, the way they construe that commitment leads them to read Kant as a constructivist, for whom morality is a human creation. I have argued, however, that Kant sees the moral law as something that we autonomously endorse, as an expression of our own essential rational nature, and yet the moral law is not human creation (and neither is it divinely created). On Rawls's reading, Kant argues from autonomy to constructivism, on the assumption that if morality is to be genuinely self-legislated, its content has to be entirely constructed by human beings. On my reading, however, Kant sees morality as having a binding force that is confirmed through our own reason. Hence, rather than arguing *from* autonomy, he instead argues *to* autonomy, since the self-legislation he envisions is a way of capturing his prior understanding of morality as something that involves a law rooted in our own reason, rather than merely in the inclinations. For Kant, the appeal to autonomy is fundamentally a way of making a point about moral motivation, rather than moral content that would otherwise be lacking.

On my reading, then, Kant avoids the false dichotomy that creates problems for constructivist accounts such as Rawls's. The choice is not between morality as a human creation and morality as something simply imposed on us from outside; rather, for Kant, morality can be understood as involving an independent order of value—indeed, one that can hold both for God and humanity—while at the same time expressing our own autonomous endorsement of those values. Through that endorsement, we appropriate moral values as our own and choose to act on them, rather than acting for merely self-interested motives. As I have shown, even Rawls's account of

Kantian constructivist procedure relies on something like an independent order of value (though he does not claim that this order of value holds for God as well as humanity), since Rawls stipulates that constructivism does not go all the way down: recall his concession that the procedure of construction relies on a moral basis that is not itself constructed (namely, a certain conception of free and equal persons). Therefore, in addition to what I see as Rawls's mistaken interpretation of Kant, I take Rawls's concession here as an indication of the incoherence of his constructivism on philosophical grounds as well.

Earlier in this paper, in developing my argument for the incoherence of Rawls's constructivism, I drew on Larmore's work. I should note here that Larmore also offers helpful articulation of how a commitment to autonomy, or self-legislation, can avoid the false dichotomy that I find in Rawls's reading of Kant. As Larmore explains,

> when we do impose principles on ourselves, we presumably do so for reasons: we suppose that it is fitting for us to adopt them, or that adopting them will advance certain of our interests. Self-legislation, when it does occur, is an activity that takes place in the light of reasons that we must antecedently recognize, and whose own authority we therefore do not institute but rather find ourselves called upon to acknowledge.[42]

Rather than assuming that values are either created by us or imposed on us, Larmore suggests that we can adopt principles as our own, in a way that expresses something of ourselves—our own nature—while recognizing that those principles are worth adopting for reasons that have an authority independent of our own choosing. Indeed, if we adopted principles without recourse to any prior authoritative reasons, then there would be a risk of utter arbitrariness (why adopt these principles and not others?), and Rawls's concession that the constructivist procedure is not itself constructed can perhaps be seen as an acknowledgment of this. Yet if arbitrariness is one sort of risk, there is also a risk of a different kind: if, instead of being our own creation, principles were just imposed on us, without any connection to our own nature, then in that case there would instead be the risk of tyranny or despotism. My suggestion is that Kant avoids both of these risks by rejecting the sort of false dichotomy seen in Rawls's constructivist account.

While Larmore's reference to self-legislation captures much of what I find appealing in Kant's own account, it is nevertheless striking that Larmore himself does not attribute that understanding to Kant. In fact, as a matter of interpretation, Larmore largely accepts Rawls's constructivist reading of Kant, while still challenging constructivism on philosophical grounds.[43] This

---

42. Larmore, *The Autonomy of Morality*, 44.
43. Ibid., 33–46, and 69–136.

occurs, I think, because Larmore sees Kant falling into the same false dichotomy found in Rawls, and like Rawls, Larmore seems to be understanding Kant to be making an argument *from* autonomy rather than *to* autonomy. However, even if I take Larmore to be mistaken as an interpreter of Kant, he still captures something crucially important about how autonomy can be coherently understood without also entailing constructivism.

Bibliography

Adams, Robert Merrihew. *Finite and Infinite Goods: A Framework for Ethics*. Oxford: Oxford University Press, 1999.
Allison, Henry E. *Kant's Theory of Freedom*. Cambridge: Cambridge University Press, 1990.
Ameriks, Karl. *Kant and the Fate of Autonomy: Problems in the Appropriation of the Critical Philosophy*. Cambridge: Cambridge University Press, 2000.
———. *Interpreting Kant's Critiques*. Oxford: Clarendon Press, 2003.
———. *Kant and the Historical Turn: Philosophy as Critical Interpretation*. Oxford: Clarendon Press, 2006.
———. *Kant's Elliptical Path*. Oxford: Clarendon Press, 2012.
Bagnoli, Carla, ed. *Constructivism in Ethics*. Cambridge: Cambridge University Press, 2013.
Evans, C. Stephen. *God and Moral Obligation*. Oxford: Oxford University Press, 2013.
Firestone, Chris L., and Stephen R. Palmquist, eds. *Kant and the New Philosophy of Religion*. Bloomington: Indiana University Press, 2006.
Förster, Eckart, ed. *Kant's Transcendental Deductions: The Three 'Critiques' and the 'Opus postumum.'* Stanford: Stanford University Press, 1989.
Hare, John E. *The Moral Gap: Kantian Ethics, Human Limits, and God's Assistance*. Oxford: Clarendon Press, 1996.
———. *God's Call: Moral Realism, God's Commands, and Human Autonomy*. Grand Rapids: Eerdmans, 2001.
———. *God and Morality: A Philosophical History*. Oxford: Blackwell, 2007.
Insole, Christopher J. *Kant and the Creation of Freedom: A Theological Problem*. Oxford: Oxford University Press, 2013.
Kant, Immanuel. *Practical Philosophy*. Translated and edited by Mary J. Gregor. Cambridge: Cambridge University Press, 1996.
———. *Religion and Rational Theology*. Translated and edited by Allen W. Wood and George di Giovanni. Cambridge: Cambridge University Press, 1996.
———. *Lectures on Ethics*. Edited by Peter Heath and J. B. Schneewind and translated by Peter Heath. Cambridge: Cambridge University Press, 1997.
Korsgaard, Christine M. *Creating the Kingdom of Ends*. Cambridge: Cambridge University Press, 1996.
———. *The Sources of Normativity*. Cambridge: Cambridge University Press, 1996.
———. *The Constitution of Agency: Essays on Practical Reason and Moral Psychology*. Oxford: Oxford University Press, 2008.
———. *Self-Constitution: Agency, Identity, and Integrity*. Oxford: Oxford University Press, 2009.
Larmore, Charles. *The Autonomy of Morality*. Cambridge: Cambridge University Press, 2008.

Lenman, James, and Yonatan Shemmer, eds. *Constructivism in Practical Philosophy.* Oxford: Oxford University Press, 2012.
Michalson, Gordon E., Jr. *Kant and the Problem of God.* Oxford: Blackwell, 1999.
O'Neill, Onora. *Acting on Principle: An Essay on Kantian Ethics.* New York: Columbia University Press, 1975.
———. *Constructions of Reason: Explorations of Kant's Practical Philosophy.* Cambridge: Cambridge University Press, 1989.
Rawls, John. *A Theory of Justice.* Cambridge: Belknap Press, 1971.
———. "Kantian Constructivism in Moral Theory." *Journal of Philosophy* 77 (1980): 515–72.
———. "Themes in Kant's Moral Philosophy." In *Kant's Transcendental Deductions: The Three 'Critiques' and the 'Opus postumum,'* edited by Eckart Förster. Stanford: Stanford University Press, 1989.
———. *Political Liberalism.* New York: Columbia University Press, 1993.
———. *Collected Papers.* Edited by Samuel Freeman. Cambridge: Harvard University Press, 1999.
———. *Lectures on the History of Moral Philosophy.* Edited by Barbara Herman. Cambridge: Harvard University Press, 2000.
Rossi, Philip J., and Michael Wreen, eds. *Kant's Philosophy of Religion Reconsidered.* Bloomington: Indiana University Press, 1991.
Schneewind, J. B. *The Invention of Autonomy: A History of Modern Moral Philosophy.* Cambridge: Cambridge University Press, 1998.
———. *Essays on the History of Moral Philosophy.* Oxford: Oxford University Press, 2010.
Stern, Robert. "Freedom, Self-Legislation and Morality in Kant and Hegel: Constructivist vs. Realist Accounts." In *German Idealism: Contemporary Perspectives,* edited by Espen Hammer. New York: Routledge, 2007.
———. *Understanding Moral Obligation: Kant, Hegel, Kierkegaard.* Cambridge: Cambridge University Press, 2012.
———. *Kantian Ethics: Value, Agency, and Obligation.* Oxford: Oxford University Press, 2015.

6 On the Moral Significance of Nature

A Comparison of Hegelian Constructivism and Natural Law[1]

David A. Clairmont

It is probably fair to say that constructivism is a serious option in contemporary metaethics and that metaethics as a field is primarily the domain of philosophers. As a point of departure, I take the basic view of constructivism offered by Carla Bagnoli that "[t]he central idea behind constructivism is that moral values and moral norms are not discovered, or revealed to us as if by the gods, but rather constructed by human agents for specific purposes. The metaphor of construction implies agents who do the constructing, materials for the construction, a method or procedure for carrying it out, and a plan."[2] As the other contributors to this volume illustrate, there are various forms of constructivism, depending on whether one emphasizes the ability of reason and rational communal deliberations to construct cross-culturally and transhistorically objective ethical standards (a broadly Kantian form of constructivism) or whether one emphasizes the socially contingent nature of ethical standards based on their negotiated acceptability to individual persons or historical communities (broadly Humean and Hegelian forms of constructivism, respectively).

In this chapter, my aim is to compare and contrast Hegelian constructivist and natural law accounts of the moral significance of nature in the hopes of shedding some light on the place of nature in religious ethics. My strategy is to examine one prominent form of constructivism in religious ethics (the Hegelian constructivism of Jeffrey Stout) as argued against a prominent natural law approach in religious ethics (the revisionist natural law ethics of Jean Porter). It is important, for the purposes of this chapter, that both thinkers are working in the field of religious ethics, since part of what I hope to show through this comparison is that one can better understand the differences between these approaches to the moral significance of nature by examining how nature is interpreted in religious frameworks.

---

1. The author wishes to thank the participants in the Wake Forest University workshop of constructivism, especially Kevin Jung and Per Sundman for their detailed comments on an early draft of this paper, and Ebenezer Akesseh for detailed comments on a later draft.
2. Carla Bagnoli, "Introduction," in *Constructivism in Ethics*, ed. Carla Bagnoli (Cambridge: Cambridge University Press, 2013), 5.

There are, admittedly, problems in selecting a representative thinker from each of these metaethical traditions and questions peculiar to each side that must be addressed. On the Hegelian constructivist side, one encounters the problem of the extent to which the label "Hegelian" may be rightly applied to thinkers that emphasize the historically contingent nature of the justification of truth claims but do not adopt many of the other views held by the German Protestant philosopher Georg Wilhelm Friedrich Hegel (1770–1831 CE). This is especially true when one is interested in the moral significance of nature since Hegel's view of nature may be more or less present in a Hegelian constructivist's view of nature's moral significance.

On the natural law side, one encounters a different problem in that natural law ethics tend to be tied closely to particular historical expressions of a religious tradition (medieval Roman Catholic thought, especially in the work of Thomas Aquinas [1225–1274 CE]) and yet is also closely linked with a philosophical tradition in metaethics. Natural law is often taken to be a form of moral realism, insofar as it acknowledges that nature (and especially human nature) has some kind of moral significance that resists attempts to equate "moral values or moral norms" with a construction either of the practical implications of human reasoning or of the socially discursive practices explicitly established or implied by certain language use. Natural law, in his view, is a species of what Robert Audi has described as "non-reductive naturalism" in ethics because, while it views moral values and norms as having a meaningful connection to the natural world (what Audi calls "naturalistic anchors"), it is not reducible to what is observable in nature or to biological or other physical processes.[3]

Putting Hegelian constructivism into dialogue with natural law has the benefit of bringing to light a number of important issues both for metaethical constructivism and for the shape of religious ethics as a field. Focusing on natural law (especially among medieval thinkers and their later interpreters) provides useful questions for constructivism as it considers the connection between nature and the roles of society in the articulation of moral values and norms. For the latter, focus on natural law helps to explain the return of central questions that were present in the early days of religious ethics as a distinct field of study (for the sake of simplicity, we can date its emergence to the inaugural issue of the *Journal of Religious Ethics* in 1973)[4] and have

---

3. See Robert Audi, "Secular and Religious Foundations of Normative Standards: Liberalism, Naturalism, and Rationalism in Political Philosophy," in *Von der religiösen zur säkularen Begründung staatlicher Normen*, ed. Ludwig Siep, Thomas Gutmann, Bernard Jakl, and Michael Stadtler (Tubingen: Mohr Siebeck, 2012), 43.
4. The *Journal of Religious Ethics* (*JRE*) was first published in 1973 to provide a forum for those working at the intersection of philosophical ethics, theological ethics, and the history of religions. Arguably, the field is much older, as some point to the publication of *Encyclopedia of Religion and Ethics*, ed. James Hastings from 1924–1927. However, as the editors described the journal's mission in 1973, "We believe the proper development of religious ethics requires a transcendence of the boundaries now dividing those engaged in the various

returned with no less force in recent years: questions such as how to balance descriptive and normative scholarly priorities, along with the integration of historical and philosophical methods, in religious ethics.[5]

---

aspects of this area of study. The JRE will seek to facilitate interaction among scholars concerned with one or another aspect of religious ethics: metaethics, normative ethics, decision-making procedures, moral policy thinking and historical ethics. We perceive an emergent openness among religious ethicists to the multiplicity of resources being generated for these projects by persons trained methodologically in the history of religions. We are also presently in an era where a sustained examination of issues and problems of mutual interest is possible with philosophical ethicists, as this issue of the JRE clearly demonstrates. Similar opportunities present themselves by virtue of the level of discussion religious ethicists currently find possible with normative political theorists, cultural anthropologists, developmental and humanistic psychologists, sociological theorists, and interpreters of the aesthetic. The JRE is keen on each of these conversations as it contributes to sharpening our understanding of the nature and vision of religious ethics." See "Editorial," *Journal of Religious Ethics* 1 (1973): 3–4. That inaugural issue contained a collection of essays on one of the most intractable methodological issues in the field: discerning the proper relation between virtue and obligation in religious ethics. The following year saw the publication of an important review article that set forth some of the central differences between philosophical and theological views of metaethics. As Glenn Graber then noted, most philosophers who are concerned with metaethics tend to focus on either the logical or linguistic relationships between religion and ethics. In these views, religious ethics

> refers to moral theories in which either or both of the following is found: (a) the basic standards of value and/or obligation have a logical basis in theological statements (as in the proposal that the statement 'Person x ought to do action y' entails, or is entailed by, the statement 'God commands that x do action y'), or (b) the fundamental terms of moral discourse acquire linguistic meaning by reference to irreducibly religious concepts (as in the view that the expression 'Person x ought to do action y' is synonymous with the expression 'God commands that x do y'). In the eyes of these philosophers (who are mostly in the 'analytic' tradition) the paradigm of a system of religious ethics (and, unfortunately, the only form discussed by the most strident critics of religious ethics) is one in which all ethical terms are defined by means of theological concepts such as the approval or the commands of God and, hence, in which we must make reference to these concepts in order to determine (or, at least, to justify) what we ought to do in every situation of moral choice. There can, it is clear, be other relationships between ethics and religions besides (a) the logical and (b) the linguistic. Frankena (1961: 421–25) specifies three additional possible relationships: (c) causal or genetic, (d) psychological, and (e) epistemological; and I would add two more: (f) ontological and (g) normative. But, in the view of most contemporary philosophers, none of these relations count towards making a moral theory a 'religious ethics.' If a given moral theory is linguistically and logically detachable from the religious context in which it is developed and presented, it would not be counted as a religious ethics even if the religious context shaped it and contains epistemological, psychological, causal, or ontological claims bearing directly on it.
> (53–4)

See Glenn C. Graber, "A Critical Bibliography of Recent Discussions of Religious Ethics by Philosophers," *Journal of Religious Ethics* 2, no. 2 (1974): 53–80. See also William K. Frankena, "Public Education and the Good Life," *Harvard Educational Review* 31 (1961): 413–26.

5. The question about the relationship of religion to ethics, as well as the relationship between the descriptive and the normative in religious ethics, was central to the special 25th anniversary issue of the *Journal of Religious Ethics*. See especially, James M. Gustafson,

Comparing a Hegelian constructivist and a natural law account of nature's moral significance also brings to light a frequent mischaracterization of natural law positions by some constructivists as either excessively physicalist (e.g., in sexual ethics) or as based on a view of practical reason as having certain universal characteristics which enable it to identify basic human goods and establish the proper principles by means of which those goods ought to be pursued. The former kind of views (i.e., purported physicalism) is commonly attributed to certain medieval Christian thinkers who often serve as resources for natural law positions in religious ethics. The latter kind of view (i.e., purported universal practical reason) are commonly attributed to the modern natural law positions of the so-called New Natural Law (or New Classical Natural Law) thinkers who derive natural law from what they take to be self-evident truths of practical reasoning, thereby seeking to show how the resources of the natural law tradition can speak to modern anxieties about threats to human dignity and respect for persons.[6] Both of these readings of natural law were also, historically, troublesome to many Protestant theologians who viewed natural law as an attempt by Catholic theologians to establish common cause with non-Christian approaches to ethics and thereby to blunt the incisive power of Christian revelation.[7] I argue that such critiques envision a distinctly modern understanding of natural law (consonant with the envisioned

---

"A Retrospective Interpretation of American Religious Ethics: 1948–1998," *Journal of Religious Ethics* 25, no. 3 (1997), 25th Anniv. Suppl.: 3–22; and John P. Reeder, Jr., "What Is a Religious Ethic?" *Journal of Religious Ethics* 25, no. 3 (1997), 25th Anniv. Suppl.: 157–81. More recently, see Aaron Stalnaker, "Judging Others: History, Ethics, and the Purposes of Comparison," *Journal of Religious Ethics* 36, no. 3 (2008): 425–44.

6. The most widely discussed position is that of Germain Grisez, Joseph Boyle, and John Finnis. See their "Practical Principles, Moral Truth, and Ultimate Ends," *American Journal of Jurisprudence* 32 (1987): 99–151. A position in some ways similar to that of Grisez, Boyle, and Finnis may be found in Martin Rhonheimer, *Natural Law and Practical Reason: A Thomist View of Moral Autonomy*, trans. Gerald Malsbury (New York: Fordham University Press, 1993). Although the work of John Finnis and his collaborators is perhaps the best known of the New Natural Law (or as Finnis would prefer to call it, the "New Classical Natural Law") thinkers, Martin Rhonheimer has developed the most pointed exchange with Jean Porter on the issues discussed in this chapter. See Martin Rhonheimer, "Review Article: Nature as Reason: A Thomistic Theory of the Natural Law," *Studies in Christian Ethics* 19, no. 3 (2006): 357–37. This article and related exchanges with Porter and on the topic of natural law are collected in Martin Rhonheimer, *The Perspective of the Acting Person: Essays in the Renewal of Thomistic Moral Philosophy*, ed. William F. Murphy, Jr. (Washington, DC: The Catholic University of America Press, 2008). For a useful comparison of natural law thinkers, especially in reference to Porter, see William C. Mattison III, "The Changing Face of Natural Law: The Necessity of Belief for Natural Law Norm Specification," *Journal of the Society of Christian Ethics* 27, no. 1 (2007): 251–77.

7. For a helpful review of the history of Protestant critiques of natural law, and the recent Protestant engagement with the natural law tradition, see Carl E. Braaten, "Protestants and Natural Law," *First Things* (January 1992): 1–16.

philosophical problems posited in modernity) that is certainly not held by all natural law thinkers today.[8]

The argument of this paper proceeds in four parts. First, I consider the Hegelian constructivism of Jeffrey Stout, examining the moral significance of nature in his own ethical project and in Hegel as one of his main constructivist sources. Along the way, I consider both how he understands Hegel as a resource for thinking about the work of modern science and its philosophical judgments about nature and how his view of science affects Stout's judgments about natural law. I pay special attention to his discussion of the connection among metaphysics, the justification of moral claims, and the moral significance of nature.[9] Opting to engage those natural law accounts that do not engage the moral significance of nature at any depth, opting instead for precisely the same kind of contextualist epistemology that fits the constructivist philosophical account Stout wishes to argue for in the first place, this leaves the moral significance of nature, as interpreted through religious frameworks that themselves raise basic metaphysical questions, largely unexplained.

Second, I turn to the work of Jean Porter, who develops an account of natural law that seeks to integrate metaphysics and historically sensitive epistemological concerns. Porter's revisionist natural law takes social context seriously when examining the nature of moral values and moral norms (as the Hegelian constructivist also would want to do) but does not dismiss the necessary metaphysical questions embedded within natural law (as traditional religious accounts highlight) or the importance of the human continuity with the natural world for thinking about moral values and moral norms. Drawing on sources from medieval Christian theology and recent studies in developmental psychology and evolutionary biology, Porter charts a path that keeps metaphysical questions in play through a rootedness in certain

---

8. While accounts of modernity and post-modernity vary, I here follow David Tracy's view that "[a] great deal of post-modern thought is directed towards exposing two illusions of modernity: the unreality of modernity's belief in self-presence in modernity's self-understanding as *the* present: and the unreality of the modern understanding of the autonomous, self-grounding self." See David Tracy, "The Post-Modern Re-Naming of God as Incomprehensible and Hidden," *Cross-Currents* (Spring/Summer 2000): 204, 240–7. In other words, modernity is characterized based on a twofold sense of what is real and therefore the proper object of any academic study: reworking Tracy's order, the certainty that the self is the criterion for truth and the conviction that the *present time* in history provides the *primary* perspective from which we can look back and assess the truth of earlier periods and ways of life, including our own understandings of ourselves. The postmodern instead focuses on the truth of the other rather than the self and on the historical (and, by extension, the contingent) rather than the present (and, by extension, the certain).
9. For a discussion of the influence of Jeffrey Stout's constructivism on comparative religious ethics, see David A. Clairmont, "Cultures of Comparisons and Traditions of Scholarship: Holism and Inculturation in Religious Ethics," in *Religious Ethics in a Time of Globalism: Shaping a Third Wave of Comparative Analysis*, ed. Elizabeth M. Bucar and Aaron Stalnaker (New York: Palgrave Macmillan, 2012), 81–112.

stable, transhistorical aspects of human biological and social life while still giving due place to historical and social context through an appeal to criteria of intelligibility. I argue that, by emphasizing the moral significance of the intelligibility of nature, combined with a distinction between the conventional and preconventional in appeals to the natural powers of human reason, Porter is able to account for constructivist concerns about the roles that social context and practical reasoning play in the generation of moral norms while also grounding that historical flexibility and dialogical sensitivity in an account of human nature and its continuity with other forms of animal life as morally significant. This allows Porter to do something like what Stout calls for in his appeal to the process of giving and exchanging reasons for moral claims, but it is to my mind a more useful and satisfying approach because it calls reason-givers to acknowledge a range of intelligible possibilities about distinctly human ends that serve as preliminary cross-cultural bases for provisional moral agreements.

Third, I examine how Stout's constructivism and Porter's natural law position approach a relevant topic in personal and social ethics: the status of homosexuality and the possibility of legal recognition of same-sex marital unions. Fourth, I offer several points of comparison between these two thinkers, suggesting ways that Porter's account might be revised slightly in light of the concerns that motivate Stout's approach, or at least to read her position as not entirely lacking attention to constructivist challenges. Through this comparison, I hope to show that there are ways of acknowledging constructivist concerns about natural law discourse without giving up on the possibility of a shared metaphysical ground (open to gradual clarification and refinement) that a natural law position requires. Neither must we give up on a meaningful dialogue between ethics and modern scientific, historical, and cultural studies that support many constructivist positions. The comparison may also prompt Hegelian constructivists to take a second look at Hegel's philosophy of nature that, although not settling debates about the extent to which a "non-metaphysical" Hegel may be a resource to religious ethics, at least can pose a question about whether a Hegelian constructivist religious ethics can be viable without a compelling account of the moral significance of nature.

I. The Moral Significance of Nature in Hegelian Constructivism

I take Hegelian constructivism to be a kind of metaethical position in which moral values and norms are negotiated through the discourse of particular historical communities and, although binding on those communities through their negotiated consensus, cannot be necessarily shown to be binding on communities of other times and places. In other words, the content of moral values and norms and their justification are historically contingent and therefore must be held open to future revision because the moral values and norms of the community may change in light of new questions or situations that arise, and so, too, might the reasons proffered in defense of those values and norms. To label a form of constructivism Hegelian (instead of merely social or historical) is certainly to emphasize the important place that contingent historical conditions—especially contingent social practices keyed to certain moral languages or culturally specific forms of moral reasoning—have in the articulation of moral values and norms and in the process of giving and exchanging reasons why individual or groups would affirm those values and norms. According to this view of Hegelian constructivism, Jeffrey Stout may be said to represent many of the insights of this metaethical option, insofar as Stout takes seriously the possibly that moral *practices* provide standards against which moral theories and their moral judgments must be checked. Indeed, he is one of the most significant voices in religious ethics from this perspective.

But what does it mean for a Hegelian constructivist position such as Stout's to be *Hegelian*? Is there a distinctly Hegelian view of nature in Stout's position or does Hegel's view of nature help us to understand a Hegelian constructivist's view of nature, or even natural law? Thankfully, Stout offers us both a reading of Hegel on nature and his own interpretation of natural law. Moreover, probing the moral significance of nature presents an interesting initial challenge to a Hegelian constructivist account of values and norms insofar as a wide range of human cultures over a range of historical periods interpret certain aspects of human life that are continuous with other forms of animal life as having some normative significance, either in terms of certain kinds of goods that should be pursued or in terms of basic forms of community that support the social context of human flourishing. In the remainder of this section, I examine Stout's view of Hegel on nature, followed by a short engagement with Hegel on nature to highlight some of the relevant similarities and differences. I conclude this section with an examination of Stout's view of natural law and the place of his reading of nature in that account.

I.1. On Stout on Hegel on Nature

Let us begin by examining Stout's discussion of Hegel on spirit and nature as developed in the *Phenomenology of Spirit*, which Stout argues is the central text to understanding the whole of Hegel's philosophical project. The central concern of that text focuses on the question of "the standard of knowledge" and on the answer to the question is "absolute spirit."[10] How does Hegel approach the question of the standard of knowledge, and what place does nature play in answering that question?

---

10. Jeffrey Stout, "What Is It That Absolute Knowing Knows?" *Journal of Religion* 95, no. 2 (2015): 163–82.

On Stout's reading, Hegel "sets himself the task of determining what the standard of knowledge is, [and] his goal is to arrive at a standard that is absolute in the sense of being self-sufficient and unsurpassable."[11] The basic starting points or building blocks for Hegel are "formations of consciousness," and *consciousness* is a term that denotes for Hegel a certain directedness of thought. So for Hegel, we can have consciousness of subjects (ourselves or others) and consciousness of objects, which means that consciousness is something we can experience. As Robert Pippin explains, "phenomenology" is for Hegel a "science of the experience of consciousness" that involves "imagining possible models of experience (models of its basic structure), primarily experience of objects and of other subjects, restricted to one or some set of competencies, or in some specific relation."[12]

There are many things about which one can have consciousness, and, as Stout explains, "[t]he formation of consciousness that the *Phenomenology* names *reason* locates the standards [of knowledge] in 'purposive activity,'" but

> [u]nderstood synchronically and individualistically . . . reason too falls short of self-sufficiency. Its successor is spirit, which is purposive activity, or reason, reinterpreted in social and diachronic terms. Spirit is a process: in which human subjects come to recognize one another as loci of responsibility; in which they observe, desire, conceptualize, employ, act upon, and create objects; and in which they make inferences, criticize and revise their commitments, and earn entitlement to commitments that survive critical review.[13]

How does this view of experience, consciousness, reason, and spirit relate to the process of discerning reliable knowledge? For Hegel, on Stout's view,

> [t]he approved standard of rationality emerges from an immanent critique of deficient conceptions of epistemic statuses, such as the somewhat permissive status of being justified in believing something given at an available stage of inquiry and the much-harder-to-achieve status of being able to vindicate one's commitments decisively against all possible alternatives to them.[14]

This process, Stout argues, is not for Hegel one of skepticism as "'a merely negative procedure'" but, rather, of determinate negation where the process of questioning leads both to more adequate knowledge and to a better

---

11. Ibid., 168.
12. Robert B. Pippin, *Hegel on Self-Consciousness: Desire and Death in the Phenomenology of Spirit* (Princeton: Princeton University Press, 2010), 9.
13. Stout, "What Is It That Absolute Knowing Knows?" 168–9.
14. Ibid., 169.

understanding of what the absolute standard of knowing ought to be: "One thing determinate negation of previous conceptions teaches us is that the self-sufficient standards must inhere in social practices in which both individual subjects and objects are caught up. *Spirit* is Hegel's name for practices of this sort."[15] This means, as Stout explains, that it is neither the qualities of the knowing subject (experiences mediated through sense impressions or the categories through which those are organized) nor the qualities of the object as it is in itself that the subject seeks to know that determine truth. Rather, it must be something which unites the subject side and the object side which can also transcend the limitations of each side. Hegel finds the solution in the social practices of assessing claims to truth that address both the subject and the object side of the knower and what is known:

> The diagnosis of failure [to locate the standard of knowledge either in the subject or the object] implies that something capable of encompassing both subjects and objects is required to make sense of the standard. The more encompassing thing is spirit, the social practical realm, or purposive activity understood socially and diachronically.[16]

What is Hegel reacting to such that he emphasizes that the standard of knowledge must be located neither exclusively in the subject nor exclusively in the object? In the latter case, Hegel "rigorously avoids backsliding into modes of justification and discovery characteristic of precritical metaphysics"[17] that focus naively on the way the things of the world are presented to consciousness while in the former case Hegel wishes to avoid a Kantian approach whereby the "subjective idealist imagines himself, his concepts, his commitments, and his evidence all trapped on the subject side of a subject-object divide, with the absolute, in the sense of objective truth, on the other side."[18] It is for this reason that spirit, understood as the "encompassing context" wherein "knowing must be understood in terms of a context of evolving social practices that encompass both the subjects of knowledge and whatever is known by them" is understood as "the condition of the possibility of knowing."[19]

When Hegel speaks of "absolute spirit" he has in mind an extension of the community of practices to all times and all places:

> Absolute spirit is the name for that context when the subjects participating in it attain mutual recognition of one another as loci of responsibility and authority. . . . In epistemological terms, absolute spirit is

---

15. Ibid., 170.
16. Ibid.
17. Ibid., 168.
18. Ibid., 172.
19. Ibid., 170.

the expanded epistemic context required to theorize the standard of knowledge self-sufficiently. It is all encompassing, because everything there is, has been, and will be is involved in determining the content, justification, and truth of what can be known. But it is also very down to earth, because it amounts to nothing other than this-worldly human practices and everything they encompass, unfolding in time.[20]

Stout goes on to argue that "Hegel's approach is transcendental in the sense of inquiring critically into conditions for the possibility of the knowledge we take ourselves to have" but that "Hegel takes the conditions for the possibility of knowledge to be neither essentially fixed nor located solely in the individual subject."[21] Moreover, for Hegel, the absolute is not supersensible: "Neither spirit, nor absolute spirit, nor the absolute (in the sense of that which determines the true) is supersensible by Hegel's reckoning. They do, however, exist, and Hegel is committed to their existence."[22] They are real in the sense that they are observable as social practices, but their status as absolute is observable only cumulatively through time. As Stout explains,

> [i]f reason, rightly understood, is essentially social and historical, then reason is spirit, as Hegel defines the term. This means that all previous formations of consciousness, including Kantian philosophy, are rightly viewed as abstractions of formations of spirit. If, however, that is correct, the conditions for the possibility of any such formation are social-historical. They belong to an unfolding dialectical process that includes all prior formations of spirit. This process is the absolute standard—in short, the absolute.[23]

So what have these discussions of spirit as social practice and absolute as the standard of that practice to do with a Hegelian view of nature? In its most basic and non-controversial description, nature is (or at least includes) physical elements in the world and the objects they compose, both individually and collectively, of various size and complexity. People, like other animals, interact with nature through their descriptions of nature and through their use of nature. Both descriptions and uses are practices. For example (combining two of Stout's images), we give descriptions of elements in the natural world such as trees, which help us to identify certain objects and differentiate them from others. The adequacy of our description depends both on the subject side and the object side of the description. If we were radically to alter our customary use of the term *tree* and suddenly use the term to refer to something that has never before been called a tree, we might

---

20. Ibid., 171–2.
21. Ibid., 174.
22. Ibid., 175.
23. Ibid.

suspect that something has gone wrong on the subject's use of the term in a practice that she or he understood to be customary and reliable. Similarly, if the objects that we had customarily referred to when using the word *tree* themselves changed radically so as to frustrate our use on the object side (e.g., if every "tree" in our environment to which we had previously applied the term *tree* suddenly began to grow heads and wings and fly around singing gospel hymns), we might be inclined to say that such an object was not a tree but something else, reserving the term *tree* for those objects that looked and reacted in ways similar to the objects we had previously labeled trees. The point here is that there is a reliability and predictability on the subject side and on the object side of our descriptions of natural things in the world. The same could be said for the use of trees. We might carve trees into baseball bats, and we would still recognize that they were once trees, but we cannot make trees into iPhones because, while trees can be used for many things, their modest modifications or even their most basic components cannot be used to send text messages (short of turning them into paper and writing text on them).

The point is that neither nature as objects in the world nor the concepts we use to describe and use nature are infinitely pliable since they are constrained by a set of practices. As Stout explains,

> [c]oncepts are what they are by virtue of the roles they play in those practice[s]. The practices are not inside the subject's mind. They transpire in the world. They also include the objects. The natural world is itself an object of inquiry and other forms of practical attention within the practices. For this reason, the practices encompass the world. The practices shape subjects into loci of responsibility and equip them with concepts. A practice in which subjects respond appropriately to trees by saying things such as 'The tree on the battlefield is blooming' cannot be adequately identified without making reference to trees, as well as to subjects and to the concepts they employ. This is not to say that we subjects get the objects of consciousness—trees, quarks, revolutions, duties, knowledge, and such—entirely right. Whenever incompatibilities arise among our commitments, the implicated concepts require rectification. Repeatedly rectified concepts are what they are and mean what they mean in part because of the actual objects we have applied to them over time.[24]

In this passage, Stout is trying to explain how the world outside of the subject nonetheless plays a role in establishing what we can reliably know about the object. It is important that the picture offered is one of gradual addition to or filling out of an incomplete picture. Through the social

---

24. Ibid., 173.

process of exchanging descriptions and reasons for believing this or that about an object in the natural world, we get a better sense of the full picture of what we aim to know.

One of the more difficult aspects of a Hegelian view of nature (and, by association, of the Hegelian constructivist's view of nature) is the relationship between nature and spirit. Going back to his example of baseball, Stout explains that, in a Hegelian view,

> [s]pirit encompasses nature in the same sense that baseball encompasses such physical objects as human bodies, fields of grass, bits of leather, and pieces of wood. By treating those things as players, outfields, gloves, and bats, respectively, baseball confers spiritual (*geistig*) significance on them.... Similarly, spirit as the general context or abode of inquiry, encompasses everything that has been or might someday be an object of inquiry and everyone who has been or might someday be engaged in inquiry.[25]

In other words, spirit is the name for the social practice(s) through which nature acquires a significant social meaning within and for a cooperative human activity. Yet Stout goes on to say that

> [i]t is also true, and perhaps initially puzzling, that nature encompasses spirit. How can this be if spirit also encompasses nature? The two sorts of encompassment differ. Spirit encompasses nature in the way any social practice encompasses the objects that are caught up in it. This is social-practical encompassment. Nature encompasses spirit in what might be called causal-nexus sense. Nature is causally prior to the realm of social-practical norms and values. For eons, if modern science has the story right, nature harbored spirit, the realm of human practices, as a yet-unrealized possibility. Had the causal story gone a bit differently, the natural world could have existed in something like its actual form without ever having given rise to spiritual beings, to subjects in the Hegelian sense. On the other hand, the concepts required to describe the natural world as comprising determinate, propertied, law-governed objects, including human bodies, depends for their intelligibility on spirit's activities, distinctions, and norms.[26]

In this account, nature has no inherent purposiveness but those to which we can put nature, and those purposes are derived from the rational (i.e., the purposive consciousness-driven) engagement with nature. What is interesting for our discussion of the moral significance of nature is the emphasis

---

25. Ibid., 178.
26. Ibid., 178–9.

140   David A. Clairmont

Stout places on the human subject as the center of an analysis of nature. As Stout tells the story, nature acquires moral significance to the extent that it can be taken up into the realm of human social practice. In the narrative of "modern science" spirit emerged accidentally, and it could have been the case that social-practice (i.e., "spiritual") beings did not emerge in which case nature would never have had a "moral significance" since the moral is an expression of the social-practical expression of reason. Although Stout need not give a wider account of Hegel on nature to assess his own claims about nature's moral significance, by way of comparison it will be useful to compare Stout's reading of Hegel on this point with other Hegel scholars who examine the wider context of Hegel's discussion of nature. What we find, I submit, is another plausible account of how nature may be said to have moral significance, be taken up into human social practice as spirit, and yet have a kind of moral integrity of its own that is both immanent and yet continuous with its significance to human beings.

I.2. On Hegel on Nature

It should not be surprising that modern commentators on Hegel, especially those who have examined carefully his account of nature, note that his account changed over time, which itself reflects the fact that Hegel was constantly reworking his philosophical system (including its references to nature) throughout his life, from his early work in the *Phenomenology of Spirit* (first published in 1807) through his *Encyclopedia of the Philosophical Sciences (1817) and Philosophy of Right (1821)*.[27] The sections on nature in the *Phenomenology* were refined further in the second part of the *Encyclopedia* in a section on *Philosophy of Nature*. What is common to all three is his concern for understanding the human being, in whom alone purposive directed consciousness resides as reason, arising from nature but also distanced from it through the exercise of freedom.

Hegel scholars identify the relation between nature and the emergence of consciousness as a significant concern for Hegel starting during his time as a private tutor in Frankfurt and continuing through his residence at the University of Jena (1801–1805), a concern that he would work through in a more systematic way in the *Phenomenology* and in the *Encyclopedia*.

---

27. In the following sections, I draw on a range of accounts of nature in recent Hegel scholarship. Since I am not by training a Hegel scholar, I make little direct reference to Hegel to sort out how he understood nature, its relationship to human and other forms of animal life and to the connection between human rationality and animal purposiveness. It seems to me best to leave these debates to those most invested in them. However, it does seem clear to me, having reviewed some of these debates in reference to Stout's Hegelian constructivism, that his references to Hegel on nature are rather modest and not inclusive of the many important points raised by those who have written on Hegel's account of nature. In fact, many of the most interesting issues raised by those scholars are fruitful in considering revisionist natural law accounts like Porter's.

At Jena, Hegel was working through a very particular problem within the consideration of nature, namely, how an individual biological entity can be aware of itself both as individual and as universal.[28] According to Italo Testa, the key to Hegel's solution to this problem is the idea of evolution of the "recognitive relation to oneself; a relation that starts from an organic self, endowed with communicative capacities that enable it to interact with its environment and other selves."[29] More specifically, the central Hegelian notion of "Spirit—the social structure of the historical world of individual agents and institutions—is constituted through recognition (*Anerkennung*), i.e. through processes of reciprocal interaction."[30] Testa goes on to argue that, for Hegel, "if spirit is constituted through recognition, then the fact that recognition somehow depends on nature will have deep consequences on how we are to conceive the genesis and the structure of the social and historical world."[31] The process whereby recognition emerges from nature is connected to the processes of nature at various levels of organization, of which Testa identified five that are primary for Hegel during this period: (1) sexual differentiation and natural individuation; (2) the pre-thematic awareness the animal possesses of its movements and environment-linking capacities (especially its capacities for proprioception and communication); (3) the practical relation of appetite and conflict as the animal seeks satisfaction of its basic appetites that it experiences as denial (negativity) and fulfillment (positivity); (4) animal voice and individuality's expressive recognition, where the organism develops pre-thematic awareness of its individuality through its capacity to communicate and be responded to by other animals; and (5) the objectivized and rational recognition of procreation, wherein the individual learns to see itself both as distinct from other animals by its ability to create something out of itself but also the universality that is expressed through its species (or, in Hegel's nomenclature, genus) continuing into the future even after its own individual existence ceases.

In each of these cases, the process of recognition is at work, a directedness of thought that links the various parts of the body through awareness of their related movements, or an awareness of the body's relation to what

---

28. Michael H. Hoffheimer, "The Influence of Schiller's Theory of Nature on Hegel's Philosophical Development," *Journal of the History of Ideas* 46, no. 2 (1985): 232. Hoffheimer describes how Hegel's early interest in nature developed at the same time as his theology studies. "Hegel had taken required science courses while a student at the state-run seminary (*Stift*) in Tübingen; his interest in science and nature at that time clearly had gone beyond the required curriculum. He had further pursued botanical studies in the summer of 1791 on his own initiative to such an extent that H. S. Harris in his study of Hegel's development remarks that 'Botany certainly interested Hegel more than theology in 1791 and 1792.'"
29. Italo Testa, "How Does Recognition Emerge from Nature? The Genesis of Consciousness in Hegel's Jena Writings," *Critical Horizons* 13, no. 2 (2012): 177–8.
30. Ibid., 176.
31. Ibid., 177.

is external, or of the organism's awareness of the continuation of its genus and species in the face of threat to its individual existence. As Testa explains,

> [o]rganic individuality is defined as the 'absolute middle term (*absolute Mitte*)' between two processes: the cycle through which the singular organism preserves and individuates itself, and the cycle through which the *Gattung* [genus of biological classification]—the universal moment—endures through sexual reproduction of individuals. The natural process is thus the beginning of a process of individuation through universalization. In this sense Hegel writes: 'The idea of organic individuality is genus, universality; it is infinitely an other to itself and in this otherness [is] itself, exists in the division of the sexes, each of which is the entire idea, but such that it, relating itself to itself as to an other, intuits itself in otherness as itself and supersedes this opposition.'[32]

It is important to note that the process of recognition is not itself teleological, although it makes use of internal teloi of biological processes to explain the process of internal differentiation, relation, and awareness of relatedness that arises from them.

Commentators on the *Phenomenology of Spirit* (1807)—the central text in reference to which Stout engages Hegel on this topic—have discerned in the text's account of nature a tension, roughly speaking, between Hegel's direct comments about nature and the role nature ought to play in his system given his understanding of reason.[33] As we said earlier, reason is not for Hegel best understood as a faculty but, rather, as a particular determination of consciousness as purposive activity which can eventually rise to the level of spirit. In the *Phenomenology*, nature is treated in the third section on reason, after the discussion of consciousness and self-consciousness and before the discussion of spirit, religion, and absolute knowing which also appear in the same third section. As Daniel Dahlstrom notes in his discussion of this section, there are three themes which are particularly important in Hegel's discussion of nature in the *Phenomenology*: "the inexhaustibility of nature, the holistic character of animal life, and the individual distinctiveness of the earth."[34]

Dahlstrom explains that there are three "senses of reason" expressed in the *Phenomenology*, which when taken together help to make sense of Hegel's account of nature: "an abstract reason and its mere certainty, actual reason as the (instinctive) search for the truth of abstract reason that amounts to its self-deconstruction, and finally, the respective outcomes of reason's transformation, ultimately, the identification of reason as spirit."[35]

---

32. Ibid., 180.
33. Kirill Chepurin, "Nature, Spirit, and Revolution: Situating Hegel's Philosophy of Nature," *Comparative and Continental Philosophy* 8, no. 3 (2016): 302.
34. Daniel O. Dahlstrom, "Challenges to the Rational Observation of Nature in the Phenomenology of Spirit," *The Owl of Minerva* 38, no. 1–2 (2006–7): 35.
35. Ibid., 43.

The goal of reason in the first form is subjective certainty about what it can know, but this does not guarantee any reliable (much less historically complete or "absolute") knowledge of the world, and so (absent some real relation to the material historical world) abstract reason goes unfulfilled:

> Such a form of rational self-consciousness leads to this "empty" idealism because it cannot explain why it is certain of its universal reach and because it attributes unity to itself in a way that compels it to suppose without being able to account for difference.[36]

However, as Dahlstrom describes, "rational self-consciousness must first turn to itself 'in its own depths' before turning to things if it is to come to see how both it and things other than it can be said to be rational."[37] Reason is transformed into spirit—that is, into a series of achievements of more adequate knowledge about itself and the world, because it is forced to go out of itself—or, as Dahlstrom puts it, Hegel "treats reason in the context of a series of progressively more adequate epistemic achievements, culminating systematically in a fully transparent self-consciousness, otherwise deemed 'absolute knowledge,' in which the discerned and the discerning consciousness completely coincide."[38]

Hegel was aware that nature—understood as the natural world of inanimate and animate objects but also of subjects with varying degrees of self-awareness—may be considered both theoretically—that is, from the perspective of reason reflecting on itself—and practically, in its particular expression of interaction with the world. In this way, Hegel continues to examine the significance of nature of the animal subject in his *Philosophy of Nature*. Mark Peterson poses the central concern of this text in the following way: "Subjectivity arises when primitive animal sentience confronts an external nature it must assimilate in order to endure."[39] Peterson describes a similar shape to Hegel's thinking in *Philosophy of Nature* to what we observed in the Jena lectures and in the *Phenomenology*, focusing on Hegel's view of how animal subjectivity emerges. "'Assimilation' is the penultimate phase of the animal organism," Peterson argues, "and initiates the dialectical transformations through which mere animal sentience (*Selbstgefühl*) begins to acquire the characteristics of subjectivity."[40] He continues (and I quote him at length):

> The process begins when the animal must interact with an external, and opposing, nature. This interaction is characterized by the

---

36. Ibid., 41.
37. Ibid., 44.
38. Ibid., 40.
39. Mark C. E. Peterson, "Animals Eating Empiricists: Assimilation and Subjectivity in Hegel's Philosophy of Nature," *The Owl of Minerva* 23, no. 1 (1991): 50.
40. Ibid.

animal's attempt to subdue the world to which it finds itself opposed or, in Hegel's language, its own negativity. The processes that make up assimilation express the animal's attempt to resolve this opposition. The animal carries out this program under three increasingly adequate modes of encounter: (1) sensation and reaction, (2) purposeful manipulation of the physical world, and (3) transformation/mediation of the world through eating and digesting it. In the language of the system these are: (1) the unity of practical and theoretical processes as instinct, (2) the particularizations of instinctive behavior, and (3) formal self-reproduction.[41]

Peterson helpfully adds that, for Hegel, nature is purposive both in its basic animal determination and in human expressions of animal nature:

> Hegel notes that 'the fundamental determination of living existence is that it is to be regarded as acting purposively' (§ 360, Remark) and this echoes the Aristotelian notion of life as that which acts toward some end. The reason that 'purpose' here must be called 'instinct' is that the animal does not think—it can only feel. It acts according to ends upon which it cannot reflect and therefore does not understand. Hegel expands on this distinction: 'The main sources of the difficulty here . . . are that the relation implied by purpose is usually imagined to be external, and that purpose is generally thought to exist only in a conscious manner. Instinct is purposive activity operating in an unconscious manner' (§ 360, Remark). This stands to reason, for, in the context of idea's development, thought has yet to come on the scene. The animal is capable only of 'feeling.' Consequently, the drive by which the animal seeks to overcome the deficiency it feels in the face of externality is a purposive activity—but an activity that is non-conscious and which must therefore be rendered as instinct.[42]

So the emergence of purposiveness in animal nature is distinct from but related to rational purposiveness. There is, in other words, a continuity between the animal that comes to understand its relationship to its world and the human being as animal that thinks about its purposes in light of a particular form of life that it selects for itself in community with others. As Hegel himself notes in the *Philosophy of Nature*,

> [n]ature is to be regarded as a system of stages, the one proceeding of necessity out of the other, and being the proximate truth of that from which it results. This is not to be thought of as a natural engendering

---

41. Ibid.
42. Ibid., 54–5.

of one out of the other however, but as an engendering within the inner Idea which constitutes the ground of nature.[43]

Yet for all of Hegel's writing on nature, he remained more interested in what nature communicated about the emergence of consciousness and reason than about nature in its own integrity. Nature remained both its own internally coherent system, which Hegel certainly admired, and, more important, a clue to the ways that purposive consciousness worked at various levels of animal development.

This is helpfully illustrated by contrasting Hegel with his onetime friend Friedrich Wilhelm Joseph von Schelling (1775–1854 CE). As Kirill Chepurin explains,

> whereas in Schelling, *Naturphilosophie* has to do directly with the real, Hegel's philosophy of nature has for its subject not nature 'as such,' but rather a new, 'spiritual' nature, nature as cognized by *Geist*; the narrative of the identity of these two natures is not something given, but something constructed by spirit itself, retroactively.[44]

To further distinguish nature in its own workings from nature as it is taken up into spirit, Michael Hoffheimer draws attention to the ways that Hegel looked to nature for its own models of exile and belonging that can be used to understand the ways that human beings are disintegrated and reintegrated with nature. In this way, although it is true as Stout claims that Hegel viewed nature as encompassed by spirit, nature also provides the interpretive models for spirit's own dynamic unfolding. The human relation to nature was not only biological and philosophical but aesthetic as well.

---

43. *Hegel's Philosophy of Nature*, 3 vols., trans. M. J. Petry (London: Allen & Unwin; New York: Humanities Press, 1970). §249 quoted in Mark C. E. Peterson, "Review of Alison Stone, Petrified Intelligence: Nature in Hegel's Philosophy," 215.
44. Kirill Chepurin, "Nature, Spirit, and Revolution: Situating Hegel's Philosophy of Nature," *Comparative and Continental Philosophy* 8, no. 3 (2016): 302. Chepurin goes on to explain that "[t]he origin of this difference between nature-as-it-is and nature-as-spirit can be traced, I will argue, to the revolutionary event that takes place at the very outset of the philosophy of spirit and institutes Hegel's anthropology, namely, his doctrine of the human soul and its exposition in the first section of the philosophy of spirit, which at once fills and maintains the gap between the real and the spiritual. The anthropology culminates for Hegel in the birth of consciousness and the creation of a philosophical 'nature,' first as an 'external' world of objects and then as the conceptual world of nature as 'we' (that is, philosophers of nature) know it. The philosophy of nature's 'nature' is essentially human nature, whereas nature-as-the-real remains, as a consequence, a non-place relegated to the margins of Hegel's *Naturphilosophie*, which the philosopher replaces instead with an anthropological foundation. The human is revolutionary for Hegel, but nature as such is not—rather the human revolutionizes, among other things, the natural status quo itself." Ibid.

In this way, Hegel was influenced by the philosophical treatment of the aesthetics of nature developed by Schiller:[45]

> [V]iewed as a harmonious whole, nature was a model for the reintegration of subject and object, man and nature. Yet this view of nature also implied that something like a subject-object dichotomy existed within nature, within the object, for the harmony of nature was seen as the consequence of antagonisms and strife within nature, a view which was happily also held by pre-Socratic Greek thinkers who viewed nature as inherently dynamic.[46]

In terms of spirit's development, Hegel noted that nature provided patterns of response to which human beings could then draw examples in light of their own historical circumstances, both natural and social.

For example, reflecting on a hiking excursion in the Alps in 1797, he notes in a journal the workings of nature and its capacity to exhibit both continuity and difference in the same outward expression:

> Through a narrow ravine the water presses above, quite narrow, and then falls down vertically in much wider waves-in waves that continually draw the spectator's glances down with them and which one nevertheless can never fix, never follow, for their image, their form, dissolves every few moments and is replaced by another, and in these falls one sees eternally the same image, and sees at the same time that it is never the same.[47]

Not only does nature encourage reflection on the internal direction of thought and its outward manifestation in action; it also offers a model of human response to the events of nature. Writing to a friend about the villagers of the country surrounding Frankfurt, Hegel marvels that

> the inhabitants of this region live in a feeling of their dependence on the power of nature and this gives them a tranquil submissiveness in its

---

45. Michael H. Hoffheimer, "The Influence of Schiller's Theory of Nature on Hegel's Philosophical Development," *Journal of the History of Ideas* 46, no. 2 (1985): 235. "For Schiller the essence of man consisted in man's refusal to accept his relation to the world—the schism between subject and object, man and nature—as permanent, for man had attempted to overcome the dichotomy. But the process of surmounting the schism involved man's acceptance of the dichotomy. Consequently, man rationally retraced the steps of his own natural development and 'has the power . . . of transforming the work of blind compulsion into a work of free choice, and of elevating physical necessity into moral necessity.' Schiller viewed man's development as a sort of circle: the originally united became separated and finally reunited."
46. Ibid., 240.
47. Ibid., 234–5.

destructive eruptions. If their cottages are smashed or buried or swept away, then they [like the Greeks?] build another on the same spot, or nearby.[48]

The issue that Hegel is addressing throughout his writings on nature is how reason, which emerged from nature but is also radically different from nature, can itself see the rationality of nature's internal workings and then discern what kind of response, appropriate to its own social manifestation, is appropriate. As Dahlstrom describes,

> [r]eason has, in other words, an impoverished view of the natural world precisely as it presents itself to us by way of our senses. Reason's way out of this impasse, Hegel submits, is to stipulate a distinction between the essential and unessential characteristics, a distinction that, while testifying to the fact that it is as concerned with its own self as with things, is not simply one of its own making since things—paradigmatically, animals—distinguish themselves from one another and, indeed, do so individually as well as particularly.[49]

I.3. On Stout on Nature, Science, and Natural Law

In what we have reviewed thus far from Stout's engagement with Hegel, we begin to see in outline Stout's view of the moral significance of nature. He agrees with Hegel that nature provides the raw material from which human beings draw basic material goods and on which they construct their social projects, which, in turn, express their basic values and norms. However, he does not look to nature as having a moral significance beyond what reason assigns to it, and this differentiates him from Hegel somewhat. Whereas Hegel discerned in nature pre-thematic modes of differentiation that prefigured and offered patterns for rational consciousness that could discern those patterns and opt for them as a model, Stout sees only the epistemic and social forms of that differentiation (the emerging criteria for absolute knowledge) rather than any clue to its proper content. Another way to put this is that, for Stout, the history of philosophical engagements with science show, in his view, that conceptions of some inherent teleology of nature must be rejected outright in light of the insights of modern scientific research, especially in the physical sciences, which show that the natural world—and all biological creatures within it, along with their purposive activities—is ultimately contingent and therefore cannot sustain any view about an internal or inherent order. So for Stout, *nature as inherent order* is a problematic approach to moral values and norms because science has moved us beyond drawing

---

48. Ibid., 235.
49. Dahlstrom, "Challenges to the Rational Observation of Nature in the Phenomenology of Spirit," 45.

moral significance from assumed inherent teleologies ordered to the perfection of different kinds of creatures. Moreover, while there exist basic goods that Stout admits characterize human life, they are morally irrelevant since they cannot be said to be part of social practices except through some link by human discourse.[50] So *nature as recognition of basic goods* is also problematic because those goods cannot be morally evaluated outside of the social practices that order them and give them meaning.

One might then ask whether there is anything normative about the environment in which human beings assemble, order, and give meaning to those basic goods through their social practices. For example, nature could be understood to mean the environment in which human practices take place, which constrain them in some way (through limits of natural resources, e.g., or as a repository of the cumulative effects of our consumer decisions). In other words, it may be the case that nature not only lacks any inherent teleology but also lacks any intelligibility at all outside of human purposes. This is because intelligibility is a feature of social practices—especially the social practice of establishing moral values and norms—rather than a feature of the biological (or even the human) world. For Stout, *nature as intelligibility based in environment* is not feasible since the environment is the raw material and context for intelligible arguments about moral values and norms rather than morally significant in its own right. This sense of nature will provide the most striking point of comparison between Stout and Porter in the next section of the paper.

So then is there any moral significance to nature at all for Stout or for Hegelian constructivists who hold similar positions to his? While having no strong conception of inherent teleology, or basic goods, or of normative environmental constraints on the pursuit of whatever goods are counted as desirable, Stout does maintain an important sense in which nature is normative. Because human beings are creatures who reason from finite perspectives, they must exhibit humility about the scope of their moral claims and

---

50. In his engagement with Alasdair MacIntyre, Stout does give some clue to his understanding of basic goods and the role they could play in a Hegelian constructivist account. It is particularly interesting to note that he admits there are some goods, recognized as such, that do not require being part of a social practice to admit them as good. Working from MacIntyre's distinction between goods internal to practice and goods external to practice, Stout says the following: "The relation between goods internal to practice and goods external to it tends to be morally problematic—a source of temptations that test our courage and temperance, as well as a source of difficulties that require wise and just resolution. Goods can be external to a practice in more than one way. *Some goods, like the satisfaction of hunger, thirst, or sexual desire, belong to no particular social practice.* One can seek and achieve them without engaging in any of the complex, cooperative, virtue-dependent forms of activity MacIntyre means to single out. Other goods are external to one social practice while internal to another. Goods internal to football may be external to the practice of preventive medicine, and vice versa. The goods of medical care overlap but sometime conflict with the goods of biomedical research." See Stout, *Ethics After Babel*, 272 (emphasis added).

the standards by which they may be justified. If there is a normatively basic good for the human creature it is a recognition of fallibility and therefore the capacity for epistemic humility. We might call this something like *nature as epistemic limit in context*. Stout argues that at the deepest level, human beings are characterized by their limits, in particular their epistemic limits manifest through practices of community agreement and disagreement, and indeed if there is anything distinctive to *human* nature it is our encounter of these limits in and through social practices. This shows Stout to be both deeply Hegelian yet also a distinctive kind of Hegelian—one for whom nature is revealed through democratic society. Is there any way that human nature in this sense can be linked with nature in a more general sense to include other kinds of creatures or even a wider environmental context? As it happens, we can best understand Stout's position here by examining his engagement with natural law and his critique of it which are closely linked with his understanding of scientific study.

Stout's critique of natural law emerged from his concern to address a central problem in philosophical ethics: to what extent is the justification of moral claims dependent on one's epistemic context?[51] In so doing, he developed an account of the justification of moral claims and the nature of moral truth that has had a wide influence on scholars in religious ethics. In addition to his defense of a contextualist account of moral justification and what he has called his "cautionary use of 'true,'"[52] he has also issued assessments of various theological forms of religious ethics for their particular moral judgments, their strategies of justification, and their accounts of moral truth. Among the positions he critiques are various kinds of natural law arguments, each of which he thinks relies on corresponding metaphysical systems to varying degrees.[53]

One kind of natural law argument that he finds particularly problematic is the one that understands natural law in terms of widespread consensus

---

51. Stout's first attempt to address natural law theories came in his second book, *Ethics After Babel: The Languages of Morals and Their Discontents* (Princeton and Oxford: Princeton University Press, 1988). A revised edition of this book was published in 2001 with a new postscript by the author. He offered a more developed account of the same critique in Jeffrey Stout, "Truth, Natural Law, and Ethical Theory," in *Natural Law Theory: Contemporary Essays*, ed. Robert P. George (Oxford: Clarendon Press, 1992), 71–102. Elements of that chapter were used in Jeffrey Stout, *Democracy and Tradition* (Princeton and Oxford: Princeton University Press, 2004), 241–5.
52. Stout, "Truth, Natural Law, and Ethical Theory," 82.
53. The longer background story for Stout's critique of foundationalism was offered in Jeffrey Stout, *The Flight from Authority: Religion, Morality, and the Quest for Autonomy* (Notre Dame: University of Notre Dame Press, 1987). For an analysis of Stout's critique of foundationalism from a moderate foundationalist position, see Kevin Jung, *Christian Ethics and Commonsense Morality: An Intuitionist Account* (New York: Routledge, 2015), 27–43. Jung also provides a helpful discussion of the similarities and differences between the variety of intuitionism he defends and various natural law approaches in his chapter on "Commonsense Tradition and Intuitionism." Ibid., 117–40.

about moral values and norms.[54] Drawing a comparison between C. S. Lewis, who holds a version of this position, and Stanley Hauerwas, who critiques it, Stout explains that

> Lewis believes in the natural law as a universal, transcultural standard of morality. Hauerwas criticizes appeals to any such standard, claiming that all moral reasoning is a radically contextual affair, situated within specific traditions and dependent upon their contingent assumptions and forms of life. Lewis plays down the extent to which people disagree on specifically moral grounds. Hauerwas plays it up.[55]

Yet he goes on to say that the issue is not so much in Lewis's empirical claim about the widespread extent of moral agreement but, rather, what one can do with the fact of extensive moral agreement or disagreement. "It does follow," Stout argues,

> that any two people who disagree about a given moral proposition will inevitably have a lot of common ground, just as Lewis claims. It does not follow that we can isolate a small set of general principles on which all societies necessarily agree, on pain of irrationality, principles of the kind Lewis seems to have in mind when he speaks of the natural law.[56]

For Stout, this is a characteristic natural law strategy: to identify a set of general principles on which all people regardless of historical location or cultural background could theoretically agree.[57] He goes on to suggest that

> [i]f 'the natural law' or 'the moral law' is just a fancy name for all the moral truths known and unknown, then neither Hauerwas nor I need object to belief in it. I do object to the idea that we can explain what it is for moral propositions to be true by saying that they correspond to the Law, since the relation of correspondence involved by such an

---

54. In none of these cases could I locate any substantial engagement with Jean Porter, so what I offer here can be no more than an outline of a conversation that either has not yet happened or has happened off the record.
55. Stout, *Ethics After Babel*, 15.
56. Ibid., 20.
57. I acknowledge the point, raised by some members of the workshop at which this paper was originally discussed, that Stout himself acknowledges that he has selected Lewis and Hauerwas not as the best representative proponents and opponents of natural law thinking, respectively, but, rather, as figures who, being public intellectuals but not professional philosophers, illustrate the nature of moral disagreement, the trouble with correspondence approaches to truth and the dynamics of being in dialogue about that disagreement given different approaches to truth, admitting as much in *Ethics After Babel* (15–16). This admission notwithstanding, it is telling that the merely incidental use of natural law as an inroad to talking about moral disagreement prefigures the oddly ahistorical reading of the natural law tradition in his later engagements.

explanation doesn't seem clear enough to explain anything. This, however, is another, quite different, issue. To say that a moral proposition corresponds to the Moral Law doesn't obviously add anything more than a well-worn figure of speech—anything of explanatory value—to saying that the proposition is true. For it to do so, we would have to be able to say what such correspondence consists in. Yet this is precisely what philosophers have had trouble saying. There would be no problem here if we knew what it would be like to look directly, without help from variable tradition-bound presuppositions, at the Moral Law and then back again at our beliefs, surveying the relations for instances or failures of correspondence. But we don't know what it would be like to do that, so talk of correspondence as an explanation of truth cannot help us.[58]

Stout draws an interesting conclusion from this critique of Lewis's approach to natural law. In response to the objection that "[c]ommon sense is committed to a culture-transcendent moral law," Stout argues that "[w]hat belongs to common sense is the idea that there are moral truths, not a conception of moral truths tailored to essentially post-Kantian epistemological purposes."[59] Although he does not link it specifically to Lewis, soon after his discussion of Lewis he entertains the objection that "[w]hat we have, then, ironically enough, is a picture of human nature, [according to which] people believe, desire, intend, and so on, criticizing and revising these attitudes as they go along."[60] Stout responds in the affirmative, so long as "we can agree to mean by this a way of describing human beings, a collection of truth-claims not dependent on the distinction between necessary and contingent truths or on the metaphysics of 'natures' and 'essences.' . . . I have urged humble acknowledgement of human fallibility, irrationality, and corruption. Even justified beliefs, I have said, often turn out to have been false all along. Even true beliefs, I have said, can be held for bad reasons."[61]

Another kind of natural law thinking that troubles Stout is the view that certain kinds of acts are contrary to nature and therefore rise to the status of moral abominations, such as the judgments about homosexual sex in the work of the medieval Christian natural law thinker Thomas Aquinas. Stout argues that

> [t]raditional Christian natural law theory may be viewed (in part) as an attempt to explain and justify specific judgments of moral abomination by explicitly defending the corresponding features of cosmology and social structure. Contrary to the standard interpretation of Aquinas's

---

58. Stout, *Ethics After Babel*, 22–3.
59. Ibid., 34.
60. Ibid., 57.
61. Ibid., 57–8.

ethics, he rarely used natural-law categories to justify specific moral judgments. But when he turned to 'unnatural vice,' including bestiality and sodomy, natural-law categories become central to his argument. Unnatural vice, he said, is especially ugly because it conflicts with 'the natural pattern of sexuality for the benefit of the species'.[62]

Stout goes on to explain that

> [w]hatever fault we find with the theory of natural law that Aquinas uses to frame his explanation [of bestiality and sodomy]—and I would be inclined to find much fault—it must be admitted that he is locating debate at the proper level. He does not merely appeal to an inarticulate sense of revulsion. He attempts to justify his revulsion in relation to his conception of the seams of the moral universe. If that conception can be sustained, the moral import of the revulsion would be established.[63]

This kind of natural law approach does not turn on the establishment of moral consensus but, rather, links particular moral judgments to the

---

62. Ibid., 158. Although one should not make too much out of footnotes, it is worth mentioning that the second line of the passage cited here directs the reader to note 14, which reads, "My interpretation of Aquinas is influenced by many conversations with my colleague, Victor Preller." Stout does not cite where the "standard interpretations" come from or why conversations rather than published work ought to be the source of an interpretation of this magnitude. Preller did, in fact, publish a book on Thomas Aquinas, interpreting his views on the nature of claims to knowledge of God in light of the developments in philosophy of language. That book, *Divine Science and the Science of God: A Reformulation of Thomas Aquinas* (Princeton: Princeton University Press, 1967), was examined by Jean Porter in one of her earlier articles on Thomas Aquinas, "Desire for God: Ground of the Moral Life in Aquinas," *Theological Studies* 47 (1986): 48–68. There she describes the implications of Preller's reading of Aquinas: "In his discussion of the revealed propositions of sacred doctrine, Preller argues that since we cannot form a concept of God, the propositions of sacred doctrine (at least, those that refer directly to God) must necessarily be conceptually meaningless. Nonetheless, the mind of the believer really is conformed to God through assent to these propositions. God Himself correlates the propositions of faith to the full knowledge of God enjoyed in the beatific vision. Through the supernatural transformation of faith, the believer is enabled to judge that the propositions of sacred doctrine really do have God as their intention, and to affirm them accordingly, even though no one is able in this life to see how these propositions are correlated with God." This is an interesting line of investigation—that the believer can be conformed to God though assent to "propositions of sacred doctrine" (Stout might say "theologically grounded truth claims" or "metaphysical propositions") that are conceptually meaningless. Porter goes on to argue that "something similar can be said about the relation of charity to the acts of the moral life" wherein "we can affirm that charity transforms the acts of the moral life in such a way as to direct them to the final fulfilment of the human person. But we cannot say how the acts of the moral life, so transformed, are ordered to the true happiness of the vision of God." Although Porter more so than Preller emphasized the centrality of natural law to Aquinas's account of virtues (especially the relationship between justice and prudence), this line of inquiry will be important in assessing Stout's views about scholastic natural law.

63. Ibid., 159.

long-term good of particular species. As we noted earlier, Stout finds this view problematic because he does not consider the good of the species, which turns on the idea of a good emerging from its inherent order or perfection as a particular kind of creature, as itself morally normative. Neither the mere existence of basic goods nor a concept of inherent order that links their proper pursuit of a characteristic fulfillment signals the proper realm of moral concern.

A final kind of natural law thinking that Stout finds problematic is based less on an account of the natural focuses rather on an understanding of law drawn from the experience of scientific experimentation and the testing of law like principles to explain occurrences in nature. Stout's approach here is to link the development of law with an understanding of moral languages on which the articulation of law and the adjudication among laws depend. In his essay "Truth, Natural Law and Ethical Theory," Stout examines different options in natural law thinking and draws

> two sets of reasons for suspecting that natural law theory, as commonly understood, may not be a good thing to pursue. The first set has to with the quest for system, the second with the doctrine of realism as natural lawyers have typically construed it.[64]

Analyzing natural law in terms of its likeness to a system of scientific laws which seeks to explain how the world works is Stout's first move.

Drawing on the work of David Lewis, Stout argues that it is helpful to think of natural law approaches as requiring some sense of "lawhood" wherein "'a contingent generalization is a *law of nature* if and only if it appears as a theorem (or axiom) in each of the true deductive systems that achieves a best combination of simplicity and strength.'"[65] Parallel to establishing the provisional test of what counts as a law of nature, Stout offers preliminary criteria by which one could evaluate systems of moral truths, arguing that

> we can define *the moral law* as precisely those generalizations appearing as theorems or axioms in each of the best moral systems. *The natural law* would be that part of the moral law we human beings can discover unassisted by divine revelation.[66]

In this case, "[l]awhood has been defined not in terms of someone's decree, nor even in terms of what one would decree or know if one were like God, but rather in terms of concepts like truth, deductive system, axiom, strength, and simplicity."[67] The problem is that when we evaluate different moral

---

64. Stout, "Truth, Natural Law, and Ethical Theory," 72. [italics in original text]
65. Ibid., 76.
66. Ibid.
67. Ibid.

systems, we are confronted inevitably with the problem of translating one moral system into another since we cannot assume at the outset that the meanings of terms in the moral systems we are attempting to compare afford us enough stability for an effective comparison. "It quickly becomes evident," Stout says,

> that the competition among moral systems will turn on which moral language to employ. When that question remains open instead of being closed off by metaphysical stipulation, it becomes central. To judge a moral system by the standards of properly balanced strength and simplicity is to judge a set of sentences *in a given language*. The conceptual resources of that language will determine the strength and simplicity of which the system in question is capable.[68]

Stout still wishes to maintain some connection to what metaphysically laden positions mean by a moral law, a natural law, and an eternal law, but he recognizes that there will be questions about his "metaphysically austere"[69] equivalents to these terms. For example, with reference to "moral law" and "natural law" he says that such terms

> have long been a rhetorically effective means of emphasizing that the all-too-human codes we confront in society are always likely to include moral falsehoods and conceptual deficiencies. This fact makes room for conscientious objection to such codes. It underscores the need for social criticism. It assures us that a lonely dissenter or critic, taking a stand against the crowd or the powers that be, might be right.[70]

On "eternal law" he says,

> On my interpretation, it goes without saying that true moral sentences correspond to the eternal law, for the conception of eternal law merely takes the concept of truth ordinarily applied to moral sentences and combines it with a vague notion of improved vocabularies and a particular ideal for the construction of deductive systems.[71]

So Stout's critique of natural law approaches, as distinct from the natural law judgments of thinkers like Lewis and Aquinas, seems to rest on two problems he has with these systems. First, features of more "metaphysically austere" systems seem to operate in more or less the same ways as metaphysically laden systems and can be evaluated, he thinks, in terms of

---

68. Ibid., 79–80.
69. Ibid., 80.
70. Ibid., 81.
71. Ibid., 87.

simplicity and strength of system just as well as (perhaps even better than) those with strong metaphysical commitments. Second, since it would appear that metaphysical additions are required only by a correspondence theory of truth, and because such theories are on Stout's view problematic because they do not explain how a correspondence relation adds anything to the meaning of truth, their purpose can only be rhetorical and social-critical rather than ethically substantive.

Summarizing Stout's position on natural law, we might say that Stout holds that most, if not all, natural law approaches are committed to the following: (1) that there are general moral principles to which most if not all societies basically agree, (2) that a correspondence theory of truth is used to support key aspects of the existence and meaning of a moral law, (3) that there are infallible truth claims about human nature and that any contingent truth claims about human nature are not finally morally significant, (4) that moral claims are justified on metaphysical grounds and therefore are justified independently of an individual's or a society's epistemic context, (5) that practical moral reasoning proceeds basically in a deductive matter, and (6) that natural law positions are basically indifferent to social criticism.[72]

In the following section, we examine Jean Porter's revisionist account of natural law and see if the characteristics of natural law positions as Stout reads them apply to Porter's account. In the meantime, it is sufficient too that all six of Stout's critiques do not really get at the reason why a natural law position would want to argue for the moral significance of nature or even the various ways that such an argument might proceeds. Moreover, as we saw above, a Hegelian account of the moral significance of nature might emphasize, as Stout does, the way that nature is encompassed by spirit (understood as social practices through time), but it might also emphasize as Hegel did the ways that the form of those practices are themselves prefigured in nature itself. Or to give another example, we might ask why natural law systems ought to be analyzed according to theoretical reflection on scientific knowledge (what is legal or "law-like" in the study of nature) rather than according to theoretical reflection on legal knowledge (what is natural in the study of law) or the various ways that nature can be understood to have a moral significance.

II. The Moral Significance of Nature in Natural Law Ethics

Let us begin with the most significant differences between Porter and Stout and then progress to those areas where they appear to be similar in some respects. My argument in this section is that Porter maintains the intelligibility of nature to be of central importance for understanding nature's moral significance but intelligibility is flexible enough to support both species-specific

---

72. I am grateful to Kevin Jung, organizer of the workshop at which this paper was first presented, for his suggestions about how to formulate a summary of Stout's position on natural law. Here and elsewhere, I have adjusted slightly the original suggestions he made to me.

norms necessary for any coherent understanding of nature's moral significance while recognizing the various ways that moral languages mediated through social practices interpret individual placement in a species-specific ethic. In this way, Porter's revisionist natural law comes close to aspects of a Hegelian constructivist account, drawing Stout's constructivism to be more coherently Hegelian in its account of nature if it is to respond to the kind of challenges Porter's natural law provides.

Consider first Porter's statement at the beginning of *Nature as Reason* where she sets forth her starting points. "In this project," she says,

> I presuppose that we are able to attain genuine, albeit imperfect, knowledge of the world around us, and to formulate and express that knowledge through concepts which adequately correspond to the kinds of things they represent. That is to say, I presuppose a kind of realism, at least concerning our knowledge of the natural world.[73]

In other words, she assumes the possibility of genuine knowledge, that such knowledge means a real connection to the truth of things as they are, and that we can accurately (though not completely) describe the different kinds of things we find in the world including creatures of different kinds. She says that "realism" in her usage is intended to follow the medieval scholastic accounts she examines, and she believes that it reflects how the scholastics understood the connection between reason and nature and natural law and human happiness.

On the first of these points, she explains that the scholastics operated with several different understandings of nature and the natural, all of which cohered for them because of their basic metaphysical commitments and their religious beliefs but which when enumerated separately or taken together might seem unfamiliar to us. The most significant of these are the ideas of "nature as nature" (which Porter develops primarily from Albertus Magnus [1200–1280 CE]) and "nature as reason" (which Porter develops primarily from Philip the Chancellor [1160–1236 CE] and Huguccio of Pisa [d. 1210 CE]). The former is the view that

> nature, in the sense relevant to moral reflection, is intelligible in its operations, and this intelligibility in turn reflects the goodness as well as the inherent reasonableness of the variety of forms of created existence which go to make up the world.[74]

The latter is the view that "reason discerns or generates moral norms, or functions in some way as a norm itself."[75] This second option is the one that,

---

73. Jean Porter, *Nature as Reason: A Thomistic Theory of the Natural Law* (Grand Rapids and Cambridge: William B. Eerdmans Publishing, 2005), 57–8.
74. Ibid., 57.
75. Ibid., 231.

on initial inspection, tracks with Stout's critique of natural law thinkers who derive moral norms from metaphysical assumptions about the meaning of natural processes (as he thinks Aquinas does, at least when the disputed question is about sex) or those thinkers who elevate reason to the status of a law in the absence of such metaphysical assumptions or about the extent to which things in themselves are knowable (as he thinks Kant does). The first option is the one that seems closest to the critique Stout thinks modern philosophy of science gives to any understanding of an ordered natural world that is anything but contingently related to the human good.

Porter explains that

> [t]hese different interpretations of nature did share one critical presupposition, however—they presupposed that nature, understood in most of the ways in which the term can be used, is intelligible, and as such can and should be analyzed in terms of its own proper principles of operation.[76]

The focus on the *intelligible*, and what the intelligible will and will not allow in terms of interpretations of the goods of prerational nature or human nature, is central to Porter's view of how the scholastics interpreted nature and natural law. For the scholastics, intelligibility is the first step in establishing a sense of purposiveness for different kinds of creatures, which then requires the additional use of reason in order to establish particular purposes by which they achieve the full expression of flourishing proper to the kinds of creatures they are. There are, then, a number of different possible purposes that could potentially lead to the flourishing the human creature, and discerning these particular purposes are the work of human reason.

As Porter explains,

> the intelligibility of nature can be understood in more than one way, depending on what kind of nature is at stake—the primary options being nature considered as an ordered whole, and the nature proper to a given kind of creature.[77]

The earlier scholastics tended to emphasize the former, while the later scholastics (including Thomas Aquinas) tended to emphasize the latter in their accounts of nature and natural law.[78] Intelligibility may be found in the order of the cosmos, in the distinctive natures of different kinds of creatures, and in the relationships among creatures of different or the same kinds.

Intelligibility, on Porter's account, is rooted in a conception of what is good for human beings as a particular kind of creature, both in their own

---

76. Ibid., 69.
77. Ibid., 49.
78. Ibid., 69.

158   David A. Clairmont

integrity and in relation to other creatures, human and other than human. As she explains,

> the human person, together with every other living creature, comes into being, pursues the activities characteristic of its specific kind, and finally passes away—all in accordance with natural principles of action. These natural principles are intrinsically intelligible, and the form of existence constituted by them is naturally good. By the same token, these principles can be regarded as normative principles, albeit in a carefully qualified sense. That is, these principles are not rules (or laws) in the primary sense of norms that are grasped as such through rational apprehension and carried out through deliberate choice. Yet they represent something more than statistical regularities or contingent of events. They are intelligible components of a form of life, and they are intrinsically good and valuable insofar as they reflect (actually or potentially) the fullest possible development of that natural form.[79]

To say that "natural principles" are "intrinsically intelligible" means that there is something about the purposive activity of creatures (in this case, human creatures) that is not reducible to social convention mediated by language (as the Hegelian constructivist would hold) or to the processes of human reason (as the Kantian constructivist would hold) or to the fulfillment of basic desires (as a Humean constructivist would hold). There exist a number of ways in which creatures can achieve the flourishing proper to the kinds of things they are, and the specification of the ways that flourishing may involve being in compliance with the dictates of practical reason (as a Kantian constructivist would hope) mediation by social convention which is given meaning through language (as a Hegelian constructivist would hope) and/or taking into account basic tendencies and desires of that creature (as a Humean constructivist would hope). Yet the move from intelligibility to purposiveness to rationally determined purposes is not reducible to any one of these, even as it attends to all three of them.

For Porter, it is certainly the case that the intelligibility of various rationally determined forms of life depends on creatures having at least somewhat stable and discernable natures and on our having at least an initial reliable access to those natures—a suggestion that would be problematic to Stout, and depending on the level of specificity to Hegel as well. As she explains,

> the scholastic approach presupposes the real existence of natures—presupposes, that is to say, that our concepts of universals or natural

---

79. Jean Porter, *Ministers of the Law: A Natural Law Theory of Legal Authority* (Grand Rapids: William B. Eerdmans Publishing, 2010), 99.

kinds correspond, at least roughly and in part, with the actual character of the world. And this kind of realism is fundamental to the theological account of the natural law that I am developing, because it provided the foundation for the teleological judgments that are central to this concept. For the scholastics, nature is normative to the extent that it is good, and it is good to the extent that it manifests intelligibility and purpose in its operations. This purpose, in turn, is to be interpreted by reference to the overall life and well-being of the creature. What this approach to natural law presupposes, in other words, is the overall goodness or value of a specific kind of life, the form of life appropriate to a given kind of creature when it is flourishing in accordance with the intrinsic principles of its existence.[80]

Porter acknowledges that such a view is often critiqued in light of the developments of modern science, especially modern views about evolution that would seem to call into question any sense of the stability of biological natures which would seem to be constantly in flux.[81]

In response to what she views as a premature consensus in this point, Porter turns to the work of philosophers of biology, particularly Richard Lewontin and Ernst Mayer, to argue that how one reads the possibility of natural kinds in light of evolution depends a great deal on the level of analysis with which one begins and how one understands the disciplinary integrity of various scientific fields. So, for example, if one begins at the level of biochemical processes and genetic material (the place where Stout begins in his account of the history of scientific understandings of law), then change is bound to appear more random than if one begins at a higher level of specificity (e.g., the level of the biological system or the organism). As Porter says,

> the question here concerns the level of description at which a living creature can be rendered intelligible, at least sufficiently so to be the object of systematic description, and fruitful hypothesizing. By implication, this question concerns the autonomy of biology as a science; could

---

80. Porter, *Nature as Reason*, 88.
81. Porter notes that "it is sometimes said that the theory of evolution implies not only that species emerge and develop over time, but also that the kinds which emerge out of this process have no real existence independently of the particular creatures that instantiate them. In other words, because the processes of evolution are construed as random interactions of chance events, therefore the products of evolution, namely, species, are likewise to be seen as sheerly contingent groupings. And this view would of course rule out any kind of appeal to the norms of flourishing intrinsic to a kind of creature, for the simple reason that it denies that there are kinds of creatures, existing as such apart from our systems of classification. That, at least, is the interpretation of evolutionary theory favored by some of its exponents. Yet this interpretation is by no means universally held, nor, as I will argue, is it the most likely interpretation." Ibid.

we, even in theory, analyze biological phenomena without remainder in terms of the operations of the most basic physical forces, or will an adequate biological science necessarily also require distinctive principles and modes of inquiry?[82]

In defending the latter position, Porter's view raises an important comparison between her position and Stout's, indeed between any natural law and any constructivist account. To what extent does a constructivist rejection of natural law depend on a prior commitment in the debate about where the appropriate level of analysis rests in a philosophy of biology or about the appropriate way to think about relating philosophy of science to philosophical or religious ethics? A Hegelian description of nature, as we saw earlier, at least accounts for the ways that nature can provide patterns through we to understand the development of rational consciousness that, while certainly not an account of biological kinds, strikes a sort of middle position.

In addition to her focus on the intelligibility of nature, Porter also develops an important distinction between the conventional and the *pre-conventional* in exploring how human reason may be said to be part of nature. As Porter explains, for the scholastic tradition leading up to and including Aquinas, there existed

> a traditional distinction between what is natural in the sense of existing prior to human customs and legal enactments, and what is conventional or established by human design. Hence, anything that can be said to exist prior to human customs and enactments, and that somehow gives rise to or structures those customs and enactments, can be included in the concept of the natural, as the scholastics understand it. Interpreted this way, the concept of the natural can encompass nature understood in both of the primary senses . . . nature as seen as the ordered totality of all creatures, and nature seen as the intrinsic characteristics of a given kind of creature. It can also refer to the human capacity for rational judgment, which gives rise to moral norms, or to God's will revealed in scripture, since the divine will certainly exists prior to all human enactments and provides their ultimate norm.[83]

Here we see an attempt to account for the kind of problem that Hegel and Stout were both considering, namely how human customs (including social conventions in their linguistic of social-structural forms) arise from nature, either by way of gradual development or radical break: "The link between prerational nature and reason is thus constituted by the intelligibility of nature, rather than the naturalness (in one sense) of reason. In virtue of its intelligibility,

---

82. Ibid., 90.
83. Jean Porter, *Natural and Divine Law: Reclaiming the Tradition for Christian Ethics* (Grand Rapids: William B. Eerdmans Publishing, 1999), 77.

nature broadly construed is open to comprehension by human reason."[84] To say that nature can be comprehended by reason means that, in its parts and as a whole, it can be rightly interpreted as having some kind of purpose that human reason discovers but also that human reason can give purpose to it by way of social convention. Human reason itself, for example, can seek to understand its world (its theoretical expression), but it can also think about how to act in the world (its practical expression). Porter continues:

> Since intelligibility implies purposiveness, human nature in particular provides reason with aims which provide starting points and goals of practical operations. In this sense, practical reason in its operations opens downward—although the metaphor is perhaps not ideal—drawing on the intelligibilities of prerational nature, which it extends and completes in a distinctively human fashion. More specifically, reason shapes our prerational inclinations into determinate social practices and institutions, through which natural aims and exigencies can be pursued. In addition, it introduces tendencies of its own, directed towards goods which cannot be attained by nonrational creatures, and it brings its own exigencies, grounded in requirements for proper functioning. Certainly, reason bestows distinctive meaning on behaviors we share with the other animals, and this in turn leads to distinctive moral precepts. Yet even in these aspects of its functioning, reason is not divorced from prerational nature.[85]

This explanation introduces some interesting features of the scholastic discussion which begin to signal some of the important differences between a revisionist natural law position such as Porter's and a Hegelian constructivist position such as Stout's. Is it true, as Porter suggests, that intelligibility implies purposiveness? Her claim seems to be that this claim is both a feature of the scholastic view (a description that Stout would probably affirm) and a feature of intelligibility as such (a description that Stout probably would not affirm unless significantly qualified). At the very least, we can say that, for Porter, the viability of a natural law approach to ethics, beyond its prevalence in those communities that have developed it (the Roman Catholic community is an example) or cautiously adopted it (as some Protestant thinkers from Calvin onward have done), is the connection between intelligibility and a wide (if admittedly general) sense of purposiveness in human nature. While Stout (and other constructivists) may not wish to affirm what Porter does, at least this aspect of natural law should be acknowledged.

How then does Porter deal with the kind of charge that Stout leveled against Aquinas, especially on the issue of particular moral judgments

---

84. Porter, *Nature as Reason*, 71.
85. Ibid., 71–2.

about certain kinds of acts such as those Stout profiled in his discussion of moral abominations? Porter does take up the issue of moral judgment in her chapter on "Nature as Reason: Act and Precept in the Natural Law," and the discussion is too extensive to review here since she returns to many of her long-standing opponents in Catholic circles who were interested in questions about moral absolutes and intrinsically evil acts (John Finnis and Martin Rhonheimer among them) while also engaging with a variety of consequentialist and Kantian positions to clarify the distinctive theoretical features of a Thomistic account. However, as relates to Stout, the issue is rather confined to how the discussion about nature, reason, and natural law relate to moral judgments about naturally occurring human inclinations, such as those to sexual union and procreation. Again, it is important to quote Porter at length:

> In order to count as a genuine expression of human nature on the scholastic view, an observed inclination must be not only innate and generally experienced, it must also be amenable to construal in terms of what is proper to, or at least characteristic of, human nature considered as such. By the same token, as the scholastics reflected on their own observations and experiences, they did change their views about what should count as an expression of human nature, and they modified their conceptions of the natural law accordingly. Scholastic appraisals of reproduction and sexuality offer an especially clear example of this process. As [Philip the Chancellor's] remarks illustrate, the scholastics were heirs to a widespread patristic view that sexual desire is intrinsically sinful. In the twelfth century, the canon lawyers in particular were inclined to endorse this view, even though they stopped short of saying that sexual desire is in itself mortally sinful. But it was apparent even then that this position is incongruent, given a more general assumption that whatever stems from human nature must in some way be good. The scholastics soon began to modify their position accordingly, either by distinguishing between sinful and morally neutral forms of sexual desire or by simply asserting that sexual desire as such is morally neutral. Aquinas is the first of the scholastics to say that sexual desire is in itself good, but this view was anticipated by his predecessor William of Auxerre, and we find it intimated thought not explicitly said, by his contemporary Bonaventure.[86]

I think what Porter has in mind here is to caution those who read scholastic natural law thinking that these thinkers have two different intellectual contexts in mind and were aware of the need to speak to both. The first is an ecclesial-theological tradition which associated certain kinds of acts

---

86. Ibid., 78.

with sin and carried on an extensive casuistic analysis to determine which acts ought to be judged sinful and which ought not to be so judged, based both on the gravity of the sin and also the level of knowledge about the act and the conditions under which the act was performed. But there is a second philosophical-scientific-legal tradition (what Porter calls the scholastics' social and intellectual context) that reflects the life of medieval courts and universities more than it reflects the pastoral context of confessionals. In this social and intellectual public context, specific judgments were always being revised based on new knowledge introduced at the time about human beings and an accumulation of cases reflecting a history of difficult prudential judgments that offered new insight into moral problems and the nature of moral actions that had not been previously considered.

This, too, is an interesting point of comparison with Stout, at least on the intellectual life of the scholastics, since on Porter's account the scholastics were anything but a group of people wedded to the predetermined parameters of a metaphysical system. Certainly they had one, but it was always in the process of being tested and expanded in light of new situations and cases. For Stout, natural law (whether in its metaphysically maximal or its metaphysically minimal form) is a hypothesis about a universal moral law, and whether such a law is possible and the conditions under which it could be possible and able to be promulgated. Porter, on the other hand, argues that the scholastics' view of natural law was a derivative of a certain understanding of the intelligibility (and therefore purposiveness) of nature as apprehended by reason. She explains that

> Aquinas holds that the will is naturally, although not necessarily, moved by the proper objects of all the capacities natural to the human person, since these are either necessary to human existence or bound up in some way with human development and well-being (I-II 10.1) In this way, the operations of the will reflect general structures of existence and causality.[87]

In other words, Porter follows Aquinas and other scholastics to argue that the moral life has a basically teleological structure. This means, in contrast to Stout's constructivist account, which sheds some of the more metaphysical aspects of Hegel's thought, human beings have a natural end that they strive to discover—albeit gradually—and that knowing and willing that end is the fulfillment of a good human life. Porter goes on to explain:

> We recall that each creature is oriented toward its perfection, understood as the full actualization of its form, and correlatively, each creature is

---

87. Jean Porter, *Justice as a Virtue: A Thomistic Perspective* (Grand Rapids: William B. Eerdmans Publishing, 2016), 150.

naturally inclined toward whatever is presupposed as a condition for that actualization and whatever follows as an expression of its natural causal powers (I 5.5). The point is that the natural inclinations of any creature move it in such a way as to pursue, develop, and express the form of existence proper to its specific kind, and as such, they are structured in accordance with an intelligible form of existence. Having established that diverse moral precepts can be analyzed in terms of one common conception of goodness, he goes on to argue that the natural inclinations of the will, which reflect the intelligible form of human existence, provide a framework for integrating the diverse precepts of the natural law.[88]

For Porter, following Aquinas, a human being that is acting rationally wills not only the particular things she or he desires but, rather, those things that also contribute to their flourishing, knowing the kinds of creatures they are and what constitutes flourishing for that kind of being. For Stout, as we said earlier, the most that can be said about nature's moral significance, at least in its human form, is that whatever aims it holds for itself must be held provisionally, since what is most characteristic of human nature is an awareness of the fallibility of its own perspective. Whereas for Hegel, there did exist a purposiveness within rational consciousness rooted in the very processes of its emergence, in Stout's Hegelian constructivist view it is the result of that rational consciousness, as it considers its own limits in its quest for certainty, that most basically and essentially defines the human creature.

This brings us to one final point worth considering when comparing Stout and Porter's views on the moral significance of nature. Porter notes that the scholastics argued for a close connection between nature and reason to an equally strong link between virtue and law. Taking Aquinas as representative of the scholastic position on this question, she says that

> [t]he concept of happiness is central to a Thomistic theory of the natural law because it provides a framework within which to integrate two dimensions of human existence, namely, human nature comprehensively understood and the distinctively human character of natural existence, that is to say, human reason. At the same time, this concept also offers a different way to bring together two approaches to moral reflection which we often take to be distinct and indeed antithetical, namely an ethic of virtue and an ethic of law.[89]

How does this help us to understand the differences between Porter and Stout?

---

88. Ibid.
89. Ibid., 143–4.

For Porter, a Thomistic account (or virtually any other scholastic account, for that matter) assumed that a picture of the human being in which she or he possesses basic rational capacities to think about her or his life. Those rational capacities, directed at both the intelligible proximate ends of human acts and also at an intelligible final end, were necessary preconditions to thinking about human reason as having a deliberative prudential use, such that it could make laws and understand the force of laws. For Stout, on the other hand, this kind of connection between a picture of the human being, more or less stable and teleologically ordered (even if not to a divine final end) is unnecessary to a minimalist conception of natural law. Why is this so? Because changes in our perspectives on science have challenged teleologically ordered conceptions of nature (human, non-human, or ecological), just as changes in our perspectives on philosophy have challenged correspondence understandings of truth that link conceptions of moral or natural law to a metaphysical system.

But is this what Porter is saying about Aquinas and the scholastics? Porter notes, for example, that if one wishes to turn to science as a model for how to understand philosophical debates about human nature, one needs to address the significant division among scientists on how to approach this question. There are two very different lines of support in evolutionary biology, for example, one of which focuses on the connection between random processes and contingent groupings (as one finds in the work of Richard Dawkins) and another that marks relevant differences between the methods and goals of molecular biology and organismic biology (as one finds in the work of Richard Lewontin).[90] Even so, Porter argues,

> we do come to a point of genuine tension between the scholastic approach to natural law and some interpretations of evolution. That is, the scholastic approach presupposes the real existence of natures—presupposes, that is to say, that our concepts of universals or natural kinds correspond, at least roughly and in part, with the actual character of the world. And this kind of realism is fundamental to the theological account of the natural law that I am developing, because it provided the foundation for the teleological judgments that are central to this concept. For the scholastics, nature is normative to the extent that it manifests intelligibility and purpose in its operations. This purpose, in turn, is to be interpreted by reference to the overall life and well-being of the creature. What this approach to the natural law presupposes, in other words, is the overall goodness or value of a specific kind of life, the form of life appropriate to a given kind of creature when it is flourishing in accordance with the intrinsic principle of its existence.[91]

---

90. Porter, *Nature as Reason*, 89.
91. Ibid., 88.

Would it be fair to pose the following question to Stout: Is there no room in his constructivist moral philosophy for the kind of affirmation we find in this last line, and if there is, what kind of qualifications would be necessary for it to fit within his view?

III. A Case Study: Marriage and the Social Good of the Species

Since both Stout and Porter have explicitly referenced human sexuality and the institution of marriage in their writings on natural law, we can illustrate the similarities and differences between Stout's constructivism and Porter's natural law by comparing their views of homosexuality and same-sex marriage.

Let us look at the distinctions previously introduced as these relate to an analysis of human sexuality and marriage. Recall Porter's distinction between nature as nature and nature as reason introduced earlier. She also discussed another scholastic notion—reason as reason—developed from Philip the Chancellor. The first of these refers to "our intelligible functioning as animals of a certain kind," noting with respect to human reproductive capacities that this intelligible functioning "prompts us toward sexual union."[92] The second of these refers to "rationality as the defining characteristic of the human animal" which with respect to—prompts the individual to mate with one and only one other individual."[93] The third of these, as Porter explains, refers to "those processes of rational social deliberation giving rise to institutional forms of social life."[94]

What is the difference between "nature as nature" and "nature as reason" in this example? While the former refers to "nature understood primarily in terms of the natures of specific kinds of creatures, regarded as the intelligible principles of their existence and their causal powers,"[95] the latter refers to the ways in which

> human existence and flourishing cannot be understood in terms of these characteristically human inclinations alone; an adequate concept will also take account of the way in which the inclinations we share with other kinds of creatures are integrated into a characteristically human way of life.[96]

In other words, where "nature as nature" identifies certain characteristics of the human species, both those that mark it as continuous with and those

---

92. Jean Porter, "The Natural Law and Innovative Forms of Marriage: A Reconsideration," *Journal of the Society of Christian Ethics* 30, no. 2 (2010): 83.
93. Ibid.
94. Ibid.
95. Porter, *Nature as Reason*, 69.
96. Ibid., 119.

that distinguish it from other forms of animal life (and reason, which can identify those very characteristics, is surely among them!), "nature as reason" refers to the way that human beings—creatures of a rational nature—think about those characteristics and how, when properly identified and pursued, they contribute to the true flourishing of a human being. It is in this way that "nature as reason" may be said to "[refer] in a summary way to the view that reason discerns and generates moral norms, or functions as a moral norm itself."[97]

In the scholastic view, Porter argues, there was no direct link between an understanding of nature and the social convention of marriage. While these medieval thinkers did rely on a view of human biology that influenced their thinking about the purposes of human procreation and marriage, this was only one of a number of questions they considered. They understood that there were various forms of marriage in the biblical record, and canon law debates in medieval society considered many different aspects of marriage itself: how is a marriage formed, with whom can and should it be contracted, what if any role does the community have in marriage.[98] "For [the scholastics], marriage is not a necessary, organic expression of human nature but a complex and in many ways contested set of institutional practices—albeit practices that stem from and give expression to the intelligibilities of our shared nature."[99] The most basic of these intelligible forms was not particular acts of procreation (the morality of these acts was certainly important to the scholastics and had their own intelligibility) but, rather, the perpetuation of the species that was a basic characteristic of the human species as such. The means for that perpetuation required not only specific sexual acts, some of which had a procreative capacity, but also the wider social context of nuclear family, extended family, and society.

The case of marriage illustrates the scholastics' thinking about the connection between nature and social convention when it comes to moral values and norms. They inherited a debate about the extent to which existing social conventions can be understood as expressions of human nature and therefore as a necessary component of human flourishing. As Porter explains,

> the scholastics were aware—as many later natural law thinkers were not—that the practices and institutions of society cannot be regarded as organic expressions of nature, which emerge spontaneously from its exigencies and derive their authority from that fact. On the contrary, they never lost sight of the fact that social practices and institutions are always more or less conventional, in some cases contrary to the law of

---

97. Ibid., 231.
98. For more on this history of marriage and marriage law in medieval and early modern Europe, see John Witte, Jr., *From Sacrament to Contract: Marriage, Religion, and Law in the Western Tradition* (Louisville: Westminster John Knox Press, 1997), 16–41.
99. Jean Porter, "The Natural Law and Innovative Forms of Marriage: A Reconsideration," *Journal of the Society of Christian Ethics* 30, no. 2 (2010): 84.

nature, at least seen from some perspectives. In this respect, they follow Cicero rather than Aristotle. That is, rather than endorsing Aristotle's view that social conventions stem immediately from natural inclinations, in such a way as to reflect human nature directly, they appropriate Cicero's view that human society reflects a long-standing process of human reflection and invention, in which natural inclinations are given expression through negotiation, legislation, and the emergence of custom.[100]

In other words, over time societies examine the extent to which social conventions at any one time do, in fact, over the long haul, contribute to human flourishing and this involves some interrogation of what appears to be natural or proper to the human being at any one time. For the scholastics, those forms come from observation of current and past societies and the interpretation of scripture that provides both the testimony of moral standards and stories about what happens to people as they live by, challenge, and refine those standards.

Examining further Philip the Chancellor's writings on the sin of adultery, Porter notes that Philip's judgment on adultery reflects the three distinct levels at which adultery violates human nature. He "regards adultery as a violation of human nature at the level of nature as nature" for the reason that

he regards it as a distortion of the human inclination toward reproduction, and not only or most fundamentally as a sin at the level of nature as reason (a sin against the monogamous union of man and woman) or reason as reason (a sin against the social and juridical institution of marriage). His analysis points to a critical presupposition about the natural law as he and his interlocutors understood it. Even considered in its preconventional aspects, human reproduction can only be understood within a context set by the characteristic way of life of the human animal. Thus, it is naturally aimed toward bringing forth human children who will mature into rational agents and members of society. Correlatively, the process of reproduction, considered in its properly human form, involves not only biological reproduction but also the care, nurture, and socialization of the child. The specific ways in which this socialization takes place and the ideals informing it will of course be conventional, but the necessity for some kind of socialization stems from aspects of our nature, including in this case our fundamentally social way of life and the relative weakness and lack of development of human children. Hence, because adultery transgresses and undermines the kinship structures necessary for the formation of children into fully functioning adults, it can be said to be contrary to the inclination to

---

100. Porter, *Nature as Reason*, 18–19.

reproduce, even considered prior to qualifications introduced by rational reflection and institutional formulation.[101]

That adultery is viewed as a sin reflects that it violates a basic moral value and a moral norm. The value in question is a good not only of the individual or society but also of the human creature as such. For Philip and other scholastics it contradicts a value at the very heart of the human creature: its natural inclination to continue as a species that requires for its completion that people remain with and care for their young in a manner appropriate to the kind of creatures they are. So the value of marriage is linked not only to the moral norm of fidelity, but that norm is also grounded in a basic value that is foundational to the kind of creature the norm governs.

For Porter the key issue this raises is the difficulty, but also the necessity, of discerning which elements of social conventions—those of the current time and those of earlier times—are rooted in the natural in a normative sense because they are proper to and necessary for the flourishing of human beings as rational creatures. "The scholastics are well aware," Porter notes,

> that indissoluble, monogamous marriage is by no means the universal form of the institution. Even apart from the practices of Muslims or the scholastics' own ancestors, the Old Testament recorded the polygamous marriages of the saints of the Old Covenant, and the Old Law made provision for divorce. These tensions did not lead them to abandon their view that monogamy and indissolubility are tenets of the natural law, but it did prompt them to elaborate the ways in which different forms of marriage are more or less compatible with the natural law.[102]

It is for this reason that Porter thinks that the scholastics, including Thomas Aquinas, although they had strong negative judgments about homosexual sexual acts, were not in theory opposed to thinking about new forms of marriage that could still honor the centrality of the procreative purpose of marriage and the importance of the procreation and education of children to the social institution of marriage.[103] "In contrast to many of our own contemporaries," Porter write,

> [the scholastics] did not attempt to defend the marital practices of their own societies as immediate, direct, or much less necessary expressions

---

101. Porter, "The Natural Law and Innovative Forms of Marriage: A Reconsideration," 83.
102. Ibid., 85.
103. While Porter's argument cannot be reviewed in detail here, she does note that there are aspects of her interpretation of the scholastics that would minimize certain theological interpretations while playing up others. For example, she notes that the view of marriage as a sacrament, especially in the theology of Hugh of St. Victor (1096–1161 CE), emphasizes a more positive view of the sexual acts of spouses in the sense that sexual union

of human nature, nor were they much interested in developing a natural law analysis of the social and sexual practices of other societies. They were, however, very interested indeed in the marital practices of their own societies, which were currently in flux, and the natural law as they construed it offered criteria by which to appraise, defend, or reform these practices.[104]

Recall that Porter is trying to argue against a prominent interpretation of natural law, shared by some of its proponents as well its critics, that natural law is either a physicalist naturalism or a natural legalism. Porter is rather trying to show natural law as a kind of middle ground that takes seriously the importance of rational discourse about the human creature and its characteristic kinds of flourishing while remaining open to the ways that social context changes thereby revealing both new ways that human beings can flourish while guarding against new threats to long-standing social institutions that have made flourishing possible.

IV. Conclusion

So we arrive at some interesting points of convergence between Porter and Stout that also reveal some deep disagreements. First, on the most basic level (and this should not be underestimated), Stout takes nature as always evolving and changing over time (i.e., as having no fixed telos or substantive form), and he also views knowledge as always something limited and piecemeal (because the justification of beliefs is contingent on the epistemic context of the knower). Thus, he is opposed to what he understands to be the basic tenets of natural law because he believes that natural

---

may be said to have a religious significance through a theology of marriage as sacrament. Porter explains: "The most striking of such reassessment occurs near the beginning of the period we are considering in the work of the monastic theologian Hugh of St. Victor, who asserts that the bodily union between the spouses is a sacrament of the relation between Christ and the church, just as the agreement between the spouses—that is, their mutual consent to marry—is a sacrament of the love between God and the soul. He goes on to say that just as husband and wife are joined in one society and one love through marriage (which is established through the mutual consent of the parties), they are joined in one flesh through the conjugal act. The latter is not added to marriage in vain, he adds, because it offers both an occasion for obedience and virtue, and tangible fruit in the form of offspring. These remarks are not quite equivalent to a claim that the sexual act serves as an expression of love. Nonetheless, they do imply that the mutual love and society established by marriage sets the proper context within which the purposes of sex are to be understood, and they imply that sexual union between the spouses is itself a direct expression of one component of the sacramental significance of marriage." Ibid., 88. Theologians in the Christian tradition from Augustine to Pope John Paul II have probed the theological symbolism of sexual acts, and although Porter accounts for this development, it is not central to her view about moral significance of marriage and sexuality. This is because Porter emphasizes the importance of reading scholastics as products of their intellectual climate rather than as spokespersons for the ecclesial institution.

104. Ibid., 84.

law fails to pass muster with our postmodern anti-metaphysical and anti-foundationalist sensibilities. Porter, by contrast, admits that knowledge is limited and piecemeal but that the acquisition of knowledge assumes a basic intelligible structure of the natural world and of human beings as one natural kind in a wider intelligible universe. This is another way of saying that Porter is trying to develop a realist account of ethics based on natural law that remains flexible enough to consider knowledge of the human as an unfolding project. Moral values and norms that can reasonable be understood to fit within the basic intelligible structure of the natural world ought to be considered, even if they expand or even challenge previously held values and norms.

Second, on a practical level, we can recall that Stout expressed concern at those positions (including those held in the medieval period) that condemned homosexual acts, suggesting that the language of moral abominations helped us to understand what was at stake in disagreements about the use moral values and norms. He explained that "the language of abomination finds use wherever distinctions between 'us' and 'them' or between masculine and feminine roles remain sharp and acquire a certain kind of social significance."[105] He further suggested that, in matters of moral disagreement, what finally needs to be examined is not the substantive nature of the disagreement on issues that would appear to be perennially irreconcilable, or of staking out some common metaphysical ground between positions that display differences in moral judgments, but, rather, our operative understandings of what it means for moral values and norms to be true.

Interestingly, Porter and Stout seem to be closer on the normative question of same-sex marriage, and one might suggest that supports Stout's position that what was important is the pragmatic agreement about particular moral judgments. While Porter herself does not claim that the scholastics (including Aquinas) would have affirmed modern judgments about same-sex relations or marriage based on the information available to them, she does think that their approach to the relationship among an understanding of nature, the natural law, and social institutions such as marriage would have allowed them to consider seriously such possibilities. As she comments,

> this line of analysis leaves open the possibility that the institution of marriage can also serve other purposes, legitimate and worthy of promotion so long as they do not undermine the orientation of the institution toward procreation, comprehensively considered to include the extended processes of education and socialization.[106]

The advantage of this approach to discerning the moral significance of nature (including its interpretation of natural) over a constructivist approach of the

---

105. Stout, *Ethics After Babel*, 285.
106. Porter, "The Natural Law and Innovative Forms of Marriage: A Reconsideration," 90.

kind exemplified by Stout is that it allows us to consider how moral values and norms can emerge from reflection on our nature as rational creatures, continuous with but different from other mammalian species, while situating that view in a social context that allows us to add to and refine our knowledge of human nature through the study of biology, social analysis, law, and history.

Third, so far as I can tell, Stout's chief objection to speaking about the moral significance of nature is that he thinks we can no longer take for granted (or even talk productively about) certain metaphysical presuppositions about nature as a coherent whole, of natural kinds of creatures, or of any teleological conception of creatures and their basic capacities. This means that nature, as well as natural law, remain for him a suspect route to productive, ethical conversations. He is willing to entertain something like a provisional understanding of a moral law, built on the leanest possible metaphysical foundation, although he does not see what those metaphysical pylons would do for practical deliberations about moral issues. He counsels a kind of epistemic "humility" when it comes to proposing metaphysical systems that could conceivably be the basis for a discussion about the moral law, although he realizes that many who engage in public discussions about moral issues will not abandon them in such discussions. Perhaps the only way that we can talk about what is morally significant about human nature is the long-term value of epistemic humility for a productive, ethical conversation. Yet I think it reasonable to say that Porter too counsels a kind of epistemic humility, but her reasons for this come not from assessments about the practices of modern democratic moral deliberation but from her own tradition's struggle to understand the nature of the human person in light of new sources of knowledge about human life, including both the discoveries of modern science but also (perhaps more so?) the history of legal deliberation about moral cases. These are related but different forms of epistemic humility: one is directed to present moral deliberation, chastened by the lessons of past moral deliberation turning violent (Stout); the other is directed to understanding how past moral deliberations held on to and refined a basic understanding of the intelligibility of nature and human purposiveness, looking for ways to make the intellectual context and spirit of medieval moral debate alive again in the Catholic Church and the modern academy.

The similarities are still significant, as can be seen in their views about the promise and limits of moral theories. For example, Porter claims that

> natural law does not provide us with a system of ethical norms which is both detailed enough to be practical and compelling to all rational and well-disposed persons. However, there are good reasons to doubt whether any moral theory can provide us with such a system, and this approach to the natural law offers us something arguably more

valuable, namely, a way of reflecting theologically on the phenomenon of human morality.[107]

In this way, she seems to move closer to some aspects of Stout's position on moral theory since she does not think that natural law is a closed system in the way Stout thinks it is, although to be fair she has engaged with other Catholic natural law thinkers whose positions would be closer to the varieties of natural law discourse that Stout finds troubling.[108]

Fourth, although I have argued for the value of Porter's account of intelligibility for an understanding of the moral significance of nature, I think there are resources in Hegelian constructivism—specifically in Hegel's account of nature—that could hold a structurally similar place in Hegel to the place that intelligibility holds for Porter and the scholastics. Since neither Porter nor Stout considers this possibility, I offer it as a potentially fruitful comparison for further study.[109] For example, in one view,

> Hegelian constructivism amounts to an intrinsically historical view of epistemology as a trial and error process situated in the social context. Knowledge emerges from a trial and error process in which we construct a cognitive framework to grasp objects constructed in and through this process.[110]

Is this not also what Porter is doing, if we add to this description a starting point: the basically intelligible structure of nature and of natural kinds within it? For Porter, this is an activity more akin a gradual metaphysical

---

107. Porter, *Nature as Reason*, 5–6.
108. To offer just one additional example from Porter's presidential address to the Society of Christian Ethics, we read, "The similarities between the Scholastics' conception of morality and our own indicate the extent to which the latter presupposes distinctive theological commitments that have since receded from view. At the same time, the points of divergence between the two suggest that our modern conception is not the fruit of pure practical reason; it might have developed differently, if other aspects of the medieval conception had been preserved or given a central place." See Porter, "Christian Ethics and the Concept of Morality: An Historical Inquiry," 5. See Jean Porter, "Christian Ethics and the Concept of Morality: An Historical Inquiry," *Journal of the Society of Christian Ethics* 26, no. 2 (2006): 3–21.
109. As far as I know, Porter's direct engagement with Stout is limited to three brief footnotes in *Moral Action and Christian Ethics* (Cambridge: Cambridge University Press, 1995), 207 n7, 208 n11 and n13. She also mentions Stout and Rorty in her discussion of Alasdair MacIntyre in Jean Porter, "Openness and Constraint: Moral Reflection as Tradition-Guided Inquiry in Alasdair MacIntyre's Recent Works," *The Journal of Religion* 73, no. 4 (1993): 525. I have not yet located any significant engagement with Hegel, although I have not yet completed a complete review of her writings as of the time of this draft.
110. Tom Rockmore, "Hegel and Epistemological Constructivism," *Idealistic Studies* 36, no. 3 (2006): 183–90.

expansion, aided by modern biological and social sciences and the ever-expanding tradition of case law, than it is an epistemological crisis or evolution. Would Stout be open to engaging Hegel more deeply on nature, especially on how the intelligibility of nature relates to the emergence of the self-aware, finite, and humble epistemological subject?

Finally, I want to raise one additional point of comparison between these two accounts of natural law and thereby introduce my own (quite tentative, at least at this point) view on the matter. In Allen Verhey's review of Stout's *Flight from Authority*, he aptly describes the connection Stout draws between epistemological questions and the issues of authority and political life:

> Religious tolerance and the origins of liberal society were not won by philosophical foundationalists but carved out of the experience of threatened minorities and weariness with religious wars. And that experience, that tradition, not any new esperanto (not even when constructed by as able a philosopher as John Rawls), provides some confidence in the nurturing of peaceable and constructive moral conversation in the midst of serious moral disagreements and different moral communities and languages.[111]

Maybe that is an interesting way to read Porter's account of natural law too, if one replaces the "experience of threatened minorities with religious wars" with "the experience of tired penitents with sin-classification wars." What Porter is trying to show, it seems to me, is that a tradition that shares certain fundamental commitments to a religious view can get by with something like the old debates about "probabilism"—if two opinions are judged by competent authorities (i.e., if the people are both "wise" judges and the arguments are strong) as equally probable, then one can in good conscience follow a probable opinion.[112] There is sufficient metaphysical agreement to ensure that the authorities are still debating within a tradition whose basic claims they share, and Porter acknowledges at least the possibility of constructing a shared conception of the basic elements of human nature across religious tradition.[113] This is my own view, as well, that there is a place for

---

111. Allen Verhey, "Review of Jeffrey Stout, *The Flight from Authority: Religion, Morality, and the Quest for Autonomy*," *Calvin Theological Journal* 25, no. 2 (1990): 264.
112. For a discussion of probabilism in the 16th century, see John Mahoney, *The Making of Moral Theology: A Study of the Roman Catholic Tradition* (Oxford: Clarendon Press, 1987), 116–73. For a critical interpretation of Stout that inclines me to suggest this comparison between Porter and her Catholic precursors, see Edmund Santurri, "The Flight to Pragmatism," *Religious Studies Review* 9, no. 4 (1983): 330–8.
113. On this issue, see Porter's positive assessment of the kind of project envisioned by Lee Yearley to undertake comparative studies of human nature and virtues across religious traditions in *Nature as Reason*, 132–3.

a comparative religious ethics grounded in a comparative religious metaphysics, gradually produced and then tested over time. It is a flexible and patiently constructed moral realism, which a metaphysically inclined casuist like Porter, counting on the long history of cases to give us a workable picture of human nature, might also endorse.

Bibliography

Audi, Robert. "Secular and Religious Foundations of Normative Standards: Liberalism, Naturalism, and Rationalism in Political Philosophy." In *Von der religiösen zur säkularen Begründung staatlicher Normen*, edited by Ludwig Siep, Thomas Gutmann, Bernard Jakl, and Michael Stadtler, 33–55. Tubingen: Mohr Siebeck, 2012.

Bagnoli, Carla. "Introduction." In *Constructivism in Ethics*, edited by Carla Bagnoli, 1–21. Cambridge: Cambridge University Press, 2013.

Boyle, Joseph, John Finnis, and Germain Grisez. "Practical Principles, Moral Truth, and Ultimate Ends." *American Journal of Jurisprudence* 32 (1987): 99–151.

Braaten, Carl E. "Protestants and Natural Law." *First Things* (January 1992): 1–16.

Chepurin, Kirill. "Nature, Spirit, and Revolution: Situating Hegel's Philosophy of Nature." *Comparative and Continental Philosophy* 8, no. 3 (2016): 302–14.

Clairmont, David A. "Cultures of Comparisons and Traditions of Scholarship: Holism and Inculturation in Religious Ethics." In *Religious Ethics in a Time of Globalism: Shaping a Third Wave of Comparative Analysis*, edited by Elizabeth M. Bucar and Aaron Stalnaker, 81–112. New York: Palgrave Macmillan, 2012.

Dahlstrom, Daniel O. "Editorial." *Journal of Religious Ethics* 1 (1973): 3–4.

———. "Challenges to the Rational Observation of Nature in the Phenomenology of Spirit." *The Owl of Minerva* 38, no. 1–2 (2006–7): 35–56.

Frankena, William K. "Public Education and the Good Life." *Harvard Educational Review* 31 (1961): 413–26.

Graber, Glenn C. "A Critical Bibliography of Recent Discussions of Religious Ethics by Philosophers." *Journal of Religious Ethics* 2, no. 2 (1974): 53–80.

Gustafson, James M. "A Retrospective Interpretation of American Religious Ethics: 1948–1998." *Journal of Religious Ethics* 25, no. 3 (1997), 25th Anniv. Suppl.: 3–22.

Hoffheimer, Michael H. "The Influence of Schiller's Theory of Nature on Hegel's Philosophical Development." *Journal of the History of Ideas* 46, no. 2 (1985): 231–44.

Jung, Kevin. *Christian Ethics and Commonsense Morality: An Intuitionist Account*. New York: Routledge, 2015.

Mahoney, John. *The Making of Moral Theology: A Study of the Roman Catholic Tradition*. Oxford: Clarendon Press, 1987.

Mattison, William C., III. "The Changing Face of Natural Law: The Necessity of Belief for Natural Law Norm Specification." *Journal of the Society of Christian Ethics* 27, no. 1 (2007): 251–77.

Peterson, Mark C. E. "Animals Eating Empiricists: Assimilation and Subjectivity in Hegel's Philosophy of Nature." *The Owl of Minerva* 23, no. 1 (1991): 49–62.

———. "Review of Alison Stone, Petrified Intelligence: Nature in Hegel's Philosophy." *The Owl of Minerva* 38, no. 1–2 (2006–7): 209–17.

Petry, M. J., trans. *Hegel's Philosophy of Nature*, 3 vols. London: Allen & Unwin; New York: Humanities Press, 1970.
Pippin, Robert B. *Hegel on Self-Consciousness: Desire and Death in the Phenomenology of Spirit*. Princeton: Princeton University Press, 2010.
Porter, Jean. "Desire for God: Ground of the Moral Life in Aquinas." *Theological Studies* 47 (1986): 48–68.
———. "Openness and Constraint: Moral Reflection as Tradition-Guided Inquiry in Alasdair MacIntyre's Recent Works." *The Journal of Religion* 73, no. 4 (1993): 514–36.
———. *Moral Action and Christian Ethics*. Cambridge: Cambridge University Press, 1995.
———. *Natural and Divine Law: Reclaiming the Tradition for Christian Ethics*. Grand Rapids: William. B. Eerdmans Publishing, 1999.
———. *Nature as Reason: A Thomistic Theory of the Natural Law*. Grand Rapids and Cambridge: William. B. Eerdmans Publishing, 2005.
———. "Christian Ethics and the Concept of Morality: An Historical Inquiry." *Journal of the Society of Christian Ethics* 26, no. 2 (2006): 3–21.
———. *Ministers of the Law: A Natural Law Theory of Legal Authority*. Grand Rapids: William. B. Eerdmans Publishing, 2010.
———. "The Natural Law and Innovative Forms of Marriage: A Reconsideration." *Journal of the Society of Christian Ethics* 30, no. 2 (2010): 79–97.
———. *Justice as a Virtue: A Thomistic Perspective*. Grand Rapids: William. B. Eerdmans Publishing, 2016.
Preller, Victor. *Divine Science and the Science of God: A Reformulation of Thomas Aquinas*. Princeton: Princeton University Press, 1967.
Reeder, John P., Jr. "What Is a Religious Ethic?" *Journal of Religious Ethics* 25, no. 3 (1997), 25th Anniv. Suppl.: 157–81.
Rhonheimer, Martin. *Natural Law and Practical Reason: A Thomist View of Moral Autonomy*. Translated by Gerald Malsbury. New York: Fordham University Press, 1993.
———. "Review Article: Nature as Reason: A Thomistic Theory of the Natural Law." *Studies in Christian Ethics* 19, no. 3 (2006): 357–78.
———. *The Perspective of the Acting Person: Essays in the Renewal of Thomistic Moral Philosophy*. Edited by William F. Murphy, Jr. Washington, DC: The Catholic University of America Press, 2008.
Rockmore, Tom. "Hegel and Epistemological Constructivism." *Idealistic Studies* 36, no. 3 (2006): 183–90.
Santurri, Edmund. "The Flight to Pragmatism." *Religious Studies Review* 9, no. 4 (1983): 330–8.
Stalnaker, Aaron. "Judging Others: History, Ethics, and the Purposes of Comparison." *Journal of Religious Ethics* 36, no. 3 (2008): 425–44.
Stout, Jeffrey. *The Flight from Authority: Religion, Morality, and the Quest for Autonomy*. Notre Dame: University of Notre Dame Press, 1987.
———. *Ethics After Babel: The Languages of Morals and Their Discontents*. Princeton and Oxford: Princeton University Press, 1988.
———. "Truth, Natural Law, and Ethical Theory." In *Natural Law Theory: Contemporary Essays*, edited by Robert P. George, 71–102. Oxford: Clarendon Press, 1992.

---. *Democracy and Tradition*. Princeton and Oxford: Princeton University Press, 2004.

---. "What Is It That Absolute Knowing Knows?" *Journal of Religion* 95, no. 2 (2015): 163–82.

Testa, Italo. "How Does Recognition Emerge from Nature? The Genesis of Consciousness in Hegel's Jena Writings." *Critical Horizons* 13, no. 2 (2012): 176–96.

Tracy, David. "The Post-Modern Re-Naming of God as Incomprehensible and Hidden." *Cross- Currents* (Spring/Summer 2000): 240–7.

Verhey, Allen. "Review of Jeffrey Stout, *The Flight from Authority: Religion, Morality, and the Quest for Autonomy*." *Calvin Theological Journal* 25, no. 2 (1990): 262–6.

Witte, John, Jr. *From Sacrament to Contract: Marriage, Religion, and Law in the Western Tradition*. Louisville: Westminster John Knox Press, 1997.

7 Grounds of Normativity
Constructivism, Realism, and Theism[1]

Kevin Jung

Can normativity be grounded in the facts about what we human beings care about? In this chapter, I consider Christine Korsgaard's Kantian and Sharon Street's Humean versions of metaethical constructivism (hereafter constructivism unless noted otherwise) in order to explore this question. Notwithstanding some important differences between the thought of the two thinkers, both Korsgaard and Street share the view that we human beings are creators of value and that the truth of normative claims is fixed by none other than the evaluative attitudes of human agents. Each in their own way develops what Street calls a "thoroughgoing" (or "unrestricted") form of constructivism in which the goal of constructivism is to give an account of the truth of normative claims in the entire normative domain rather than only in some limited subset of normative claims.[2]

Although constructivism as a metaethical theory need not be incompatible with theism,[3] I take both Korsgaard's and Street's accounts of constructivism as two non-theistic attempts to ground normativity exclusively in human points of view. Still, for some theists, such a constructivist understanding of value can pose certain problems. One such problem lies in the fact that this constructivist view requires theists to conceive of a God who is either unable or unwilling to evaluate any states of affairs in the world by

1. I would like to thank all who attended the Wake Forest workshop and Christian Miller for their helpful comments on earlier versions of this chapter.
2. Sharon Streets contrasts "restricted constructivism in ethics" with "thoroughgoing or metaethical constructivist views." The former "specify some restricted set of normative claims and say that the truth of a claim falling within that set consists in that claim's being entailed from within the practical point of view, where the practical point of view is given some substantive characterization." According to the latter, "the truth of a normative claim consists in that claim's being entailed from within the practical point of view, where the practical point of view is given a formal characterization." Sharon Street, "Constructivism About Reasons," *Oxford Studies in Metaethics* 3 (2008): 208; "What Is Constructivism in Ethics and Metaethics?" *Philosophy Compass* 5, no. 5 (May 1, 2010): 367, 369. See also James Lenman and Yonatan Shemmer, "Introduction," in *Constructivism in Practical Philosophy* (Oxford: Oxford University Press, 2012), 3–4.
3. For instance, in this volume Christian Miller provides a sketch of how constructivism can be made compatible with theism.

God's own standards.[4] It raises the question why God would let us ground all normative facts in *our* evaluative attitudes instead of God's if God is understood as omnipotent, omniscient, and benevolent enough to care about what we ought to value and do. Assuming, on the one hand, that God does make normative (both evaluative and deontic) judgments on states of affairs and, on the other, that God's normative judgments are incomparably better than ours, theists may have difficulty in accepting and reconciling *thoroughgoing* forms of constructivism with their theistic views, for reasons having to do with lack of objectivity and some features of divine power.

The main purpose of this chapter is twofold. I offer a critique of the two thoroughgoing constructivist accounts of value and present an alternative realist account of value that is compatible with theism. In section 1, I sketch Korsgaard's Kantian and Street's Humean versions of constructivism, in turn, outlining the main features of each account. In section 2, I discuss some possible objections to their accounts of normativity. In section 3, I provide a realist framework of value as an alternative for explaining how to ground the normativity of evaluative judgments. In section 4, I explain how such a framework could be best understood by theists who believe that there is a place for the divine will in morality.

I. Two Versions of Constructivism

I.1. Korsgaard's Kantian Constructivism

Korsgaard, one of the most influential Kantian constructivists in contemporary philosophy, maintains that we can derive *substantive* normative truths from what is constitutive of our practical identity as human beings by scrutinizing our capacity for normative self-constitution (or self-government). To understand how this may be possible, she suggests that we look at how the problem of normativity begins in the first place.

Korsgaard believes that the problem of normativity is rooted in our rational nature, specifically in the reflective structure of human consciousness. Unlike other animals that are merely conscious of and responsive to external objects, human beings do not simply act on their perceptions or desires; they need a *reason* to believe and act. They must decide based on reflection which perception to believe and which desire to act on. This is so because

> we human animals turn our attention on to our perceptions and desires themselves, on to our own mental activities, and we are conscious of them.... For our capacity to turn our attention on to our own mental

---

4. For a contemporary theological articulation of God as the judge of all human valuation, see H. Richard Niebuhr, *Radical Monotheism and Western Culture: With Supplementary Essays* (Louisville: Westminster John Knox Press, 1993).

activities is also a capacity to distance ourselves from them, and to call them into question.[5]

In other words, the problem of normativity comes from the need for reflective endorsement: What reason ought I to *endorse* for belief and action?

On Korsgaard's account, nothing is intrinsically normative unless we legislate the moral law or recognize something as valuable. In this respect, it may be helpful to read Korsgaard as a *reasons internalist* (or internalist about reasons) who holds that having normative reasons to do something requires some motivational fact internal to the agent. According to reasons internalism, in order for something to be a reason, the reason should be in what Bernard Williams calls the "subjective motivational set."[6] Putative normative reasons that are independent of one's subjective motivational set are insufficient for motivation, and hence, one does not actually possess those reasons. Following Kant, however, she thinks that inclinations cannot be a rational basis for endorsing or rejecting a reason because using them as normative reasons implies that the will is not free and is only conditionally good as the result of being determined by the laws of nature.[7]

It bears mentioning, though, that Korsgaard does not see the reasons internalism thesis as requiring "that rational considerations always succeed in motivating us. All it requires is that rational considerations succeed in motivating us insofar as we are rational."[8] Someone who is skeptical about the possibility of human action being directed by pure practical reason mistakenly assumes that "pure practical reason will exist if and only if we are capable of being motivated by the conclusions of the operations of pure practical reason as such."[9] But she rejects the notion that, unless the principles of pure practical reason motivate us, they cannot be normative. In her view, the fact that one might or might not be motivated to choose a certain course of action by the principles of practical reason does not show that rational considerations cannot motivate us and thus cannot be normative. Whether we are motivationally responsive to rational considerations has nothing to do with their bearing on one's deliberation and choice. Instead, the following appears to be true: "if we can be motivated by considerations stemming from pure practical reason, then that capacity belongs to

---

5. Christine M. Korsgaard, *The Sources of Normativity* (Cambridge and New York: Cambridge University Press, 1996), 93.
6. The subjective motivational set is usually explained in terms of desires, but it also includes "such things as dispositions of evaluation, patterns of emotional reaction, personal loyalties, and various projects, as they may be abstractly called, embodying commitments of the agent." Bernard Williams, "Internal and External Reasons," in *Moral Luck* (Cambridge and New York: Cambridge University Press, 1982), 105.
7. Korsgaard, *The Sources of Normativity*, 97–8.
8. Christine M. Korsgaard, "Skepticism About Practical Reason," in *Creating the Kingdom of Ends* (New York: Cambridge University Press, 1996), 321.
9. Ibid., 327–8.

the subjective motivational set of every rational being."[10] Insofar as we are rational, we can be motivated by rational considerations.

Rational considerations are solutions for normative problems that require reflective endorsement. Korsgaard does not think, however, that reflective endorsement requires either non-natural or supernatural entities. Taking a cue from John Rawls, who develops a Kantian constructivist moral theory based on "a particular conception of the person as an element in a reasonable procedure of construction,"[11] Korsgaard seeks to derive substantive moral principles from what she calls our "practical identities." She argues that we usually choose a course of action under some description of who we are, that is, of our self-understanding. We are governed by a practical identity that provides us with reasons for action, and our actions, in turn, constitute us.

However, Korsgaard denies that it is our *particular* practical identities (e.g., I am a teacher, a mother, or a soldier) that have unconditional authority in the practical domain. This is because she believes that there is a different form of practical identity that precedes and overrules any particular practical identities, an identity every rational agent necessarily endorses by virtue of being a valuing agent: our practical identity as *human beings*. She explains as follows:

> But *this* reason for conforming to your particular practical identities is not a reason that *springs from* one of those particular practical identities. It is a reason that springs from your humanity itself, from your identity simply as *a human being*, a reflective animal who needs reasons to act and to live. And so it is a reason you have only if you treat humanity as a practical, normative, form of identity, that is, if you value yourself as a human being.[12]

That we give or ask for reasons for action is a sign of rationality that we possess as *human beings* rather than as particular individuals. Rationality is, in fact, defined as a normative capacity different from intelligence in that the former lies "in what Kant took to be the unique human ability to reflect on the reasons for our beliefs and actions, and decide whether they are good reasons or bad ones."[13] Every time we try to justify an action by giving or asking for a reason, we are *necessarily valuing ourselves* as human beings who have this normative capacity. Thus, Korsgaard argues that it is our practical identity as valuing agents that gives reasons for our action.

10. Ibid., 328.
11. John Rawls, "Kantian Constructivism in Moral Theory," *Journal of Philosophy* 77, no. 9 (1980): 516.
12. Korsgaard, *The Sources of Normativity*, 121.
13. Christine M. Korsgaard, "A Kantian Case for Animal Rights," in *Animal Law—Tier Und Recht.: Developments and Perspectives in the 21st Century. Entwicklungen Und Perspektiven Im 21. Jahrhundert*, ed. Margot Michel, Daniela Kühne, and Julia Hänni, Bilingual ed. (Zurich: Berlin: Dike Publishers, 2012), 5.

It follows from her view that acting from our practical identity as human beings is to have a *moral* identity since valuing (or appreciating) human beings is part and parcel of what it means to be rational human beings. An agent must then think of *oneself* as a citizen of the kingdom of ends because one is foremost to be identified as a human being prior to being a means to someone else's particular end. This means that each agent's reasons for action must be guided by one's moral identity as a human being. This is why respect for humanity must be the moral law since our practical identity as human beings places normative constraints on action. The Formula of Humanity as an End in Itself is the substantive moral law on which all other moral principles rest since no rational agents who understand the process of practical reasoning can deny, on pain of contradiction, that we have a normative capacity.

In *Self-Constitution*, Korsgaard goes one step further by explaining why respect for humanity is a necessary condition of what she calls effective action and is the law of successful self-constitution. She advances the view that we human beings constitute our practical identities through action, as we *make* ourselves the authors of our actions.[14] We attribute an action to an agent considered as an integrated whole, not to a mere part of the agent. But some actions unify their agents better than others if the actions are not merely our products but "expressive of principles we ourselves have chosen, principles we have adopted as the laws of our own causality."[15] Only the actions performed on the basis of the principles of practical reason that we have freely chosen genuinely constitute our practical identities because what counts as "effective" actions are the movements that are not just caused by us but that have been identified as *ours*.[16] Effective actions are movements that render their agents both efficacious and autonomous. But this implies that we have to respect humanity in us in the first place. This is so because

> without respect for the humanity in your own person, it is impossible to will the laws of your own causality, to make something of yourself, to be a person; and unless you make something of yourself, unless you constitute yourself as a person, it will be impossible for you to act all.[17]

Respect for humanity makes it possible for effective action and successful self-constitution; it is "the law of unified self-constitution."[18]

It is worth noting here how Korsgaard explains that autonomy, not some metaphysical reality independent of human interests, is the source of

---

14. Christine M. Korsgaard, *Self-Constitution: Agency, Identity, and Integrity* (Oxford and New York: Oxford University Press, 2009), 45.
15. Ibid., 131.
16. Ibid., 84.
17. Ibid., 206.
18. Ibid.

normativity. Taking the form of a transcendental argument, the basic structure of her argument is deceptively simple. She explains it this way:

> rational action exists, so we know it is possible. How is it possible? ... I show you that rational action is possible only if human beings find their own humanity to be valuable. But rational action is possible, and we are the human beings in question. Therefore we find ourselves to be valuable. Therefore, of course, we are valuable.[19]

Her transcendental argument starts from a premise—some widely accepted aspect of experience—and then reasons to a conclusion that is a necessary condition of the premise. Let's start with the premise, which Korsgaard believes, that all reasonable human agents cannot deny from within their first-person perspective. The premise is that rational action is possible. In order for our actions to be rational, we must take some conception of our practical identity to be normative. Otherwise, there would be no reasons for action since it is a conception of practical identity that furnishes us with reasons for action. If no reasons for action, then no action at all since we as reflective agents "cannot act without reasons."[20] Thus, the necessary condition for the premise is this: a conception of practical identity is normative.

It should be added, however, that the conception of our practical identity that is normative is not any contingent conception of practical identity but must be a fundamental conception of our identity *as human beings* since it springs from our humanity itself and as such precedes all particular practical identities. Hence, our humanity must be the source of normative reasons; we must value our own humanity if we were to act at all.

But how does Korsgaard move from the claim that we must value our own humanity to the claim that we are valuable? The key is to consider these claims from a first-person perspective. She argues that "value, like freedom, is only directly accessible from within the standpoint of reflective consciousness."[21] She then goes on to say that

> when we are in the first-person perspective we find ourselves to be valuable, rather than simply that we are valuable. There is nothing surprising in this. Trying to actually see the value of humanity from the third-person perspective is like trying to see the colours someone sees by cracking open his skull.[22]

What she is getting at is that value is not something that we can apprehend apart from our reflective scrutiny of moral sentiments and dispositions. If

---

19. Korsgaard, *The Sources of Normativity*, 124.
20. Ibid., 123.
21. Ibid., 124.
22. Ibid.

our reflective distancing from competing desires creates the problem of normativity for action, it is our reflective *endorsement* from which normative reasons arise and our reflective *rejection* from which obligation arises.[23]

That we can *choose* any course of action by stepping back from our desires or motives and *reflectively endorsing* certain desires or motives implies that we have autonomy, the very capacity for reflective endorsement and self-legislation, untethered to our natural impulses. Thus, she writes,

> Behind the assumption that if every rational being could acknowledge something to be good ... then it is good ... is the idea that it is rational beings who determine what is good; rational nature confers value on the objects of its choices and is itself the source of all value.[24]

This explains why we can speak of value as *our* own construction. Since it is we as rational agents who confer value on objects and by virtue of this capacity we are intrinsically valuable, Korsgaard claims that objective goodness is not a mysterious ontological attribute: "The things that are important to us can be good: good because of our desires and interests and loves and because of the physiological, psychological, economic, historical, symbolic and other conditions under which human beings live."[25] Consider, for instance, Korsgaard's justification for animal rights. She argues that we must regard animals as ends in themselves. Animals should be regarded as "extrinsically good yet valuable as an end" because we necessarily value our own humanity, and "there is an animal—yourself—whose suffering you declare to be morally objectionable."[26] The normative claim that we ought to extend respect to animals who share animality with us is grounded in the fact that our own animality matters *to us*. Notice that this fact on which the normative reason for respecting animals supposedly depends is not a fact about value (i.e., a fact that makes an act good or bad, independently of our interests or desires) but a *fact about us* (i.e., a fact about what we prefer or desire).

I.2. Street's Humean Constructivism

We now turn to Street's Humean version of constructivism. Like Kantian constructivists, Street holds that normative facts cannot be obtained independently of reflective deliberation. However, she disagrees with the Kantian constructivist claim that *substantive* moral conclusions follow from a

---

23. Ibid., 102.
24. Christine M. Korsgaard, "Source of Value," in *Creating the Kingdom of Ends* (New York: Cambridge University Press, 1996), 241.
25. Christine M. Korsgaard, "Two Distinctions in Goodness," in *Creating the Kingdom of Ends* (New York: Cambridge University Press, 1996), 273.
26. Ibid.; Christine M. Korsgaard, "Facing the Animal You See in the Mirror," *The Harvard Review of Philosophy* 16, no. 1 (2009): 5.

purely formal understanding of the attitude of valuing as such. Whereas Korsgaard holds that certain normative facts are entailed from within the standpoint of *any* valuing agent, Street denies that substantive normative content such as moral values can be derived from the practical point of view of *any* agent as such.

Street challenges Korsgaard's view that reasons merely provided by particular identities are insufficient for normativity. Why does it matter whether we take something or other to be a reason, if we honor the basic tenet of constructivism that "there are no facts about normative reasons apart from the standpoint of an agent who is already taking things to be reasons"?[27] In Street's view of constructivism, the standards for determining one's reasons cannot be divorced from one's own judgments about what matters or what counts as reasons. If this is the case, claims that "it is illegitimate to stand apart from all of one's judgments about what counts as reasons, and then to ask whether one has some further reason."[28] If we all agree that value is ultimately conferred on things by each of us, why should we stop and require that there be some further reason to endorse our own normative judgments about reasons?

If Korsgaard is right, substantive moral facts are entailed from within the standpoint of any valuing agent, whether or not the agent is aware of her own particular identity. Street finds this unpersuasive. In Korsgaard's account, we have "the standpoint of an agent *as such*—i.e. the standpoint of a creature who is able to distance itself from its unreflective evaluative tendencies" and who *needs* some further reason for the *problem* of how to answer the normative question, "What should I do?"[29] Street criticizes Korsgaard's account for presupposing the necessity of "a certain universal standpoint" in determining the truth of normative judgments. She writes,

> What makes this idea of the standpoint of 'agency as such' sound plausible is the use of words such as *need* and *problem*. Such language makes it sound as though there is indeed a certain universal standpoint that one can identify with, a standpoint that is identified not by any particular normative commitment but rather by the general commitment to having some normative commitment or other.[30]

But why does constructivism have to require such a universal standpoint if it is still committed to a rejection of realism? It seems that such a question is quite valid considering the central tenet of constructivism, which holds that

---

27. Sharon Street, "Coming to Terms with Contingency: Humean Constructivism About Practical Reason," in *Constructivism in Practical Philosophy*, ed. James Lenman and Yonatan Shemmer (New York: Oxford University Press, 2012), 48.
28. Ibid., 49.
29. Ibid., 50; italics in the original.
30. Ibid.; italics in the original.

the only facts that matter to our normative judgments are the facts about what matters to us. In Street's reading of constructivism,

> [e]ither you take something or other to matter or you don't; either you take something or other to be a reason or you. . . . If you do, then something matters for you; then you have reasons. If you don't, then nothing matters for you; then you have no reasons.[31]

You don't need a conception of your identity abstracted from all of your particular normative commitments.

While Street denies that substantive moral judgments are entailed from within the standpoint of pure practical reason as such, she distinguishes an agent's merely contingent evaluative attitudes from those of his that can withstand reflective scrutiny. True, in her view, "the substantive content of a given agent's reasons is a function of his or her particular, contingently given, evaluative starting points," but those evaluative starting points that cannot withstand one's own reflective scrutiny should not serve ultimately as the standard of the correctness for normative judgments.[32] Acceptable substantive moral judgments must be entailed from the agent's evaluative judgments in "reflective equilibrium."[33] This means that there should be reflective scrutiny of one's entire set of judgments about one's reasons. Such a scrutiny involves comparing a particular normative judgment with the rest of the normative judgments (or evaluative attitudes) for consistency. There should be no doubt, though, that we are still talking about reflective scrutiny of one's own particular, contingently given judgments.

This requirement of reflective scrutiny is also the reason why Street does not want to reduce normative judgments to mere desires. She writes that if desire means "a feeling of being pleasantly attracted," the attitude of valuing refers to the state of mind of valuing an end, which "constitutively involves valuing what one is fully aware is the necessary means to that end."[34] Normative judgments can be *instrumentally* entailed from within one's practical point of view in reflective equilibrium without necessarily generating some feeling of attraction. In this view, the truth of normative judgments then is neither a matter of representing the way of the world (contra realists) nor a matter of merely expressing certain states of mind that are characteristically noncognitive (contra expressivists).[35] Rather, it is a function of one's

---

31. Ibid., 49–50.
32. Street, "What Is Constructivism in Ethics and Metaethics?" 370.
33. Sharon Street, "A Darwinian Dilemma for Realist Theories of Value," *Philosophical Studies* 127, no. 1 (2006): 154.
34. Street, "Coming to Terms with Contingency: Humean Constructivism About Practical Reason," 44.
35. Street, "What Is Constructivism in Ethics and Metaethics?" 375–8.

Grounds of Normativity 187

evaluative attitudes, more specifically, a matter of one's particular evaluative attitudes being in sync with the rest of one's evaluative attitudes, according to which the truth or the correctness of these attitudes is determined according to the standard set by oneself.[36]

As stated earlier, normative judgments can only come from within the contingent facts of our lives: "there are no facts about what is valuable apart from facts about a certain point of view on the world and what is entailed from within that point of view."[37] As she puts it, "to get substance out, we need substance in."[38] The standards of correctness, when it comes to normative truths, must be sought from within the contingent facts about each agent's evaluative stances. Thus, Street defends a subjectivist view of normative truths.

To see the significance of her subjectivist view, let's consider Street's example of an ideally coherent Caligula. Suppose that Caligula enjoys torturing others for fun in a way "utterly consistent with his own other values plus the non-normative facts." Is this ideally coherent Caligula making a mistake in his judgment? According to Street, the answer is no. In Street's view, such an ideally coherent Caligula is making no error in his normative judgment since there are no "standards independent of the evaluative point of view that could make it the case that Caligula's evaluative starting points are mistaken."[39]

Is Street's version of constructivism liable to the charge of relativism about normative reasons and about moral reasons, in particular? Street does not deny that her Humean constructivism lacks the kind of objectivity that realism or Kantian constructivism claims to provide. But she tries to downplay the relativistic consequences by appealing to the existence of similar normative judgments across cultures and societies. The existence of these similar normative judgments is, however, no mere coincidence. For the content of human evaluative judgments has been, to a large degree, influenced by the forces of natural selection as well as other forces (e.g., social, cultural, and historical). Despite a broad range of diversity in normative judgments that we have as a species, there are also noticeable cross-cultural and cross-historical patterns in normative judgments that can be traced to the forces of natural selection. These forces include strong selective pressures to increase our chances of survival and reproduction, which contributed to the development of an "unreflective capacity" to experience certain things (e.g., things that promote their survival rather than demise) to be "calling for" or "counting in favor of" certain reactions on our part.[40] On Street's

---

36. Street, "A Darwinian Dilemma for Realist Theories of Value," 153.
37. Street, "What Is Constructivism in Ethics and Metaethics?" 371.
38. Ibid., 370.
39. Street, "What Is Constructivism in Ethics and Metaethics?" 371.
40. Street, "A Darwinian Dilemma for Realist Theories of Value," 117.

account, the relation between selective pressures and evaluative truths can be summed up as follows:

> evaluative truth is a function of how all the evaluative judgments that selective pressures (along with all kinds of other causes) have imparted to us stand up to scrutiny in terms of each other; it is a function of what would emerge from those evaluative judgments in reflective equilibrium.[41]

Thus, joining the chorus of antirealists who stress the importance of the role of evolution in shaping our moral behavior,[42] Street contends that the patterns of normative judgments observable in human beings today largely depend on contingent facts of human evolutionary history such as our reproductively helpful dispositions (e.g., self-survival, kin altruism, and reciprocal altruism). The larger point that she is making is not just that realist theories of value cannot accommodate the forces of natural selection on the content of human values but also that if "there is no relation between evolutionary influences on our evaluative judgements and independent evaluative truth," barring a lucky coincidence between them, we must conclude that "many or most of our evaluative judgements are off track" since these judgments are independent of evaluative truths.[43]

II. Objections

II.1. Korsgaard on Autonomy and Normativity

What exactly does Korsgaard mean by 'autonomy,' when she writes that "autonomy is the only possible source of intrinsic normativity, and so of obligation"?[44] For her, *autonomy* roughly refers to a capacity for reflective endorsement in choosing an object of value without any external causal influence; it is a capacity essential to self-legislation. It is worth mentioning, however, that a number of Kantian realists have objected to the way Korsgaard and other Kantian constructivists have interpreted Kant's notion of autonomy.[45] I shall not rehearse their arguments here, as it is outside the purview of this chapter.

---

41. Ibid., 154.
42. Contemporary moral philosophers who adopted a Humean ethical outlook under the influence of evolutionary biology include Richard Brandt, Allan Gibbard, Simon Blackburn, and Patricia Churchland.
43. Street, "A Darwinian Dilemma for Realist Theories of Value," 122.
44. Christine M. Korsgaard, "Kant's Analysis of Obligation: The Argument of *Groundwork* I*,"* in *Creating the Kingdom of Ends* (New York: Cambridge University Press, 1996), 65.
45. For Kantian realists' reading of Kant on autonomy, see Karl Ameriks, *Kant and the Fate of Autonomy: Problems in the Appropriation of the Critical Philosophy* (New York: Cambridge University Press, 2000); Paul Guyer, "The Value of Agency: The Practice of Moral Judgment," *Ethics* 106, no. 2 (1996): 404–23; Allen Wood, "Humanity as End in Itself,"

For my purposes, I instead want to focus on Korsgaard's claim that our reflective endorsement makes a reason normative and constitutes an obligation. If this view is correct, reasons for action and obligations are grounded, in the final analysis, in the facts about the subject's evaluative attitudes, more precisely, in what the subject reflectively decides to endorse. The problem, as expressivists remind us, is that to say reflective endorsement or autonomy is the source of all valuing is not the same as to claim that what is valued is intrinsically valuable.[46]

We may start with a not-so-controversial fact. What Korsgaard calls normative reasons are "subject-given" reasons, to use Derek Parfit's term. In Parfit's view, subjectivists about *reasons* (hereafter subjectivists) claim that it is our desires or evaluative commitments that give us reasons to act, whereas objectivists about reasons (hereafter objectivists) see certain facts as giving us "reasons both to have certain desires and aims, and to do whatever might achieve these aims."[47] Subjectivists maintain that it is facts about the *subject's attitudes* toward objects that give us normative reasons, while objectivists focus on mind-independent facts that can render the ends of our desires and aims *objectively* good. In fact, Korsgaard herself makes this point clear:

> We can value something only if it has some form of natural appeal to us, where 'natural appeal' is to be understood broadly—it satisfies one of our needs, it is the kind of thing we are capable of being interested in, it may have aesthetic appeal. Something in us has to answer to something in the object in order for the object to be valuable.[48]

Plainly speaking, this means that our normative reasons for action are grounded in what *we* as agents value or care about. Therefore, normative reasons are all subject-given reasons.

But, as Allan Gibbard points out, it is one thing that "an expressivist can agree that the will is the source of thinking oneself obligated; that to think oneself obligated is to reflectively accept a demand or requirement. It's quite another claim that the will is the source of validly being

---

Proceedings of the Eighth International Kant Congress 1 (1995): 301–19; Robert Stern, "Constructivism and the Argument From Autonomy," in *Constructivism in Practical Philosophy*, ed. Jimmy Lenman and Yonatan Shemmer (Oxford University Press, 2012), 119–37; John E. Hare, *God's Call: Moral Realism, God's Commands, and Human Autonomy* (Grand Rapids: Wm. B. Eerdmans Publishing Co., 2001).

46. Allan Gibbard notes "[t]hat humanity is the source of all valuing is fine, but does valuing make for value? An argument like this conflates the two." Allan Gibbard, "Morality as Consistency in Living: Korsgaard's Kantian Lectures," *Ethics* 110, no. 1 (1999): 150.
47. Derek Parfit, *On What Matters: Volume One* (Oxford: Oxford University Press, 2013), 45.
48. Christine M. Korsgaard, "Internalism and the Sources of Normativity," in *Constructions of Practical Reason: Interviews on Moral and Political Philosophy*, ed. Herlinde Pauer-Studer, 1st ed. (Stanford: Stanford University Press, 2002), 65.

obligated."[49] In other words, there is a meaningful difference between *thinking* oneself obligated in virtue of one's reflective endorsement—the view that expressivists would accept—and one, in fact, being obligated in virtue of her reflective endorsement—a view that expressivists would not accept. The former could simply be understood by expressivists to mean that normative claims express the subject's noncognitive attitudes of acceptance of some rules or norms,[50] while the latter makes the *truth* of normative claims dependent on the attitudes of the subject. Gibbard's point is that Korsgaard conflates the source of *valuing* with the source of *value*. The latter does not logically follow from the former.

Is Gibbard right here? From the fact that I value a particular object, does it follow (1) that I necessarily value myself as a reflective valuer and (2) that any human being as a reflective valuer is intrinsically valuable? Concerning (1), there may be a subtle but important difference between "I value some things" and "I necessarily think of myself as valuable since I value some things." The former is a *prudential* or *contingent* judgment made *for my pursuit of my own purposes*, while the latter is a *moral* judgment on *my existence*.[51] Korsgaard seems to be saying that this moral judgment is entailed by the prudential judgment, but it is hard to see how that is the case. Suppose that a person is buying a gun to kill himself. He regards the purchase of this gun to be valuable for his practical purposes. Does this entail that he also necessarily values his existence? I think not.

Now let's consider (2). Does it follow from "I necessarily *think* of myself as valuable" that "I am intrinsically valuable"? It seems that the transition from the first statement to the second statement requires the acceptance of a metaethical assumption that the truth of normative judgments depends on the subject's attitudes. But it is not clear why one must accept this assumption. To see this, imagine that self-learning artificial intelligences have evolved to think of themselves as intrinsically valuable. Do we human beings have good reason to believe that they are indeed intrinsically valuable? It seems that Korsgaard's argument only works if one accepts the truth of the assumption that the source of "value" (as opposed to "valuing") lies with any self-thinking being that values itself. But it's not clear why this assumption is true.

Next, we shall look at Korsgaard's and other constructivists' idea of *procedure* as a heuristic device to deliver normative truths. The idea is elegantly simple: if we all have agreed to a procedure to deliver the truth of certain claims, we also have to accept the outcome of the procedure. In Korsgaard's case, this means that we idealize the procedure of reflective

---

49. Gibbard, "Morality as Consistency in Living," 149.
50. For norm-expressivism, see Allan F. Gibbard, *Thinking How to Live* (Cambridge: Harvard University Press, 2003).
51. I borrow this distinction between prudential and moral judgments from Alan Gewirth. See *Reason and Morality* (Chicago: University of Chicago Press, 1978), 145–6.

deliberation—which she believes we rational agents are logically committed to by virtue of exercising our agency—in order to track the outcome of the procedure, namely, normative truths. This procedure should be *idealized* because it is based on a hypothetical conception of rational agency (obviously, most of us do not think about the process of our practical reasoning when choosing and acting). For this reason, it is often likened to an idealized process of creating rules for a game by those who are would-be players.

Using "game" as an analogy to explain the idealized procedure of reflective deliberation is, however, not without problems. As many constructivists would readily admit, the analogy is not perfect. For most games, people need *a reason* to play a game, and they can opt out if they do not want to play it anymore. Thus, we are told that the kind of idealized procedure of reflective deliberation is different. Kantian constructivists tell us that, since we do not necessarily need a reason to be agents, the idealized procedure is one in which we do not need a reason to participate. The procedure is part and parcel of our rational agency. This implies that no one can opt out of the idealized procedure of reflective deliberation that we engage as rational beings. Even your decision to end your own life would be an act of exercising your agency and thus affirming its value. In this sense, as Korsgaard puts it, "[h]uman beings are *condemned* to choice and action."[52]

But does the fact that we cannot escape the game of reflective deliberation show that we must abide by its outcome? On reflection, it is less than obvious why every agent who must play the game of rational agency must also be committed to playing by its rules. We can imagine, as David Enoch does, someone who decries the very aims of such a game: "I cannot opt out of the game of agency, but I can certainly play it half-heartedly, indeed under protest, without accepting the aims purportedly constitutive of it as mine."[53] Enoch speculates that there could exist another possibility for the agent, besides just having to play the game as it is intended to be played. An agent who values something could be a "shmagent—nonagent who is very similar to agents but who lacks the aim (constitutive of agency but not of "shmagency") of self-constitution."[54]

Let me illustrate Enoch's point with an example. A young man volunteers to join the army because that is what he wants to do for his country in a time of war. He accepts all military rules and swears to obey them, including the order to kill enemy combatants on the battlefield at a moment's notice. But his experiences during the war cause him to lose his faith in the war. He grows depressed and disillusioned with the reality of war. He doesn't want to desert the army either because it is impossible to get out or he doesn't want to be called AWOL (absent without leave), but he also isn't particularly

---

52. Korsgaard, *Self-Constitution*, 1.
53. David Enoch, "Agency, Shmagency: Why Normativity Won't Come from What Is Constitutive of Action," *The Philosophical Review* 115, no. 2 (2006): 50.
54. Ibid., 41.

motivated to fight. Should we call this young man irrational because he no longer has a clear sense of duty? Far from being irrational, the young man may have good reasons not to hold fast to his earlier commitments.

Enoch's "shmagent" is this kind of agent, whom we are more likely to find in the real world than the idealized rational agents in Korsgaard's account. Just because one has no choice but to participate in a game of rational agency, it does not follow that one must play it according to its rules or aims. Rather, the *commitment* to playing the game requires more than logical necessity. The agent needs to see "that the relevant desire is worth having, or that its object is worth pursuing, or that the relevant game is worth playing."[55] If this is correct, the inescapability of rational agency alone does not constitute a normative reason for action. Hence, there is nothing irrational about an agent who is unable to quit the game of rational deliberation but is not committed to playing the game.

II.2. Normative Errors

Can Street's Humean constructivism account for error in evaluative judgment? Given her view that the truth of an evaluative judgment is a function of one's evaluative attitudes, how can one ever be wrong in one's evaluative judgment? To this question, Street replies that even though "the standards determining what counts as an error are understood ultimately to be 'set' by our own evaluative attitudes," there is room for normative error.[56] Such an error happens when a judgment is not among the subject's evaluative judgments in reflective equilibrium.

But this seems an odd way of accounting for normative error. Should the truth of a judgment by a coherent Caligula be solely determined by its overall coherence with his other considered judgments?[57] As I see it, the problem is not so much that there would be some coherent rapists, murderers, or dictators if their evaluative judgments were logically or instrumentally entailed by their other evaluative attitudes. In fact, Street is willing to grant this much; "an ideally coherent Caligula" is possible.[58] Rather, the problem lies in the fact that there is no way to account for an ideally coherent Caligula's normative error *at the time of the error*.

To see why evaluative facts cannot simply follow from within an agent's contingent evaluative attitudes, consider the following example. A teenager

---

55. Ibid., 52.
56. Street, "A Darwinian Dilemma for Realist Theories of Value," 153.
57. In his critique of Street, Thomas Scanlon says that the question we should be asking is not "Will this judgment be among those I would arrive at if I reached reflective equilibrium?" but rather "Is this judgment correct?" See Thomas M. Scanlon, "The Appeal and Limits of Constructivism," in *Constructivism in Practical Philosophy*, ed. Jimmy Lenman and Yonatan Shemmer (New York: Oxford University Press, 2012), 241.
58. Street, "What Is Constructivism in Ethics and Metaethics?" 377.

rebels against her parents since they constantly deny the objects of her desires. She wants to fit in with her peers by doing what they ask her to do. But her evaluative judgments are repeatedly called into question by her parents, who want to keep their child out of harm's way. Many years have passed since then, and now the woman better understands why her parents were not amenable to her demands. As a mother of her own children, she now deeply regrets her teenage evaluative judgments. I imagine such a story is not uncommon. Sometimes, people reflect on their past evaluative judgments and wish they had made different judgments. But why would they wish that? Is it because they believe that their past judgments didn't follow from their evaluative attitudes in reflective equilibrium at that time? Or is it because they believe that they could have made different evaluative judgments despite their past contingent evaluative attitudes?

As I see it, the answer does not have to be "either–or." It is possible that we sometimes make a normative error because we have not reflectively scrutinized our (first-order) desires from within their own practical standpoint. It is also possible, as R. Jay Wallace points out, that when making a normative error, we knew the truth of the relevant counterfactual judgment but failed to revise our actual judgment accordingly, due to some motivational want.[59] Suppose that the teenager mentioned earlier had a strong ego and did not want to admit that she was wrong in her evaluative judgments, though she knew quite well that she was. That would hardly be a case of procedural error in which one comes to endorse mistaken conclusions from her actual evaluative attitudes (or normative commitments). Rather, it is a case of what I would call *volitional irrationality* in which one intentionally resists changing her evaluative judgment, fully conscious of the fact that her judgment is wrong.

However, the typical constructive response to the problem of normative error is simply to regard it as a procedural error. Street is no exception. She considers normative error a failure of logical or instrumental entailment. In this view, our correct normative judgments are ones that we would have arrived at as a result of reflective scrutiny of our own evaluative attitudes. But the problem, as I mentioned earlier, is that not all normative errors may be a result of a procedural error. If this is true, our own evaluative attitudes may not reliably track all normative errors.

---

59. R. Jay Wallace raises several interesting objections from the problem of error against constructivists. One of his objections, leveled against Korsgaard, problematizes a kind of normative error called "recalcitrant irrationality." For this type of error, an agent "*actually acknowledges* that the truth of the relevant counterfactual judgment, but fails in fact to revise their [his and his group's actual] attitudes accordingly." In other words, Wallace is pointing out that not all normative errors are due to procedural errors. R. Jay Wallace, "Constructivism About Normativity: Some Pitfalls," in *Constructivism in Practical Philosophy*, ed. James Lenman and Yonatan Shemmer (New York: Oxford University Press, 2012), 36–7; italics mine.

From a different angle, we may also see that the problem of normative error is related to the problem of normative truth since an error in judgment implies getting the truth wrong. On Street's antirealist, constructivist view, normative truths depend on evaluative standards entailed by our actual evaluative attitudes. Thus, normative truths must conform to our evaluative attitudes.

But then where do our evaluative attitudes really come from? As discussed earlier, Street explains that they come primarily from our motivational system, which is shaped by evolutionary history, or more specifically, the process of natural selection. As I see it, the real force of Street's constructivist view is not so much its rejection of non-natural or supernatural *entities* by virtue of which evaluative judgments are thought to be made true or false. Rather, the real force is in its challenge to both non-naturalist and naturalist kinds of value realists to explain, if mind-independent moral facts exist at all, what these facts are really for. Given the availability of good scientific explanations for evaluative attitudes, according to which Darwinian selective pressures have imparted to us to scrutinize what we value and what we take to be true for our reproductive fitness, we must ask not only what causal explanations realists can offer but also how their explanations are compatible with such scientific explanations. The problem, Street argues, is that realists do not offer any such causal explanations. Realists must then "view the causes described by these explanations as distorting, choosing the path that leads to normative skepticism or the claim of an incredible coincidence."[60]

There isn't enough space here to provide a full discussion of Street's criticism of rival views, but let's consider one critical point of her claim that there is a relation between evolutionary influences on our evaluative attitudes and evaluative truths. In my view, however, it is one thing to say that there are evolutionary influences on the shaping of our evaluative attitudes but quite another to argue that all evaluative truths can only be explained by evolutionary biology *because* we are all products of natural selection. From the fact that we are products of biological evolution, it does not follow that all of our cognitive and other mental functions can be sufficiently explained by evolutionary biology. Even if the process of natural selection along with the development of language contributed to human cognitive capacities, I am skeptical of the claim that an evolutionary theory of human cognition can sufficiently explain reason's ability to grasp the truth of various kinds of judgments (e.g., scientific, mathematical, and logical).

My skepticism stems in part from the fact that our early ancestors, just like us, seem to have recognized the self-evidence, though defeasible, of their sensory and intellectual perception, with or without a relationship with their survival. The claim that only through the recognition of the processes

---

60. Street, "A Darwinian Dilemma for Realist Theories of Value," 155.

of natural selection have we come to accept the reliability of our cognitive capacities (including our sensory and intellectual perceptions) seems counterintuitive, given that we tend to trust our senses and reason in detecting and avoiding danger in the first place. As Thomas Nagel notes, "[e]ventually the attempt to understand oneself in evolutionary, naturalistic terms must bottom out in something that is grasped as valid in itself—something without which the evolutionary understanding would not be possible."[61] Of course, this objection isn't by any means a wholesale rejection of Darwin's theory of evolution. It simply means that there is a limit to which we can use such a theory to explain how the truth of various judgments is to be determined.

Instead, we may conceive a two-track approach to moral facts, one via pure practical reason and the other via the emotions shaped by our evolutionary history. On this approach, the former is viewed as providing cognitive access to mind-independent moral facts, while the latter is considered important for its independent ability to render evidential support for moral judgments. Very briefly, the basic idea is that emotions could provide, under appropriate circumstances, non-inferential evidential justification for moral judgments.[62] For instance, our intuition about the wrongness and badness of murder could receive additional evidential support if we have a strong negative emotional response to murder. In this sense, moral intuitions and emotions are not necessarily opposed to each other, though it is certainly possible that they may sometimes come into conflict. Nor do the existence and the importance of emotions make moral intuitions unnecessary or vice versa. We may liken the relationship between intuitions and emotions to getting an informed opinion from two different doctors. Just as seeking a second opinion from another doctor, when diagnosed with a serious disease, is always a good idea, intuitions and emotions can provide independent evidential support for our moral judgments and thus can possibly strengthen our confidence in the judgments. So understood, Street's claim that evolutionary biology renders the purpose of mind-independent moral facts gratuitous appears to be shortsighted.

In sum, both Korsgaard and Street argue that normative judgments are not made true in virtue of some mind-independent facts but by the outcome of a correct deliberative procedure, involving solely what is constitutive of agency from the first-person point of view. In response, I have been making a case that constructivists' efforts to ground normativity in facts about our evaluative attitudes are not without serious problems. In the next section, I offer an alternative framework for understanding normativity that is characteristically realist about value and objectivist in nature.

---

61. Thomas Nagel, *Mind & Cosmos: Why the Materialist Neo-Darwinian Conception of Nature Is Almost Certainly False* (New York: Oxford University Press, 2012), 81.
62. Robert Audi, *Moral Perception* (Princeton: Princeton University Press, 2013), 136–40.

III. Grounding Normative Facts: A Realist Account of Value

Now let me offer a brief sketch of a realist account of *evaluative* judgments.[63] According to this account, normativity can and should be grounded in facts that are independent of the valuing subject's practical point of view. As I will explain shortly, there are at least two ways of grounding the normativity of evaluative judgments: an axiological grounding and a theological grounding. Let's consider each in turn.

III.1. An Axiological Grounding of Evaluative Facts

Contrary to Korsgaard's claim, my position is that it is not our evaluative attitudes as valuing agents that confer "objective goodness" on certain objects. Instead, what possesses objective goodness has this goodness in virtue of its inherent properties. In this picture, we human beings are *not* in the position of determining what properties should belong to an object. The question of whether a thing has certain inherent properties is independent of whatever attitudes we have toward it or the reason we de facto value any other particular objects. Moreover, I take the primary bearers of intrinsic value to be some concrete experiences of the objects that are good in themselves, and I take it that these objects have intrinsic value in virtue of their inherent good-making properties.[64]

Analogically speaking, consider the aesthetic value of beauty. Suppose we agree that beauty is an intrinsic value, which makes the thing that possesses it choice worthy or commendable. One may, for example, find beauty in the images of stars and galaxies captured by the Hubble Space Telescope. A subjectivist and an objectivist about value, each informed by scientific knowledge, may respond to these images in different ways. A subjectivist might say that the beauty of the universe is in the eye of the human appraiser, contingent on her actual mood or her invested interest in astrophysics, but an objectivist could explain its aesthetic value as grounded in the many properties of the universe such as the symmetry, gravity, and conservation of the energy in the universe that produce a positive experience of the universe. Although it is human beings who discover many facts about the universe and attribute certain properties to it, the truth is that these properties would have been there even if no one discovered them. For instance, one may call hydrogen with a different name, but it will not change its distinct features or its existence. More important, the universe has beauty in virtue of these

---

63. Normative judgments involve evaluative (including character judgments), and deontic judgments; some normative judgments are about the good, and others are about the right or obligation. The focus of my discussion in this chapter is confined to the discussion of normativity in evaluative judgments. I shall leave the discussion on deontic judgments for another time.
64. See Robert Audi, *Reasons, Rights, and Values* (Cambridge: Cambridge University Press, 2015), 42–45.

properties, as the properties were concretely realized in the creation and are still being realized in the ongoing expansion of the universe.

Likewise, there is a dependence relation between what is intrinsically good and its inherent properties. Just as what is beautiful is experienced as such in virtue of its inherent properties (e.g., harmony or tonal color), what is intrinsically good also is experienced as such in virtue of its inherent, good-making properties (e.g., the agent's intention). This implies that whatever is intrinsically good cannot be considered intrinsically good without its being experienced by us in some way *and* without its being appropriately grounded in some subvenient properties. For instance, not all pleasurable experiences would be intrinsically good if some of these experiences involve actions that lack good will on the part of the agent who experiences the pleasure. For instance, the pleasure one experiences in torturing another cannot be intrinsically good since it is not appropriately grounded in some necessary subvenient properties such as the agent's good will. This is an important point because it means that what is intrinsically good is not reducible to some pleasurable mental states.

There remains another point which must be mentioned regarding the relationship between what is intrinsically good and its inherent properties. As G. E. Moore explains, when a thing that has intrinsic value has various parts, the sum of their values is not the same as the value of the thing in question as a whole.[65] Just as the beauty of a painting is dependent on its inherent properties (e.g., color transparency, luminosity, etc.) but is irreducible to each or the sum of these properties, intrinsic value is not quantitative but "organic" in nature.[66] A state of affairs may involve one's experiencing a steady stream of intense pleasure, but such a pleasurable experience alone does not make the state of affairs intrinsically good. For it is quite possible for such a pleasurable experience to be *unfitting* or *inappropriate* for its object (e.g., necrophilia or pedophilia). The assumption is that some feelings or emotions may be deemed, on due reflection, unfitting or inappropriate to an object, depending on their adequacy or congruence to the object.[67] Thus, as Robert Audi points out, "the *content* of a pleasure is one of the conditions

---

65. G. E. Moore, *Principia Ethica* (Cambridge University Press, 1993), 36.
66. Ibid.
67. Franz Brentano, for instance, speaks of "congruence" between the concept of an object and the love that is experienced as correct on the contemplation of the concept of the object. Franz Clemens Brentano, "Loving and Hating," in *The Origin of Our Knowledge of Right and Wrong*, trans. Roderick M. Chisholm (London: Routledge & Kegan Paul, 1969), 147. Roderick Chisholm explains the correctness of an emotion as fittingness. He formulates the idea this way: "To say that a pro attitude is *fitting* or *appropriate* to an object A is to say that the contemplation of A requires a pro attitude toward A." Roderick M. Chisholm, *Brentano and Intrinsic Value* (New York: Cambridge University Press, 1986), 52–3; italics in the original.

important for determining whether its presence adds to or subtracts from the overall intrinsic value of an experience of which it is an element."[68]

Now suppose we agree that there exist things that have intrinsic value. What does this mean in practice? The short answer is that, if there is something that is intrinsically good, it implies that this thing has normative force since the concept of good itself is action-guiding. But some might say that it is normative only for those who have the desire for it, denying that things that have intrinsic value can provide reasons for action for everyone. The skeptics of intrinsic value often argue that what makes something intrinsically valuable is ultimately our own caring about it, that is, our own valuing it.[69] It is through such a caring that we "infuse the world with importance" and provide ourselves with reasons for action.[70]

But I beg to differ. The skeptics often fail to see, on the one hand, that what is intrinsically good is indeed good for everyone and, on the other, that what is intrinsically good provides a reason for action, not in the absolute, exceptionless sense but in a *prima facie* sense. Intrinsic value has special significance for practical reason because one's experience of the thing that has intrinsic value is *choice-worthy*. Things (e.g., pleasure, knowledge, or health) that have intrinsic value are to be valued for their own sake because they make the life that have them choice-worthy, meaning that it is always preferable, other things being equal, to choose our having them to our not having them. The general idea is that no matter whose life is concerned, a life with intrinsically good things is more worthwhile than a life without them. But why is that? It is because the experiences of intrinsically valuable things contribute to human flourishing (but not limited to only humans). Health is not intrinsically good only for those who care about their health; it is essential to everyone's well-being. To regard intrinsic value merely as a function of our evaluative attitudes is to overlook an important connection between what is intrinsically good and the necessary conditions of human well-being.

Granted that what is intrinsically good is intrinsically normative, does it follow from this that we must bring it about, regardless of our circumstances? It should be noted that what is intrinsically good (or bad) provides a reason for action, but this reason is not indefeasible.[71] That is to say, what is intrinsically good provides a prima facie, rather than an "absolute," reason for action. For instance, having a pleasurable experience, other things being equal, can be a basic reason for action. But being an intrinsically good thing by itself does not necessarily constitute a *moral* reason for action.

---

68. Robert Audi, *The Good in the Right: A Theory of Intuition and Intrinsic Value* (Princeton: Princeton University Press, 2005), 128; italics mine.
69. Harry G. Frankfurt, *The Reasons of Love* (Princeton: Princeton University Press, 2009), 12–13, 23–6.
70. Ibid., 23.
71. Audi, *Reasons, Rights, and Values*, 66.

Imagine that you are finally bringing someone to justice in court for many years of abuse during your childhood. This experience would be painful since it would involve reliving painful memories through the recounting of your abuse. To the extent that extremely painful experience is an instance of intrinsic disvalue, you have a reason to avoid taking legal action. But you also have other moral reasons (e.g., justice, or protection of other minors) that would strongly support your action. The point is that considerations of the intrinsically good/bad can and should be a basis of reasons for action without necessarily being moral reasons.

III.2. A Theological Grounding of Evaluative Facts

In this section, I would like to explore another way of grounding evaluative facts with a particular focus on the domain of morality. This option is available for theists who believe there are object-given facts about moral value. I understand that not all theists need be realists about moral value, as different conceptions of God might entail different views on the source and nature of moral value.[72] But *if* one is a moral realist *and* affirms a traditional theological understanding of God—according to which God is not only omnipotent, omniscient, and benevolent but also very much involved in the governance of everything that God created—then there is good reason to connect the ground of moral goodness to God's will.[73] For it is commonly believed by many theists—especially those who belong to the three monotheistic religions, viz., Judaism, Christianity, and Islam—that what we ought to value must conform to the will of God, rather than to our own will. Such religious practices as prayer, confession of sins, and penance can illustrate this belief.

The question for theists is how they should understand the dependence relation, if any, between moral goodness and divine will. Here I would briefly explore one possibility of such a relation. We may start sketching the dependence relation between moral goodness and conforming to divine will by distinguishing what God wills for Godself and what God wills for us to will and then relating the latter to moral goodness. One reason for this distinction is *not* to characterize moral goodness as consisting in simply conforming to God's will as such. John Hare uses John Duns Scotus's example

---

72. Some theists are physicalists who believe that everything is physical or supervenes on the physical. They often seek naturalistic accounts of morality, using insights from evolutionary theory and cultural anthropology. Nancey Murphy, for instance, says, "I argue that our capacity for religious experience is enabled by culture and by our complex neural systems, just as is our capacity for morality." Nancey C. Murphy, *Bodies and Souls, or Spirited Bodies?* (Cambridge: Cambridge University Press, 2006), 5–6.
73. Some theists are simply antirealists about value, though they may accept traditional characteristics of God as described here. Other theists could be reductive realists who reduce moral properties to natural properties.

of Christ's death to show why the distinction between the two kinds of divine willing is necessary. Hare writes,

> He [Scotus] gives the example of those who willed that Christ should suffer and die, something that Christ himself also willed (since his Father did not let that cup pass from him). Nonetheless, those who willed this sinned, as Christ showed by asking his Father to forgive them. What we are to repeat is not just God's willing but God's willing for our willing.[74]

In Hare's view, Scotus's distinction between "God's willing" and "God's willing for our willing" is to underline an important difference between moral goodness and conforming to God's will. For example, God, according to God's providence unknowable to us, may will that our loved one be brought back to God much sooner than we would like. Yet, other things being equal, it would be morally bad if we wish the same. We have to be open to the possibility that the end of God's willing may be different from the end of God's willing for our willing. That is to say, what God wills for Godself and what God wills us to will may not be identical.[75] God may will that one get injured for some unknowable reason, but God may still will that we do not intentionally injure anyone and that we take good care of any injured person, when possible.

Having distinguished God's willing and God's willing for our willing, I contend that theists could understand the latter to include God's intentional *endorsement* of things that are intrinsically good or bad. But unlike subjectivist theories about value, I take it that what is intrinsically good does not depend on what human subjects would prefer (even under ideal situations)[76] but on the facts about what would be good for us, independent of our contingent preferences or attitudes. In section III.1, I explained how we might ground normative judgments objectively without an appeal to our own evaluative attitudes. What is added here is a metaphysical claim that

---

74. Hare, *God's Call*, 74.
75. Now it might be asked why God would will two different ends, one for Godself and the other for us, regarding the same event. We will never be able to fully answer this question, but one may still speculate on the reasons for the possibility of two different ends in divine willing. First, one may note that God, being who God is, has no obligation to serve our interests. But God may have a vested interest in the general well-being of human and other beings under God's providence or within the context of God's greater goals for all of God's creation. Second, the difference between God's willing and God's willing for our willing may sometimes be due to the difference between what Leibniz calls God's antecedent (what God desires to occur) and consequent wills (what God allows to occur). That is to say, as a matter of God's antecedent will, God may will that we always try to respect things that have intrinsic value, but as a matter of God's consequent will, God may permit some evils in the world for the best, even though it may seem difficult to reconcile with God's antecedent will. See Gottfried Wilhelm Freiherr von Leibniz, *The Philosophical Works of Leibniz* (New Haven: Tuttle, Morehouse & Taylor, 1908), 289–90.
76. See Miller's essay in this volume for problems with non-theistic versions of constructivism.

the objective, axiological grounds of moral goodness are indeed the same grounds on which God wills us to will.

One way to understand this claim is to hold the following: it is for the good of the whole creation that God wills us to will things that are necessary for the flourishing of all creation. According to a traditional Christian doctrine, God is the Creator of all finite beings whose existence is completely dependent upon God's will. God is also understood as the Lawgiver and Judge who has the ultimate authority over the whole of creation, including all human agents. But God does not simply issue some moral commands; God also values things. In Genesis 1, God is depicted as valuing God's own creation: "God saw everything that he had made, and indeed, it was very good" (Gen. 1:31). In fact, *after* each day of God's creative work, it is repeatedly said that "God saw that it was good" (Gen. 1:4. 1:10, 12, 18, 21, 25). This seems to imply that there was something about what had just been created that pleased or satisfied God. If we suppose that God's evaluative practice is similar to how a potter evaluates his own creations from clay (Isa. 64:8), God may render evaluative judgments by considering how created things measure up to God's particular purposes for them. If so, God's evaluative judgments involve more than merely God's approval or God's character. God evaluates an object on the basis of its inherent qualities in light of God's particular purposes.

To be sure, this does not remove the possibility that God responds to things because God already has certain dispositions towards or providential plans for God's created order. Nevertheless, it does show that God's evaluative judgments also have independent grounds of evaluative judgments in addition to God's dispositions or character. Thus, it may be said that when it comes to moral goodness, God makes evaluative judgments at least partly in virtue of these independent grounds.

What might those grounds be? I submit that they are natural facts concerning the flourishing of life in general. Granting that God is omniscient and omnibenevolent, God would know the natural and social conditions under which human life and other forms of life can flourish, and God would desire that we also desire the same conditions. In this view, moral goodness is not ontologically equivalent to a theological property such as God's will or character. Nor is moral goodness ontologically reducible to certain natural facts. Rather, moral goodness is grounded in natural facts whereby the former is in consequence of, rather than collapsed into, the latter. It is in virtue of natural facts (e.g., feeding the hungry) that moral goodness is ascribed to the character and actions of human beings.

Consider, for instance, the parable of the Good Samaritan in the New Testament. In this biblical narrative (Luke 10:25–37), Jesus helps his disciples see that the neighbor is the one who showed mercy to the victim of robbery by bandaging his wounds, taking him to an inn, paying for his stay, and making sure that he would be taken care of by the innkeeper. Notice here that Jesus explains what a morally good action is without appealing to

God's will or equating the nature of the action to some particular natural facts. This parable illustrates not only how moral goodness can be grounded in natural facts but also how these facts can disclose the content of what God wills us to will.

In short, I contend that there is a way to ground moral goodness in God's willing for our willing without undermining the realist view about the existence of evaluative truths independent of human attitudes.

IV. Conclusion

In this chapter, I have considered two versions of constructivism that take normative facts to be the logical or instrumental entailment from within the practical standpoint of a valuing agent. For Korsgaard and Street, the procedure involves some kind of reflective deliberation through which one arrives at normative truths as something to be logically or instrumentally entailed from an agent's own practical point of view. Though Korsgaard and Street disagree as to whether such a procedure itself can deliver substantive (as opposed to purely formal) normative judgments, both hold to the view that there can be no normative facts apart from the valuing agent. I have then raised doubts about the plausibility of normativity derived from one's evaluative attitudes.

Though my chapter was clearly intended to challenge a central tenet of constructivism that normative facts, including moral facts, are a human construction, I am *not* committed to the view that all parts of reality exist independently of human construction. From games to literary works, there are things that we humans construct in order to make our life more fun or enjoyable. But, we need not be a constructivist about value. I maintain that there are value-based reasons for action, grounded in the good-making inherent properties of objects. My view is that these object-given reasons ought to guide our actions because they tell us what is objectively good for all human beings. Furthermore, I think that there is good reason for theists to accept such a realist account of value instead of constructivist kinds. For a traditional theological conception of God, it may be the case that God has a vested interest in our welfare neither because God simply chooses to value us nor because we bear some qualitative resemblance to God but because God sees our welfare as contributing to God's larger plan for all creation.

Bibliography

Ameriks, Karl. *Kant and the Fate of Autonomy: Problems in the Appropriation of the Critical Philosophy.* New York: Cambridge University Press, 2000.

Audi, Robert. *The Good in the Right: A Theory of Intuition and Intrinsic Value.* Princeton: Princeton University Press, 2005.

———. *Moral Perception.* Princeton: Princeton University Press, 2013.

———. *Reasons, Rights, and Values.* Cambridge: Cambridge University Press, 2015.

Brentano, Franz Clemens. "Loving and Hating." In *The Origin of Our Knowledge of Right and Wrong*, translated by Roderick M. Chisholm. London: Routledge & Kegan Paul, 1969.

Chisholm, Roderick M. *Brentano and Intrinsic Value*. New York: Cambridge University Press, 1986.

Enoch, David. "Agency, Shmagency: Why Normativity Won't Come from What Is Constitutive of Action." *The Philosophical Review* 115, no. 2 (2006): 169–98.

Frankfurt, Harry G. *The Reasons of Love*. Princeton: Princeton University Press, 2009.

Gewirth, Alan. *Reason and Morality*. Chicago: University of Chicago Press, 1978.

Gibbard, Allan. "Morality as Consistency in Living: Korsgaard's Kantian Lectures." *Ethics* 110, no. 1 (1999): 140–64.

———. *Thinking How to Live*. Cambridge: Harvard University Press, 2003.

Guyer, Paul. "The Value of Agency: The Practice of Moral Judgment." *Ethics* 106, no. 2 (1996): 404–23.

Hare, John E. *God's Call: Moral Realism, God's Commands, and Human Autonomy*. Grand Rapids: Wm. B. Eerdmans Publishing Co., 2001.

Korsgaard, Christine M. "Aristotle and Kant on the Source of Value." In *Creating the Kingdom of Ends*. New York: Cambridge University Press, 1996.

———. "An Introduction to the Ethical, Political, and Religious Thought of Kant." In *Creating the Kingdom of Ends*. New York: Cambridge University Press, 1996.

———. "Kant's Analysis of Obligation: The Argument of Groundwork I." In *Creating the Kingdom of Ends*. New York: Cambridge University Press, 1996.

———. "Skepticism About Practical Reason." In *Creating the Kingdom of Ends*. New York: Cambridge University Press, 1996.

———. "Source of Value." In *Creating the Kingdom of Ends*. New York: Cambridge University Press, 1996.

———. *The Sources of Normativity*. Cambridge and New York: Cambridge University Press, 1996.

———. "Two Distinctions in Goodness." In *Creating the Kingdom of Ends*. New York: Cambridge University Press, 1996.

———. "Internalism and the Sources of Normativity." In *Constructions of Practical Reason: Interviews on Moral and Political Philosophy*, edited by Herlinde Pauer-Studer, 1st ed. Stanford: Stanford University Press, 2002.

———. "Facing the Animal You See in the Mirror." *The Harvard Review of Philosophy* 16, no. 1 (2009): 4–9.

———. *Self-Constitution: Agency, Identity, and Integrity*. New York: Oxford University Press, 2009.

———. "A Kantian Case for Animal Rights." In *Animal Law—Tier Und Recht: Developments and Perspectives in the 21st Century. Entwicklungen Und Perspektiven Im 21. Jahrhundert*, edited by Margot Michel, Daniela Kühne, and Julia Hänni, Bilingual ed. Zurich: Berlin: Dike Publishers, 2012.

Leibniz, Gottfried Wilhelm Freiherr von. *The Philosophical Works of Leibnitz*. New Haven: Tuttle, Morehouse & Taylor, 1908.

Lenman, James, and Yonatan Shemmer. "Introduction." In *Constructivism in Practical Philosophy*. Oxford: Oxford University Press, 2012.

Miller, Christian. "Motivational Internalism." *Philosophical Studies* 139, no. 2 (2008): 233–55.

Moore, G. E. *Principia Ethica*. Cambridge: Cambridge University Press, 1993.

Murphy, Nancey C. *Bodies and Souls, or Spirited Bodies?* Cambridge: Cambridge University Press, 2006.
Nagel, Thomas. *Mind & Cosmos: Why the Materialist Neo-Darwinian Conception of Nature Is Almost Certainly False.* New York: Oxford University Press, 2012.
Niebuhr, H. Richard. *Radical Monotheism and Western Culture: With Supplementary Essays.* Louisville: Westminster John Knox Press, 1993.
Parfit, Derek. *On What Matters: Volume One.* Oxford: Oxford University Press, 2013.
Rawls, John. "Kantian Constructivism in Moral Theory." *Journal of Philosophy* 77, no. 9 (1980): 515–72.
Scanlon, Thomas M. "The Appeal and Limits of Constructivism." In *Constructivism in Practical Philosophy*, edited by Jimmy Lenman and Yonatan Shemmer, 226–42. New York: Oxford University Press, 2012.
Stern, Robert. "Constructivism and the Argument from Autonomy." In *Constructivism in Practical Philosophy*, edited by Jimmy Lenman and Yonatan Shemmer, 119–37. Oxford: Oxford University Press, 2012.
Street, Sharon. "A Darwinian Dilemma for Realist Theories of Value." *Philosophical Studies* 127, no. 1 (2006): 109–66.
———. "Constructivism About Reasons." *Oxford Studies in Metaethics* 3 (2008): 207–45.
———. "What Is Constructivism in Ethics and Metaethics?" *Philosophy Compass* 5, no. 5 (May 1, 2010): 363–84.
———. "Coming to Terms with Contingency: Humean Constructivism About Practical Reason." In *Constructivism in Practical Philosophy*, edited by James Lenman and Yonatan Shemmer, 40–59. New York: Oxford University Press, 2012.
———. "Challenges to Moral and Religious Belief: Disagreement and Evolution." In *Challenges to Moral and Religious Belief: Disagreement and Evolution*, edited by Michael Bergmann and Patrick Kain. New York: Oxford University Press, 2014.
Wallace, R. Jay. "Constructivism About Normativity: Some Pitfalls." In *Constructivism in Practical Philosophy*, edited by James Lenman and Yonatan Shemmer, 18–39. New York: Oxford University Press, 2012.
Williams, Bernard. "Internal and External Reasons." In *Moral Luck*, 101–13. Cambridge and New York: Cambridge University Press, 1982.
Wood, Allen. "Humanity as End in Itself." *Proceedings of the Eighth International Kant Congress* 1 (1995): 301–19.

Contributors

David A. Clairmont (PhD, University of Chicago) is an associate professor of theological ethics in the Department of Theology at the University of Notre Dame. He is the author of *Moral Struggle and Religious Ethics: On the Person as Classic in Comparative Theological Contexts* (Wiley-Blackwell, 2011) and co-editor (with Don S. Browning) of *American Religions and the Family: How Faith Traditions Cope with Modernization and Democracy* (Columbia University Press, 2007). His articles on comparative theological ethics and the traditions of Catholic and Buddhist ethics and spirituality have appeared in the *Journal of the Society of Christian Ethics*, the *Journal of the American Academy of Religion*, and the *Journal of Religious Ethics*. Since 2012, Clairmont has served as the director of the Master of Theological Studies program at Notre Dame.

Molly Farneth (PhD, Princeton University) is an assistant professor of religion at Haverford College. Her teaching and research focus on modern Western religious thought, with particular attention to the relationship between religion and politics and the ways that members of religiously diverse communities confront ethical conflicts across their differences. Her book, *Hegel's Social Ethics: Religion, Conflict, and Rituals of Reconciliation* (Princeton University Press, 2017), reconsiders Hegel's view of conflict and reconciliation and argues for its relevance for contemporary democracies.

Kevin Jung (PhD, University of Chicago) is an associate professor of Christian ethics at Wake Forest University School of Divinity. He is the author of *Christian Ethics and Commonsense Morality: An Intuitionist Account* (Routledge, 2014) and *Ethical Theory and Responsibility Ethics* (Peter Lang, 2011), as well as other journal articles. He is also the co-editor of *Doing Justice to Mercy: Religion, Law, and Criminal Justice* (University of Virginia Press, 2007) and *Humanity Before God: Contemporary Faces of Jewish, Christian, and Islamic Ethics* (Fortress Press, 2006). Jung works at the intersection of moral philosophy and religious ethics, with research interests in moral epistemology, moral ontology, and action theory.

Kevin Kinghorn (PhD, University of Oxford) is a professor of philosophy and religion at Asbury Theological Seminary. Prior to that appointment he served as a tutor in philosophy and philosophical theology at Wycliffe Hall, University of Oxford. He has published articles primarily in the fields of philosophy of religion and moral philosophy and is the author of *The Decision of Faith: Can Christian Beliefs Be Freely Chosen* (T & T Clark, 2005) and *A Framework for the Good* (University of Notre Dame, 2016).

Charles Lockwood (PhD, Harvard University) is a research fellow at the Institute for Religion and Critical Inquiry at Australian Catholic University. His research and teaching interests lie at the intersection of theology, philosophy of religion, and ethics in the modern West. His current research focuses on the theological and philosophical legacies of Immanuel Kant's notion of autonomy, situated in relation to debates about modernity, secularization, and religion's role in public life. His articles and reviews have appeared in *Harvard Theological Review* and *The Journal of Religion*, and he is also a contributor to the forthcoming *Oxford Handbook of Political Theology*.

Christian B. Miller (PhD, University of Notre Dame) is A.C. Reid Professor of Philosophy at Wake Forest University and Director of the Character Project (www.thecharacterproject.com), which was funded by $5.6 million in grants from the John Templeton Foundation and Templeton World Charity Foundation. He is the author of more than 75 papers as well as three books with Oxford University Press, *Moral Character: An Empirical Theory* (2013), *Character and Moral Psychology* (2014), and *The Character Gap: How Good Are We?* (2017). He is also the editor or co-editor of *Essays in the Philosophy of Religion* (Oxford University Press, 2006); *Character: New Directions from Philosophy, Psychology, and Theology* (Oxford University Press, 2015); *Moral Psychology, Volume V: Virtue and Character* (MIT Press, 2017); *Integrity, Honesty, and Truth-Seeking* (Oxford University Press, forthcoming); and *The Continuum Companion to Ethics* (Continuum Press, 2011).

Paul Weithman (PhD, Harvard University) is Glynn Family Honors Collegiate Professor of Philosophy at the University of Notre Dame, where he has taught since 1990. He is director of the Honors Program and the Program in Philosophy, Politics and Economics. His most recent book is *Rawls, Political Liberalism and Reasonable Faith* (Cambridge University Press, 2016). He is also the author of *Religion and the Obligations of Citizenship* (Cambridge University Press, 2002), which won the North American Society for Social Philosophy's best book award, and of *Why Political Liberalism? On John Rawls's Political Turn* (Oxford University Press, 2010), which won the David and Elaine Spitz Prize for the best book in liberal and democratic theory published in its year. He has also written many articles in moral and political philosophy.

Index

absolute spirit 16, 79, 134, 136–7
Adams, Robert 44, 82, 97, 99, 121–3
Allison, Henry 112
Ameriks, Karl 110n20, 120, 188n45
animal rights 181n13, 184
antirealism *see* realism
Aquinas, Thomas 28, 29n9, 129, 151–2, 154, 157, 160–5, 169, 171
Aristotle 28, 168
Audi, Robert 129, 195n62, 196n64, 197, 198n68, 198n71
autonomy 14–15, 18, 64, 104–7, 109–26, 159, 182, 184, 188–9, 206
axiological grounding of evaluative facts 196; *see also* theological grounding of evaluative facts

badness 10, 40, 42–3, 52, 54, 58, 195
Baggett, David 53n9, 55, 58
Bagnoli, Carla 6, 7n28, 63–4, 105n2, 128
Brandom, Robert 6n25, 6n26, 7, 8n31, 12, 65, 68, 70, 74n19, 75–7

categorical imperative 15, 35n25, 48, 67, 70, 106, 113–16, 118–19; *see also* hypothetical imperative
cognitivism 3n11, 4; *see also* noncognitivism
constructivism: Hegelian 6n23, 11, 13, 16, 65–6, 128–9, 132–4, 173; Humean 5n21, 184, 187, 192; hypothetical 88–92; Kantian 9, 21–2, 63–4, 73, 76n22, 80, 104–5, 107n12, 109, 179, 187; ludic 10, 23, 25–6, 30; proceduralist 2, 83n1; restricted 7n28, 93, 178n2; theistic 3, 13–14, 87–94, 96–9, 101; unrestricted 7n28, 7n29, 84, 94, 97, 178
contentful concepts 71

contextualist epistemology 132
conventionalism 12, 74–8

Dahlstrom, Daniel 142–3, 147
distributive justice 9–10, 21–2, 26–7, 29–32, 35n24, 37–8
divine command (God's commands) 11, 13–14, 44n7, 59–60, 86, 99, 121–4, 33, 59–60, 99, 110n20, 122–3, 189n45
divine command theory: divine desire theory 14, 99–100; divine intention theory 14, 99; divine virtue theory 99
divine normative properties argument 88, 90, 92, 94, 96
divine will: God's willing 19, 200, 202; God's willing for our willing 19, 200, 202
Duns Scotus, John 19, 199
duties: imperfect 118; perfect 118
Dworkin, Ronald 30

emotivism 3n10, 4, 69n14
Enoch, David 191–2
error theory *see* moral error theory
Evans, C. Stephen 82, 87n10, 121–2
evolutionary biology 132, 165, 188n42, 194–5
expressivism 3–4, 69n14, 190n50

feasibility condition 10, 34–7
Firth, Roderick 82, 86n8, 92
Frankfurt, Harry G. 140, 146, 198n69

Gibbard, Allan 3n10, 4n16, 41n3, 83n1, 188n42, 189, 190
Good Samaritan (parable of) 201

Hare, John 15, 82, 110n20, 120, 121n31, 123, 189n45, 199–200
Harman, Gilbert 54

Index

Hauerwas, Stanley 8n32, 150
Hegelian constructivism *see* constructivism
Hegelian semantics 63, 65n7
heteronomy 14, 105, 114–17, 124
Hobbes, Thomas 29
Huguccio of Pisa 156
Humean constructivism *see* constructivism
hypothetical constructivism *see* constructivism
hypothetical imperative 48, 113–16, 119; *see also* categorical imperative

ideal observer theory 82, 92
inescapability condition 18
intrinsic value 11, 18, 196–8, 200n75
I–we construal of social practices 75, 76n22

Korsgaard, Christine 2n7, 6n24, 7n28, 17–18, 21n1, 28n6, 29, 33n22, 37n30, 82, 96n34, 105, 178–85, 188–93, 195–6, 202
Kristjánsson, Kristján 56–7

Larmore, Charles 107–9, 125–6
Lewis, C. S. 55–6, 58, 150–1
Lewis, David 85, 153
Lewontin, Richard 159, 165
Locke, John 29
ludic constructivism *see* constructivism

Magnus, Albertus 156
marriage 166–71
meaning, normative 7; *see also* Hegelian semantics
mental statism 42
Moore, G. E. 197
moral error theory 3
moral realism *see* realism
moral relativism 2
Murphy, Mark 82, 98n39, 99n42, 100n46, 100n48

Nagel, Thomas 35n25, 195
natural law: New Natural Law 16, 131; revisionist account of 17, 155
nature: as epistemic limit in context 149; as inherent order 147; as intelligibility based in environment 148; as nature 17, 156, 166, 168; as reason 17, 156, 162, 166–8; as recognition of basic goods 148

New Natural Law *see* natural law
noncognitivism 3n11, 4; *see also* cognitivism
non-reductive naturalism in ethics 129
normative error 18–19, 192–4
normative realism *see* realism
normativity 7n28, 8, 10, 13, 15, 18–19, 21, 25, 29, 64–7, 72n15, 77, 79, 89, 97, 178–96, 202
norm-expressivism 3n10, 190n50

objectivity 2, 5–6, 14, 76n22, 179, 187

Parfit, Derek 189
Philip the Chancellor 156, 162, 166, 168
Pippin, Robert 65n9, 77–8, 135
Porter, Jean 16–17, 21n1, 128, 131n6, 132–3, 140, 148, 150n54, 152n62, 155–75
practical identity 18, 179, 181–3
prescriptivism 3n10, 4, 69

quasi-realism 3n10, 4n15
Quinn, Philip 82, 90n12, 98, 100n46, 100n48

rational entitlement 11–13, 64, 70, 72, 73, 75, 79–80
Rawls, John 14–15, 22, 24n3, 26n4, 28n7, 29, 31–7, 63–4, 76n22, 82, 84, 104–10, 116, 118–19, 124–6, 174, 181
realism: anti- 3, 8, 44; moral 3n9, 9, 14–16, 33, 129, 175; normative 84, 87
reason as testing laws 70
reasons internalism 180
reflective equilibrium 186, 188, 192–3
restricted constructivism *see* constructivism
revisionist account of natural law *see* natural law

Scanlon, Thomas 7n28, 29, 31n17, 82, 192n57
self-constitution 6, 179, 182, 191
Smith, Michael 83–4, 86
social constructivism 6n23
social cooperation game 10, 26–30, 32
Stern, Robert 110n20, 121n32, 122n33, 123, 189n45

Stout, Jeffrey 8n32, 12, 16–17, 63n1, 65n7, 72n15, 76, 128, 132–40, 142, 145, 147–66, 170–4
Street, Sharon 2n8, 5, 7n28, 7n29, 17–18, 41, 64n6, 82–5, 94–6, 178–9, 184–8, 192–5, 202
subjectivist view of normative truths 187

Testa, Italo 66n9, 141–2
theistic constructivism *see* constructivism
theological grounding of evaluative facts 199; *see also* axiological grounding of evaluative facts
Tiberius, Valerie 82, 93–4
truth: cautionary use of 'true' 149; deflationary 4, 75–6; minimalist account of 13, 75–6; ordinary use of the concept 'true' 12–13, 76; theories of 4n16, 4n18, 8

unrestricted (thoroughgoing) constructivism *see* constructivism

Verhey, Allen 174
volitional irrationality 193
von Schelling, Friedrich Wilhelm Joseph 145

Wallace, R. Jay 193
Walls, Jerry 53n9, 55, 58
welfarism (about the good) 42
will: *Wille* 112, 114–15, 119; *Willkür* 112–15, 119
Williams, Bernard 29n14, 180
wise judgment constructivism 93
Wittgenstein, Ludwig 26, 31, 68n13
wrongness: the meaning of 43–5; the nature of 44–6, 49, 51, 53–4

Zagzebski, Linda 99

Printed in the United States
By Bookmasters